How to Write your Undergraduate Dissertation

Palgrave Study Skills

Business Degree Success
Career Skills
Cite Them Right (8th edn)
Critical Thinking Skills (2nd edn)
e-Learning Skills (2nd edn)
The Exam Skills Handbook (2nd edn)
Great Ways to Learn Anatomy and Physiology
How to Begin Studying English Literature (3rd edn)
How to Manage Your Distance and Open Learning Course
How to Manage Your Postgraduate Course
How to Study Foreign Languages
How to Study Linguistics (2nd edn)
How to Use Your Reading in Your Essays
How to Write Better Essays (2nd edn)
How to Write Your Undergraduate Dissertation
Information Skills
The International Student Handbook
IT Skills for Successful Study
The Mature Student's Guide to Writing (3rd edn)
The Mature Student's Handbook
The Palgrave Student Planner
Practical Criticism
Presentation Skills for Students (2nd edn)

The Principles of Writing in Psychology
Professional writing (2nd edn)
Researching Online
Skills for Success (2nd edn)
The Student's Guide to Writing (3rd edn)
Study Skills Connected
Study Skills for International Postgraduates
The Study Skills Handbook (3rd edn)
Study Skills for Speakers of English as a Second Language
Studying History (3rd edn)
Studying Law (3rd edn)
Studying Modern Drama (2nd edn)
Studying Psychology (2nd edn)
Teaching Study Skills and Supporting Learning
The Undergraduate Research Handbook
The Work-Based Learning Student Handbook
Work Placements – A Survival Guide for Students
Write it Right (2nd edn)
Writing for Engineers (3rd edn)
Writing for Law
Writing for Nursing and Midwifery Students (2nd edn)
You2Uni

Pocket Study Skills

14 Days to Exam Success
Blogs, Wikis, Podcasts and More
Brilliant Writing Tips for Students
Completing Your PhD
Doing Research
Getting Critical
Planning Your Essay
Planning Your PhD
Reading and Making Notes

Referencing and Understanding Plagiarism
Reflective Writing
Report Writing
Science Study Skills
Studying with Dyslexia
Success in Groupwork
Time Management
Writing for University

Palgrave Research Skills

Authoring a PhD
The Foundations of Research (2nd edn)
The Good Supervisor (2nd edn)
The Postgraduate Research Handbook (2nd edn)
Structuring Your Research Thesis

For a complete listing of all our titles in this area please visit www.palgrave.com/studyskills

How to Write your Undergraduate Dissertation

Bryan Greetham

palgrave
macmillan

First published 2009 by
PALGRAVE MACMILLAN

Palgrave Macmillan in the UK is an imprint of Macmillan Publishers Limited, registered in England, company number 785998, of Houndmills, Basingstoke, Hampshire RG21 6XS.

Palgrave Macmillan in the US is a division of St Martin's Press LLC, 175 Fifth Avenue, New York, NY 10010.

Palgrave Macmillan is the global academic imprint of the above companies and has companies and representatives throughout the world.

Palgrave® and Macmillan® are registered trademarks in the United States, the United Kingdom, Europe and other countries.

ISBN-13: 978–0–230–21875–8
ISBN-10: 0–230–21875–X

This book is printed on paper suitable for recycling and made from fully managed and sustained forest sources. Logging, pulping and manufacturing processes are expected to conform to the environmental regulations of the country of origin.

A catalogue record for this book is available from the British Library.

A catalog record for this book is available from the Library of Congress.

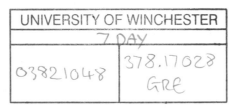

To my former supervisor Dr Joe Mintoff, for his thoroughness, attention to detail and passion for his subject. And to Pat, whose undiminished courage to accept each new challenge makes our life together so fascinating.

Contents

Preface

Like dissertations, a large part of this book is about thinking. As I've said a number of times throughout it, dissertations are set as assignments to give teachers a window into the minds of their students, to see *how* they think, not just *what* they think. It is for this reason that I have avoided burdening the text with too many references. Not only does this tend to break up the text, making it difficult to read with any fluency, but if these arguments are to show you how to think, they should be convincing enough on their own merits without appeals to outside help.

Of course, dissertations are also about more practical matters. All of these are here too. Indeed, every aspect and every stage of producing a dissertation is explained in these pages, from generating your first ideas about what you might like to research, to binding and submitting your work. You will learn how to get the most out of your relationship with your supervisor, how to generate your best ideas and develop them into interesting, original research projects, how to plan your research, manage your time and read and take notes more effectively, and how to work with primary and secondary sources, choosing from the complete range of quantitative and qualitative research techniques.

And, of course, it is also about writing – the most difficult form of thinking. You will learn how to plan every detail of each chapter, how to construct sound arguments, use language consistently and deploy your evidence convincingly, and how to convey your ideas simply and economically with a light effective style to produce a memorable, thought-provoking piece of work. Then, finally, you will learn how to revise and edit your dissertation, so that the quality of your work and the extent of your achievements really shine through.

I hope you find this book not just helpful, but perhaps most of all a source of insights and inspiration, from which you will gain confidence. Researching and writing a dissertation is a daunting challenge. But it is only daunting because it is new, something you've not done before, not because it is beyond you.

Acknowledgements

As this book is largely the product of my own academic experience, I would like to acknowledge the debt I owe to all my teachers, whose skills to inspire and motivate their students were never far from my thoughts. However, this is also the appropriate place to acknowledge all the gifted teachers working in schools, colleges and universities. Aldous Huxley once said, 'Most of one's life . . . is one prolonged effort to prevent oneself thinking.'[1] It is not easy to teach students to think; far easier just to teach them to recycle your ideas. But there are some teachers out there who spend years teaching their students to embrace the challenge of genuine thinking, rather than avoid it.

Among these are some of my colleagues. In particular, I owe a considerable debt to Professor Cliff Hooker at the University of Newcastle in Australia. The subtlety and complexity of his thought enriched my understanding of the nature of thinking. I am also grateful to Dr David Dockrill of the University of Newcastle and Shaun Theobald of the University of Kent for their friendship and support over the years.

As for my students, I owe them a debt that cannot even be measured, let alone repaid. To all those in Britain, Europe, Australia and the US who have been generous enough to accept me as their tutor, I thank you. At times I think you have taught me more than I have taught you.

To Suzannah Burywood, my editor at Palgrave, I owe a special debt of gratitude for investing such confidence in me and for her quiet patience, professionalism and unfailingly sound judgement. I would also like to thank my reviewers for their kind and encouraging words and for permission to use examples that one of them offered. I must also thank Palgrave Macmillan for allowing me to use two figures from Patrick Dunleavy's book *Studying for a Degree in the Humanities and Social Sciences* (Basingstoke: Macmillan, 1986).

Finally, I would like to thank my partner, Patricia Rowe, and my dear friend AH for enriching my life with their optimism and sense of fun and for giving me the stability to get on with my work.

---

1 Aldous Huxley, 'Green Tunnels', in *Mortal Coils* (1922; Harmondsworth: Penguin, 1955), p. 114.

Introduction

The moment any of us are presented with a project as large as a dissertation we're inclined to think this is too much for us to handle. But our confidence grows as soon as we have broken it down into smaller stages, planned them carefully and taken the advice to deal with one thing at a time. After that, if we can avoid frightening ourselves by looking at the whole project, we can get on with the manageable challenges that each new stage presents.

● Why this book?

This is exactly what we will do in this book. You will be shown how to break the task down into small manageable stages, plan each one and then work through them carefully. You will learn simple skills, techniques and methods you can adopt, along with useful systems that will help you organise yourself to take away most, if not all, of the worry about completing such a large project.

All of this is important to producing a dissertation that will earn a high mark. And yet still more important are the internal processes of thinking and writing, which we are rarely, if ever, taught. In this book you will learn how to generate your own ideas and then develop out of them the sort of fascinating questions and hypotheses that will sustain your interest, guide your research and help you produce an insightful piece of work. Later we will turn to the other aspect of these internal processes: how to critically evaluate what we read, analyse concepts and create consistent persuasive arguments of our own.

Thinking and writing: the internal processes
1 Generating your own ideas
2 Developing them – research questions and hypotheses
3 Critically evaluating arguments and evidence
4 Analysing concepts
5 Creating consistent, persuasive arguments of your own

Unfortunately, we all know just how difficult this sort of writing and thinking can be. Even though he wrote the monumental *On the Origin of Species* and many other books and papers, Charles Darwin freely admitted how difficult he found it to express his ideas on paper:

> As long as it consists solely of description it is pretty easy; but where reasoning comes into play, to make a proper connection, a clearness & a moderate fluency, is to me . . . a difficulty of which I had no idea.[1]

In this book you will learn how to develop your thinking and write your ideas simply and clearly. We will go through each stage and each component of the dissertation, along with those things we all worry about – style, punctuation, sentences, words, plagiarism and referencing – to cover all the uncertainties, so that we can get our ideas down fluently, coherently, and in a way that engages readers and holds their attention until the end.

● Writing as thinking

As this suggests, we cannot easily separate thinking from writing. Indeed, the importance of writing a dissertation lies in the fact that writing is just a form of thinking: the most difficult, yet the most effective, form. As we break down the task it seems natural to divide it into two different assignments – the research project and the report at the end of it. But they are intimately interwoven. Writing places us at the heart of our ideas. It forces us to pin our ideas down, clarify our thinking, check the consistency of our arguments and then capture all of this in language that conveys it accurately.

> Writing is the most difficult form of thinking.

It's a way of finding out what we think about something. As we write, it tells us what we know, what we still need to pin down clearly, and what we don't know and need to find out. You might gather a mass of information, read widely, analyse the issues involved and give it all sustained deep thought, but not until you write to explain it to someone else will you realise just how clear you are about it and whether it all makes consistent sense.

● Writing – a continuous, unbroken process

Equally significant, writing is an organic process: ideas grow and develop over time. Our job is to record this development. Each time we do this we plant the seeds of ideas that will develop of their own accord. Coming up with ideas is a continuous, unbroken process. Good or bad, they breed other ideas. We may produce an idea that clearly wouldn't work, but it is very likely to produce others that will.

A piece of writing that glides effortlessly across the page in light, elegant prose as if the writer is there next to you explaining with consummate clarity the most complex idea, doesn't occur all in one session. It doesn't come off the computer seamlessly as one piece of thought. It will be pieced together from different notebook jottings, journal entries and those red-hot moments when ideas just come fully formed with glaring clarity to be written feverishly into a notebook. Then, having put it all together, the author will revise, re-revise and re-revise again, cutting bits out, changing the order and re-writing whole sections, until it does finally glide across the page effortlessly.

> • Ideas develop over time
> • Our job is to record the development
> • Good writing is pieced together from these different records

So resist the temptation to split the dissertation into these two parts, telling yourself that you'll 'write it up' later. Start writing as soon as the ideas come to you, and keep writing. Be professional about your work. Tell yourself that you will write every day, even if it is just two to three paragraphs in your journal, and that you will organise yourself to catch every stray idea whenever it comes and wherever you are.

Write up sections of the dissertation as soon as possible. That way you'll reveal early any flaws in your reasoning. At the very least, commit your ideas to paper in preparation for supervisions and then, afterwards, write up the ideas you discussed with your supervisor before they lose their focus or are submerged beneath other less relevant thoughts. Supervisors never tire of telling students to go away and write it up.

Summary

1   Writing is just a form of thinking: the most difficult, yet the most effective, form.

2   It is an organic process: ideas grow and develop over time.

3   Start writing as soon as the ideas come to you, and keep writing.

4   Organise yourself to catch every stray idea whenever it comes and wherever you are.

5   Write up sections of the dissertation as soon as possible.

6   Commit your ideas to paper in preparation for supervisions and write them up afterwards.

● What next?

In the next chapter we will look at the differences between essays and dissertations and what we must do to meet the expectations of the examiners marking our work.

● Website

If you have any questions as you work through this book, use the forum on my website to get an answer either from me or from other contributors (www.bryangreetham.org.uk). You will also find there short courses that tackle most problems.

● Note

1   Charles Darwin in a letter to his sisters dated 1836, quoted in Adrian Desmond and James Moore, Darwin (London: Michael Joseph, 1991), p. 183.

Part One

Examiners and supervisors

1 Examiners: What are they looking for?

In this chapter you will learn . . .

1 the key differences between an essay and a dissertation;
2 exactly what examiners are looking for;
3 what is meant by originality and how to achieve it;
4 the range of abilities examiners are assessing.

A dissertation is quite different from anything you've been asked to do before. So your success will depend upon how well you make the adjustment.

● The differences between essays and dissertations

The most obvious difference is size. Essays are relatively short, say, 2,000–3,000 words, whereas an undergraduate dissertation can be 8,000–12,000 words, perhaps more in some cases. This means we must analyse more extensively a larger body of material, critically evaluating it using more detailed and subtle arguments.

Genuine thinking

But along with its larger scope, a dissertation also affords us the opportunity to work more independently, so we can explore our own original ideas. This may sound odd, but it's designed as an opportunity to do some genuine thinking. Many of the courses in higher education allow students to slip into the comfortable, undemanding role as mere recyclers of received opinions, while teachers opt for the corresponding and easier task of teaching students *what* to think, rather than *how* to think.

After all, teachers are appointed for their research, so they are seen as the experts, the gold standard in ideas. Therefore, it seems sensible to reproduce their ideas, rather than think for yourself. Consequently, when many students are asked to express themselves they are not expressing *their* ideas, but what they think their teachers think they ought to think. They are not involved in what they are writing at a deeper level. They do not share the needs of a genuine thinker.

> **Genuine thinking**
>
> **1** You're using *your* ideas.
>
> **2** You're not just recycling the ideas of others.
>
> **3** You are guided by the evidence whichever way it points.
>
> **4** You're thinking about your thinking.
>
> **5** You choose the focus, direction and organisation of your work.

Your dissertation may be the first time you've been asked to do some genuine thinking. It gives you the opportunity not only to choose the topic and questions you want to investigate, but also to develop your abilities to interpret texts, weigh up empirical evidence and come to your own measured judgement. You are not just setting out a simple catalogue of what you believe to be right answers, nor are you just laying down a thesis and defending it. A mature thinker is guided by the evidence, whichever way it points. She doesn't just decide what she believes to be the case and then search around for the evidence to support it.

The process not just the product

Genuine thinking is also characterised by the ability to think about our thinking: to be aware of the process of thought, not just the product. So dissertations are equally concerned with showing how we validate our results; that we understand and can justify the research methods we've chosen in order to gather and evaluate our evidence. It must be possible for anyone else to read the same passages from the literary, philosophical or historical texts we have chosen as our material and come to their own interpretation to compare with ours, or conduct the same empirical research to see how their results compare with our own.

> A dissertation will involve you thinking about your thinking.

You decide on the focus, direction and organisation of your work. You choose the questions for which you want answers or the hypothesis you want to test. It gives you the opportunity to produce a substantial piece of independent work, which reflects a wider range of your skills and abilities. In the process, you will show that you can manage a large research project, organise your own schedule, set targets, maintain your motivation throughout and produce a well reasoned and organised presentation of the results. In short, you will show yourself, your examiners and future employers that you have the personal resources to take on a large project and succeed.

If this sounds daunting, it is only because the demands are new. They are not beyond your grasp.

Dissertations
1 Work independently.
2 Original ideas.
3 Genuine thinking.
4 You choose the topic.
5 Justify your research methods.

● Examiners

But, of course, in practical terms, if we're going to do something well, we need to know why we are doing it: we need to know what examiners are looking for. In each stage of producing the dissertation, examiners will be looking for evidence that we can do all of the following:

1 **Identify a problem** – that raises particularly interesting issues worth researching.
2 **Analyse it** – produce significant, interesting questions that are capable of sustaining an in-depth investigation.
3 **Explore the literature** – in an organised, systematic way to show that our research is underpinned by existing theory. In effect we are showing examiners that we can educate ourselves about the topic.
4 **Design a research strategy** – that uses the most appropriate research methods to gather the evidence that answers our questions.
5 **Devise the most effective data-collection tools** – instruments, like questionnaires and interview questions, which are valid and reliable in gathering the evidence we need.
6 **Process the material** – analyse the evidence we gather and critically assess it.
7 **Draw conclusions** – on the basis of this material.

8   **Write the dissertation** – present our findings in accordance with the established academic practices.

The main purpose of dissertations is not just to communicate the results of your research, but, equally important, to show examiners that the methods underpinning your research have been chosen well and used skilfully.

> The purpose of dissertations =
>
> To communicate the results
>
>   +
>
> To show you have chosen the most appropriate methods and used them skilfully.

Originality

However, your dissertation should show examiners not only that you have the abilities to convey complex ideas clearly and develop arguments consistently, but that you have come to new and interesting conclusions: you have broken new ground. For many students this is the most frightening of all their concerns. Your dissertation might not have the originality of a PhD thesis, but, still, it's assumed that it will advance, even in a small way, our knowledge and understanding of certain ideas, issues and methodology. It's a common feature of almost all research that progress is very often the cumulative effect of such small steps taken by many researchers.

If this seems daunting, it need not be. Although you're not just recycling the received opinions of those regarded as authorities in your subject, you will still need to show that your research builds on published research and uses established methods, so you don't have to start from nothing. And besides, there are many ways in which your work can be original: in terms of

> Originality
>
> **1** The subject you choose.
>
> **2** Your approach.
>
> **3** The client group or material.
>
> **4** The data collected.

the subject you choose, in the way you approach it, the client group or material you focus on, and the particular data you collect. Remember, you don't have to show that what you plan to do has never been done before. In many cases what's original is that you have done it for yourself, rather than rely on other people's research.

- You might apply an existing theory to a new area, or test other people's findings and ideas for yourself using different subjects.

Example: Intellectual history

You might know of a number of studies that have compared the work of the nineteenth-century English philosopher John Stuart Mill and the Scottish essayist Thomas Carlyle, but you know of no studies that have compared their respective theories of history.

- Your research might build on existing studies to follow up new leads, or to refine or qualify the findings of earlier studies.

Example: The media

There are studies that have explored the way media representation of women has changed over the last two decades, so you might decide to explore this, focusing on one particular type of publication, say, women's magazines.

- The instruments you design might yield new, surprising evidence.

Example: Questionnaires and interviews

You might design a questionnaire that asks questions not posed before, or examines a group not previously examined. You might conduct interviews using a series of well-crafted questions that reveal new, fascinating insights into a problem.

- You might devise exercises for subjects to complete, which produce evidence of behaviour from a perspective not seen before.

Example: Study skills

You might decide to test the belief that the study skills problems experienced by most students at universities are due largely to the neglect of these skills in schools. So you design tests and a questionnaire from which you discover that there appears to be not one cause but a number.

Abilities

Beyond originality, of course, examiners are looking to see how well you have developed a certain range of abilities. To give you a clearer idea of this, look at the table below.

Understanding	Show a clear grasp of the issues involved.
Analysis	Reveal the implications of the concepts used to define the problem and the possible causes that might explain it.
Creative abilities	Devise questions and hypotheses and the means of answering and testing them, respectively.
Problem solving	Recognise problems and their possible solutions.
Comparison	Identify differences and similarities.
Criticism	Critically assess evidence and arguments.
Inductive and deductive abilities	Come to conclusions based on relevant, consistent arguments and reliable evidence.
Self-organisation Self-motivation	Manage and sustain a large research project.
Writing skills	Present findings in clear, well planned written work.

Every research project uses these abilities, albeit in different measures. A certain range of abilities will dominate some projects, while they are less obvious in others. For example, projects like the following are philosophical and literary in nature:

'The Theories of History of J. S. Mill and Thomas Carlyle'

'Novelistic sympathy and distance in the novels of George Eliot'

'Literary influences on the Pre-Raphaelite Brotherhood'

Although you would be using all the abilities in some measure, your work would be dominated by your analytic, comparative and deductive abilities.

In contrast, if you were working on projects like the following, which depend upon methods of gathering empirical evidence, your work would be largely taken up with your creative, problem-solving and inductive abilities.

'The main causes of the study skills problems of university students.'

'The effects of the smoking ban on pubs and restaurants in Bolton.'

'Young people's attitudes to, and experience of, racism.'

In the following chapters you will see the importance of designing your project to ensure it not only interests you, but uses those abilities you enjoy using and are good at. To some extent the subject you're studying will dictate this, but a lot is left to your own preferences. At an early stage it's worth consulting your supervisor, whose experience will be invaluable in designing a project that matches perfectly your abilities and preferences.

Summary

1 A dissertation is your opportunity to show that you can genuinely think.

2 You have to think about the process as well as the product of your thought.

3 You can show your work is original in a number of simple ways.

4 Choose a project that matches your interests and abilities.

● What next?

In designing such a large project that suits your particular abilities and sustains your interest you will have to draw upon the advice and experience of your supervisor. In the next chapter we will look at how you can get the best out of this important relationship.

2 Working with your supervisor

In this chapter you will learn . . .

1 the importance of being clear about the formal requirements from the start, rather than storing up problems for later;
2 how to get the most out of each supervision;
3 the importance of outlining for your supervisor how you work best;
4 four principles for managing your relationship effectively.

At first, as you assemble your ideas and think about what you might like to do, it's natural to feel lost and apprehensive. So it will pay you, at an early stage, to begin talking to your supervisor. This relationship will have a significant influence on almost every aspect of the project.

● Checking the formal requirements

But first, check the formal requirements governing assessment by dissertation. You will find various aspects are governed by important rules issued by your university or college, and then, in addition, more detailed instructions from your department or school. At this stage these might seem your least important concern as you struggle with the decision about what topic to do. But it takes little time to pin these details down and it is always better to avoid storing up problems for later. So, before the work gets under way in earnest, while you have the time, clarify the situation; make sure you're perfectly clear about the rules.

They will cover things like the length and format of the dissertation, the deadline for the final submission and any interim deadlines you may have to meet, the extent to which you can collaborate with others, the system for approving your choice of subject, and the supervision arrangements you will need to make with your supervisor. Some will even have the marking criteria: what examiners are expecting you to do and the abilities they will assess. If you're not given this, ask your supervisor. After all, you need to know exactly what you're expected to do and the range of abilities you're expected to use.

Formal requirements
1 Length
2 Format
3 Final presentation
4 Deadline
5 Collaboration
6 Choosing your subject
7 Supervision arrangements
8 Marking criteria

● Supervisors

If you fail to make clear exactly what's expected of you and when, it will become a major distraction, disrupting your emotional equilibrium just when you need to maintain a sharp focus on what you're doing. Where you need help, don't hesitate to ask your supervisor. Most of them are willing to do all they can to help you at each stage of your work.

Rules governing supervisions
The relationship with supervisors varies from one person and one institution to another. In some universities you're given unspecified time, while in others you will have a definite timetabled allocation or even just the initial supervision and no more. So make sure you're clear about the arrangement and contact your supervisor early. Don't wait to be contacted. Knock on your supervisor's door and arrange a time.

Still, the success of any relationship depends upon the personalities involved. Some supervisors adopt a flexible approach, making themselves available any time, while others will have clear times when they're available and levels of support they're prepared to give. So find out what your supervisor thinks is his or her role, how they like to work, how much time they will or can give you and what they expect of you. There may be pre-arranged weekly meetings already timetabled or it may be up to you to arrange supervisions when you want them.

It's a good idea to have regular supervisions and to agree to produce a certain amount of work for each one, which will help you monitor your progress. You will get a lot more out of those for which you've produced some written work. Without it they tend to be an ineffective use of your time.

> Find out early . . .
> 1 what your supervisor thinks is his or her role;
> 2 how they like to work;
> 3 how much time they will or can give you;
> 4 what they expect of you.

Different personalities

Your supervisor's

Some supervisors give you nothing but praise, while others seem disposed towards unrelieved criticism and negativity. They appear to think you must go through a traditional rite of fire and, if you can survive that, you have a toehold on academic achievement. But as a flower grows from being put in the light, so a student's work improves from praise that builds his or her confidence.

The ideal, of course, is to have a balance between the two. The supervisor who goes through your work with conscientious thoroughness, critically identifying where the problems lie, is priceless. Your analysis will become sharper, your ideas more grounded in reality and your arguments more rigorously consistent. Combine that with the willingness to acknowledge the improvement you've shown, and your confidence will grow along with the possibilities of what you can achieve.

With some supervisors you may feel you're not getting enough direction. Producing a dissertation is a new approach to learning, which poses new problems and challenges, so you might want more support and help than you are getting. If this is the case, consider forming a support group with your fellow students, or even just pair up with another person, so you can meet regularly and talk about problems, and how best to tackle them. It will certainly help with the feeling of isolation, which is a necessary condition of doing any sustained research and writing.

> Think about . . .
> . . . forming a support group with students or pairing up with someone.

Even so, it's easy to confuse the help and support you need as you embark on this large project with the frustration of not getting detailed instructions from your supervisor about what you should be doing exactly. As we said earlier, unlike previous assignments, with dissertations the control has shifted. Now *you* make the important decisions about which topic to research, the research methods you use, how you organise your retrieval system and your time, and how you set about writing. Supervisors are there to advise you; they're facilitators helping you achieve what you want to achieve. They can help you see all the factors you need to consider as you make your decisions, but they cannot make them for you.

Your own personality

The other factor in this relationship, of course, is your own personality. You may be the sort of student who can confidently work quite independently of a supervisor. It's worth outlining to your supervisor the way in which you generally work best, so you can negotiate the best possible arrangement. Let them know how much supervision you think would be best, the type of contact you want and at what stages you are most likely to want help.

Let them advise you. No matter what our experience, we are all likely to overlook things that a wise and experienced supervisor will see. There are very few of us who can't learn from their experience. And it's worth

---

Supervisions – checklist

Tick below the sort of help you think you might need and show the list to your supervisor.

1 Advice on how your work will be assessed

2 Deciding on the topic

3 Searching the literature

4 Formulating a research question or hypothesis

5 Advice on the research design – the methodology

6 Help in solving problems as they arise

7 Designing questionnaires, interview questions, tests or exercises, and how to analyse the results

8 Regular deadlines and checks on your progress

9 Organising and presenting the dissertation

10 Comments on draft chapters and sections

---

remembering that most failures or non-submissions involve those students who have decided to work alone without their supervisor's advice.

Help at different times
At some stages you will need more help than at others. You'll need your supervisor's help, if not approval, for your choice of topic. Your supervisor will be able to advise you about its suitability and how useful it will be in the development of your skills and knowledge. You may have chosen a topic that's far too large and challenging for an undergraduate dissertation or one that is too small and not challenging enough. Then, as you begin your literature search, you'll need your supervisor's advice on the most useful databases, texts and journals and how to find your way around them.

Similarly, you will draw heavily on your supervisor's advice as you choose the most appropriate research methods. Indeed, if it involves fieldwork, you may need your supervisor's approval to ensure it is carried out in an ethical manner. Early supervisions are often taken up with asking students to justify the research methods they have chosen.

Then, when it comes to designing the research instruments that you'll use, like questionnaires and interview schedules, you'll lean heavily on your supervisor's experience. The same applies to drafting out chapters and sections of your dissertation. Letting your supervisor read them before you meet and then, afterwards, writing up the points you have discussed, is likely to yield some of your best work.

Managing your relationship
So, as you can see, managing this vital relationship will be important to the success of your project. It's worth keeping in mind four principles:

1 **Be flexible.**
2 **Agree deadlines.**
3 **Prepare for each supervision.**
4 **Make the best use of feedback.**

1   Flexibility
You will get a lot more from supervision if you can communicate with your supervisor not just face-to-face, but through emails and phone calls, as long as you don't bury him or her under a mountain of enquiries, accumulating day by day. It can be difficult for supervisors to find time to have a conversation that's more than just a rushed, ill-considered exchange as you both hurry along a crowded corridor. Our problems usually need more careful deliberation. A short conversation on the phone when things have settled

down can usually solve a problem, rather than it being left to gnaw away at your confidence and increase your anxiety.

2   *Agree deadlines*

You will find you have much more control over your work, if you can agree with your supervisor a list of tasks with the dates on which they should be completed. Then, around these dates, you can organise supervisions. This gives you a well organised schedule to manage your work and a means of checking your progress. You will have an early warning system, so both of you will know in good time if an unforeseen problem is slowing your progress or you're going off course. You can easily waste a week or two without these regular checks.

3   *Preparation*

Of course, to get the best out of each supervision you will need to prepare for it. Identify areas you need to discuss and points you want to raise. Some supervisors will ask you to submit work prior to the meeting, but if they don't, still submit copies of sections or chapters well in advance, so your supervisor has enough time to read and comment on them. Remember, supervisors can only work with what you submit to them.

4   *Feedback*

Finally, make the best use of the feedback you get from your meeting. Take notes during it and set aside time afterwards, when you can write up the ideas you discussed and follow up every lead your supervisor gave you. You will also find it helps to write up reminders of things you will want to raise at your next supervision.

The important thing is not to leave any of this to go cold. You will need to record the ideas that come out of the supervision as soon as you can. Empty out your mind in your notebook. Don't put it off; otherwise you'll struggle to capture exactly what made them so interesting and important at the time. Once lost, they are very difficult to recapture.

- Take notes.
- Write up reminders.
- Don't let the ideas go cold.

Summary

1   Check the formal requirements early, rather than store up problems for later.

2   Check the arrangements for supervisions and how your supervisor likes to work.

3   Organise regular supervisions and prepare work for each one.

4   Let your supervisor know the way you generally work best.

5   Keep in mind the four principles for managing your relationship with your supervisor.

● What next?

Now we must examine how we choose between the different research methods to ensure that our project will not only maintain our interest, but will make the most of our abilities.

Part Two

Generating and developing original ideas

3 What activities suit you best?

In this chapter you will learn . . .

1 how to create your own research design, your methodology, using different research methods;
2 the importance of playing to your strengths and choosing a subject that most interests you;
3 that to do well you must design your research so that it involves activities you enjoy and are good at;
4 the importance of the research question in driving your research and bringing into play the methods that involve these activities.

The Austrian Zoologist Konrad Lorenz suggested that 'It is a good morning exercise for a research scientist to discard a pet hypothesis every day before breakfast.'[1] The point is that the significance of our research lies as much in what we discard as it does in what we discover. This is not a simple process of coming up with a thesis and then setting about to defend it. It involves clearing away all the weeds, the undergrowth of untenable ideas, so we can discover new things beneath. As we change our ideas or hypotheses in line with the evidence, we edge closer to the truth.

Of course, there are many different forms or styles of research ranging from the scientific and technical to the abstract philosophical and artistic. Between these two, sharing characteristics of them both, there are, among others, social, economic, psychological, natural and anthropological research. Some have their own unique research methods that are taught as an integral part of any undergraduate degree. If you are a scientist you have lived with this as a daily reality from the moment you began your studies, conducting experiments and writing up lab reports. The same is true of humanities subjects, like literature, philosophy and history. Part of the process of studying these subjects is learning to analyse, interpret and critically evaluate imaginative literature, philosophical texts and historical documents.

For these subjects, of course, it has been unnecessary to devote chapters to explaining their specific research methods, but for those whose emphasis is more on practice than research, like professional subjects, and who share common techniques and instruments, like questionnaires, interviews and case studies, it has been.

● **Activities**

But first, as you start to think about the topic you would like to research, you must take into account two things: those things that you are interested in and those activities you like to do and are good at.

> Think about ...
> 1 What you're interested in
> 2 What you like to do and are good at

As in everything you do, the key is to play to your strengths. You will obviously do better working on a topic that interests you. You're already likely to have ideas on it before you start and the motivation that will sustain you over the months of work ahead. Consequently, throughout the project you're likely to generate more ideas of your own and synthesise them into interesting, new ways of looking at the topic, resulting in a dissertation that is richer in ideas and insights. In Chapter 5 you will see how best to narrow down the subjects that most interest you.

Equally important are the activities you like to do and are good at.

> So ask yourself . . .
> . . . What sort of work do I most like doing?

Of course, to a large extent this will be dictated by your subject or discipline, but in many cases there is still room to choose your own methods of research, the 'style' or 'approach' that most suits you. Indeed, most projects are a mixture of different methods.

Example: Social sciences

If yours is a social science topic, you may choose to begin by using a descriptive research method as you embark on a historical enquiry into the circumstances that led to a particular situation. Then you might adopt a philosophical approach as you analyse and evaluate the concepts and theories that are normally used to describe this type of situation and the issues being investigated.

Still, if you do have a preference for one method alone, and you know that this is where your strengths lie, in most cases you can still do this. In the social sciences you might choose a project that employs a wholly empirical approach or one that is entirely theoretical and textual. For example, you may have realised that your preferences and abilities lie in reviewing the literature on a particular theory, how it has been discussed in the past, the different concepts and principles employed. Your strength may lie in the analysis and critical evaluation of this sort of theoretical discussion of concepts and principles, rather than in exclusively empirical work.

Example: Humanities

In the humanities, too, although exclusively theoretical and textual, you can still choose between the different activities this involves. You may be better at critical analysis and evaluation of an author's work. In philosophy you might decide to analyse the arguments R. M. Hare develops to support his account of moral thinking and then critically evaluate them. In literature you might decide to analyse the role of the narrator in the novels of George Eliot to see if the author is consistent in the way she develops it. Alternatively, your preference may be for comparative work, tracing similarities and correlations, rather than critically analysing a body of work. You might compare how different historians describe and explain certain events or how different poets responded to their experiences in the First World War.

● **Work backwards**

To make sure that your project will involve you in the activities you prefer and are good at, you will have to work backwards from these and carefully frame your question to ensure that to answer it you will have to use the research method that involves them.

The research question
The central question that you ask or hypothesis you frame drives your research: it defines your purpose. You may be critically reviewing the work of an author; testing a theory, model or hypothesis; evaluating a proposal, a

policy or a technique; or finding the solution to a particular problem. Whichever it is, your research question will bring into play the type of research methods you will use. So it is important to spend time thinking carefully about the issues that underlie and shape your question.

Ontological assumptions

When we compose the research question our thinking focuses on two key concerns. First we have to be clear about what we think exists, what in our view are the important elements of the situation or problem we want to research. These are the ontological assumptions at the heart of our research. If you were undertaking a historical or social science project, they would amount to those assumptions you make about the nature of the social and political reality you're investigating: how it's made up and how its parts interact.

Ontological assumptions

1 What is the nature of the reality we're investigating?

2 How is it made up?

3 How do its parts interact?

We all have contrasting ways of understanding what we believe to be the reality of what we are setting out to research, whether it's about how societies are made up or how we interpret the meaning of language, literature or social customs. Each way is shaped by our experiences of the world, which we bring to the research process. So, take nothing for granted and examine them carefully, otherwise you may find yourself making assumptions you would rather not have made.

The way we understand this reality is likely to lead to certain assumptions about how we should set about our research and the different methods we should employ. You might see society as the product of continual conflict between social classes or as a loose collection of isolated individuals. Either way will define what you think are the important aspects of the situation and, in turn, influence the nature of your research question and the type of research methods you employ.

- Our experiences of the world influence the way we understand the reality of our research problem.
- Take nothing for granted – examine it carefully.

In the following chapters, as we generate our ideas on possible research topics, you will see how you can list the components of any situation – the people and organisations that affect or are affected by it – and how you can then map out their interrelations. In this way you'll be clearer about the ontological assumptions you're making, which you might otherwise overlook.

Epistemological assumptions

Our second key concern is our epistemological assumptions about what we believe should count as knowledge in this context: the sort of evidence that would count as an answer to our question and how we are to come by it.

Epistemological assumptions
1 The sort of evidence that would count as an answer.
2 How we are to find it.

So, as you frame your question you will have to ask yourself, what sort of problem is this and what sort of evidence will I need to gather to answer it? Is it a question that hangs on the contrasting interpretations of documents or literary texts; is it an organisational problem the answer to which lies within the different levels of the organisation out of which policy emerges; or is it an issue that has arisen as a result of individuals interacting, which might call for an empathetic approach to understand the choices they have made?

There are, of course, many types of problems and as many strategies for gathering evidence to answer them. In Chapter 13 we will examine the practical steps you will need to take as you plan your research and then in Chapters 18 to 23 we will look in detail at the different sources of material

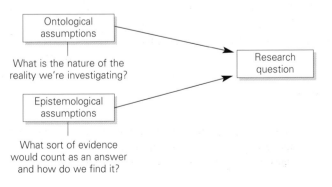

and the methods of examining them. As you can see, these epistemological questions will determine how you frame your research question, which will, in turn, determine the methods you will need to employ. It is not the methods that shape the sort of questions we can ask, but the reverse.

Methods and methodology

Once you've carefully framed your research question it will bring into play a certain combination of research methods, each of which involves certain activities, procedures and techniques. These will shape the way we go about our research: the way we frame our sub-questions implied in our original question, the different instruments we need to design, like questionnaires and interview schedules, and the best way of analysing our data.

Putting together these different research methods is the process of designing your research, the approach you are adopting in your study, often described as the 'methodology'. Although an alien term in many subjects, particularly in the humanities, it describes the way we put together the different research methods, with their own distinctive activities and techniques, to achieve what we want to achieve. In the process, we critically evaluate the different research methods to see if they will help us answer our research question.[2]

Designing your research   =   Putting together the most appropriate
(the methodology)   research methods

So to design your research to include methods that involve activities you're good at and enjoy most, you must get your research question right. In the following chapters you will learn simple ways of revealing the assumptions that shape your questions, so that you can design better ones to match these preferences.

Summary

1   Before you decide on a research strategy, think about those things you're interested in and those activities you like to do and are good at.

2   Work backwards from these activities and carefully frame

your question to ensure that to answer it you will have to use the research method that involves them.

3 Your research question drives your research: it brings into play the type of research methods you will use.

4 Make sure you've asked yourself what in your view are the important elements of the situation or problem you want to research and what sort of evidence you will need in order to answer your research question – the ontological and epistemological questions, respectively.

5 Putting together different research methods is the process of designing your research, often described as the 'methodology'.

● What next?

Now that we know the importance of the research question and the assumptions we make that will most influence it, we can begin to look in detail at the different research methods we might use. We can then design our question so that it calls upon the methods that involve the activities we most enjoy and are good at.

● Notes

1 Konrad Lorenz, *On Aggression* (1963; London and New York: Routledge, 1996), p. 8.
2 For a more detailed explanation of the nature of research methodology and ontological and epistemological assumptions, look at Jonathan Grix's excellent book, *The Foundations of Research* (Basingstoke: Palgrave Macmillan, 2004), pp. 30–4, 57–75.

4 Types of research

In this chapter you will learn . . .

1 what each research method involves;
2 about the importance of making sure your research design involves those activities you're good at and enjoy;
3 how to assess your abilities so that you play to your strengths in your project.

In the last chapter we saw the importance of our research question and how it brings into play those research methods that will involve activities we're good at and enjoy. Now we can look at each of these in detail to see which are likely to play to our strengths.

● Research methods

At times, designing your research strategy can seem a confusing business, so it helps to have a few broad categories describing the different research methods, so you can see more clearly what you have to choose from. But one word of warning: these are not mutually exclusive; they overlap and you will find yourself choosing what you want from different methods, until you've created the design that meets your needs. To see this more clearly we'll work through the following spectrum of different research methods.

Experimental ➤ Naturalistic ➤ Practical ➤ Descriptive ➤ Historical ➤ Comparative ➤ Evaluative

Experimental

Although this method is used in some measure in most forms of research, except in the humanities, it is generally associated with the natural sciences. It involves in one form or another intervening in a system to see what happens when we change certain things. In the natural sciences the ideal form of this is the controlled experiment, where we observe the influence of specific factors by isolating one element and manipulating it while we control the rest. Research based on this model involves identifying a problem, analysing it, formulating a hypothesis and then testing it. If the results falsify the hypothesis, then we amend it, perhaps by adding auxiliary hypotheses, and then testing it again. If, however, the hypothesis cannot be saved in this way and is finally falsified, then we are forced to abandon it, which is, of course, in itself a useful finding.

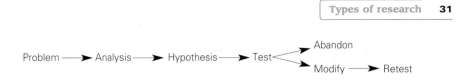

Problem ⟶ Analysis ⟶ Hypothesis ⟶ Test ⟨ Abandon / Modify ⟶ Retest

Although in the past this has been described as an inductive process of gathering evidence through observation and then allowing a hypothesis to 'emerge' naturally without scientists imposing their own to explain events, it is, in fact, more a deductive system. In what is known as the 'hypothetico-deductive system', scientists invent hypotheses, and then design experiments to help them choose between competing possibilities. As the Nobel prize-winning immunologist Sir Peter Medawar describes it, it is an imaginative and inspirational process at every level. We should think of it, he argues, as a logically articulated structure of justifiable beliefs, which begins as a story about a possible world which we 'invent and criticize and modify as we go along, so that it ends by being, as nearly as we can make it, a story about real life'.[1]

Naturalistic

Unlike the experimental method, this assumes that all situations are unique and cannot be subsumed under general laws from which we can make predictions that can be tested by controlled experiments. Often described as the 'phenomenological' method, it abandons all prior assumptions, which would otherwise distort what we observe, and adopts a descriptive approach using qualitative methods, like case studies, to gather evidence. Then, once we have our evidence, say, in a historical or social science study, we can analyse and compare the different patterns of behaviour to reach tentative explanations.

> Your presence as an observer may distort what you observe.

The key to this method is to accept that your presence as the observer in any situation is likely to distort what you observe. So you must neutralise this, for example, by not introducing twenty-first-century values into a historical study, or by ensuring that you observe the behaviour of a group by unobtrusive means.

Practical

Quite simply, this method involves applying theories and seeing how useful they are. You might have identified a problem and have some idea what the solution might be, so you intervene and make the appropriate changes to the situation and then monitor the effects. If the results are not as successful as you had hoped, you would intervene again, introducing more modifications, and then monitor the effects of these changes in a series of such interactions.

Example: Study skills

You might be the head of department at a school, responsible for improving exam results in years 11 and 12. You're convinced that the main cause of poor results has been the failure to introduce study skills courses, so you set up a programme, test its effects after six months and then intervene in response to these findings. After another six months you test again and make further changes, and so on.

Descriptive

This method involves simply finding out what things are like. You might come to realise that this sort of research just hasn't been done about something you're interested in; that we simply don't know enough about it. So you set out to identify the main features, classifying them, measuring them and revealing their internal organisation.

> Finding out what things are like.

It's the sort of research you might do that has as its subject matter natural objects, living things, organisations, like businesses and professional bodies, and even ideas, like the beliefs and values of a particular group campaigning for a change in government policy. Your intention might be to provide the groundwork from which certain inferences can be drawn and policies formed. You might even suspect that so far we have overlooked things which need to be taken into account.

Historical

Although this method is identified closely with one academic discipline, like the experimental method it is not confined to that. It's relevant whenever you want to throw light on a contemporary problem. By using historical and documentary evidence you might show just how neglected it has been or how ineffectual have been government policies addressing it. It's particularly useful in setting the context for a case study, which might otherwise lack wider significance. But it has to have a point: you're not just describing documentary evidence. It has to be set within a well-developed structure of questions you set out to answer or categories you intend to analyse.

Comparative

This method, too, can be applied widely throughout different subjects. Your aim is to identify differences and similarities between things. This could be between the work of different philosophers or novelists, or between the performance of different organisations or their methods, techniques, values or organisational structure. In history you might compare different revolutions to see if there is one common model and a common set of factors that lead to them.

> Your aim is to identify differences and similarities.

As you can see, it can be applied to most things: objects, events, ideas, organisations. Your aim is to see how closely one thing correlates with another. You might develop a clear concept of 'Romanticism' in the eighteenth century and then see how closely a particular poet or artist fits this.

But, unlike the experimental method, where you can study the relationship between certain variables by manipulating them, in this method you can only recognise them when you discover them. All you can suggest is that these relationships exist and they may indicate a certain type of influence. You cannot go on to argue that the correlation shows causation, though you might suggest this, leaving it to other researchers to pursue. So, for example, you might show that there is a high correlation between divorce rates and shift work, but on its own this cannot show causation.

Evaluative

The main focus in this method is to examine something and then judge it against a criterion: how successful, profitable or efficient a business is; how logically consistent a particular argument might be; how ethical might be the treatment of patients in a hospital ward; how effective has been a social policy or investment in a local initiative. Its effectiveness depends on establishing clearly and convincingly a standard of judgement by which you can come to your evaluation. It works best when it is highly structured so you can demonstrate precision in your judgement.

It also depends heavily on the skills of the researcher. If you are evaluating the arguments of a philosopher or historian, you must have the skills to analyse concepts and arguments, and deduce consequences, before you can then go on to evaluate them. If you're evaluating the performance of a company, you must similarly have the skills to analyse thoroughly its balance sheets before you can come to your judgement.

It depends on:

1 a clear, convincing standard of judgement;

2 that is highly structured;

3 the skills of the researcher.

● Preferences

Which methods you choose and how you combine them depends largely on your preferences as to what you like to do and what you think you're good at. You may be the type of person who prefers to work on your own in your study or in the library. For you a more abstract and theoretical approach is likely to be more suitable.

Theoretical approach

No matter what the subject, understanding anything involves using concepts and theories.

> So, ask yourself . . .
> . . . How useful are the concepts and theories that appear most often in my work?

There is usually plenty of argument in the journals about what exactly they mean, their implications and how useful they are in understanding your subject.

In some subjects, like philosophy, sociology and psychology, where there are well developed competing theories and a vibrant debate surrounding them and the principles and concepts they use, it's not difficult to find topics. But even in subjects that have a more practical orientation, like education, healthcare, social work, architecture and design, and business and administration, there are theoretical issues that can be examined and discussed at the abstract level.

Example: Healthcare

You might examine the way limited medical resources are rationed to meet the needs of patients attending dialysis units. Here you would no doubt have to combine different methods, analysing the concept of 'needs', evaluating the arguments presented in policy documents, contrasting the different positions of those most affected and comparing the approaches of different healthcare systems.

Empirical approach

Alternatively, you may be the type of person who likes to meet and talk to people and would be quite happy persuading them to be part of your research project by completing a questionnaire or agreeing to be interviewed. The sort of project you could choose might involve seeing how the theories that are so influential in your subject can be applied to the real world. What are their implications, how useful are they and do they work? By taking a case study approach you could examine whether they actually deliver what they claim to do.

Example: Smoking in public places

You could take a government policy, like the banning of smoking in public places, and the theoretical arguments that underwrite it, to see if it does in fact have the effects that ministers and officials had expected. By researching a case study, such as the effects on pubs and restaurants in Bolton, you could gather evidence that would show whether people did respond according to the behaviour patterns that the theory suggested.

⬤ Listing your preferences

So, as you design your preferred research strategy, list the sort of activities you most enjoy. To help you, go through the list of activities on p. 36 and tick those you prefer. At the end of the exercise you will have developed a profile of yourself and your preferences that you should keep in front of you as you begin to choose the topic of your research.

Do you like . . .

1 Working with texts, abstract concepts and ideas?

2 Conducting experiments?

3 Meeting people?

4 Analysing data?

5 Analysing concepts?

6 Analysing arguments?

7 Figuring out how something works?

8 Comparing things – identifying their differences and similarities?

9 Pattern recognition – seeing how things are interrelated?

10 Intervening in things: changing something to see what the effect might be, or to see if it makes it more efficient?

11 Describing things: finding out what things are like, or were like in the past?

12 Working with documents or records?

13 Trying to understand why an event occurred and how things developed as they have?

14 Practical work: applying theories to see how useful they are?

15 Synthesising ideas: bringing them together from different sources to create a new way of looking at something?

16 Evaluating things: arguments, policies for their effectiveness, companies for their profitability, etc.?

17 Working in depth with a narrow focus?

18 Searching for relationships between objects and events?

19 Analysing things into their parts to discover their nature?

20 Finding solutions to problems?

● Abilities and skills

As for matching a research strategy to your abilities and skills, by now you'll probably know where your strengths lie as clearly as you know your preferences. But, like preferences, it's as well to pin them down clearly by deliberately asking yourself some fairly obvious questions. First, take the same categories we used with preferences and ask yourself whether you're better at theoretical or empirical work.

Theoretical work

Of course, all projects involve some theoretical work. Whatever you choose, you will have to search and review the background literature to connect your research with the broader theoretical issues in your subject. And even if your strengths lie in theoretical work, you will still have to ask yourself one or two questions. If you think of the five main orientations of theoretical work –

1 Description
2 Analysis
3 Synthesis
4 Comparison
5 Evaluation

– it will be difficult to find a project that is exclusively one of these. You will have to ask yourself where your abilities lie, so that you can ensure your project draws mainly on one or a blend of abilities in which you're strongest. Use the following checklist of questions to get the blend right. Give yourself a score out of ten for each ability.

From this you should be able to see where your strengths lie. If you have one clear winner, then obviously this should dominate your project as far as it can, although remember that any project will employ the others to some measure. If more than 50 per cent of the points you've awarded yourself are for two or three abilities, you'll have a clear indication of where the general orientation of your project should be. However, if there are no clear winners, then, obvious as it may seem, you will do best with a project that uses them all in roughly equal measure.

Are you best at . . .

1 Describing an argument, a series of events or a particular situation?

2. Analysing concepts and abstract arguments to reveal their underlying assumptions, beliefs and values?

3 Synthesising ideas and arguments to create new ways of looking at a problem?

4 Contrasting and comparing two or more things to trace their similarities and differences?

5 Critically evaluating and discussing an argument or a theory's strengths and weaknesses?

Empirical work

If, however, your abilities lie in empirical work, your key concerns will be how good you are at collecting and analysing data. Collecting data raises its own unique problems, largely related to how good we are at meeting and working with strangers. Analysing data, too, calls for certain skills, particularly if sophisticated analysis is necessary. So ask yourself the following questions and, again, give yourself a score out of ten for each ability.

Are you best at . . .

1 Running controlled experiments?

2 Meeting and working with people?

3 Interviewing them?

4 Observing their behaviour?

5 Describing what you find?

6 Analysing data statistically?

7 Applying theories to see how useful they are?

8 Recognising patterns of relationships in data?

This time you're more likely to see a range of abilities appear dominant. If 2, 3, 4, 5 and 8 achieve high scores, while 6 only a low score, the research methods that best suit your abilities are likely to be those that collect qualitative data and use research instruments, like interviews and observations, that don't depend upon sophisticated statistical analysis. If, however, 1, 6, 7 and 8 score high, then the research methods you choose should be designed to yield quantitative data, which you can analyse statistically to draw your conclusions.

Summary

1   These research methods are not mutually exclusive – you will have to choose what you want from each one until you have created the design that suits your needs.

2   First, create a profile of yourself and your preferences – the sort of activities you most enjoy. Keep this in front of you as you begin to choose the topic of your research.

3   Second, try to match activities to your abilities by asking yourself whether you're better at theoretical or empirical work.

4   Then, within each one try to narrow down the type of work that clearly plays to your strengths, by working through the checklists, giving yourself points out of ten.

● What next?

We began the last chapter by pointing out that there are many different forms or styles of research ranging from the scientific and technical to the abstract philosophical and artistic. Now that we are clearer about what each involves and what we believe we most enjoy and are good at, we can begin to think about the topic we want to research. In the following chapters we will learn how to generate our own ideas and develop them into a feasible research project. But first we must start with what we're interested in.

● Note

1   P. B. Medawar, *Induction and Intuition in Scientific Thought* (London: Methuen, 1969), p. 59.

5 What interests you most?

In this chapter you will learn . . .

1. what makes the best topic for a dissertation;
2. how to find one that will interest and motivate you over the long term;
3. how to explore systematically your own unique experience and interests to find ideas.

Most of the books we read on how to write essays and dissertations deal with the mechanics of the task: how to manage your time, how to plan interviews, write questionnaires, organise case studies, and how to cite references and compile a bibliography. But few deal with the really difficult problem we all want help with: how to think. How do we generate our own original ideas, how do we develop them and how can we learn to argue consistently?

Without doubt a dissertation is the most challenging, yet most rewarding, task you will face in your undergraduate studies. So you want to produce the very best work you can, not just for the mark you will get at the end, but for your own sense of what you can achieve. You must try to exceed your expectations; surprise yourself. For this you must generate your most imaginative and creative ideas.

● How do I find the right topic?

For many students the most confusing and difficult aspect of doing a dissertation is finding the right topic to research. It must be original and interesting: something that will not only strike the examiners as worth researching, but be interesting enough to maintain your motivation over the long term. It must be *broad* enough to connect with the background theory and the ideas you find in the literature of your subject, and *narrow* enough to deal with in depth in the time and words available.

- **Interesting** enough to maintain your motivation
- **Broad** enough to connect with the background theory
- **Narrow** enough to research in depth in the time and words available

Equally important, there must be a sharply defined question at the heart of your project that will direct and control your thinking as you search for answers. Psychologists believe that thinking in all its forms is consciously or unconsciously goal-directed. So, to come up with clear, relevant answers that achieve your goal you must have clear and sharp questions that define it. These will determine how you select facts, reconstruct events and present the arguments from both sides of a dispute.

In the natural and social sciences there is more likely to be a thesis out of which you develop a hypothesis, a belief you want to test. In the humanities there may be an underlying proposition out of which you develop the key question and sub-questions to which you want answers. Whichever it is, these questions, which will guide and control your thinking, must be sharply and concisely framed to be kept by your side in the months ahead as you collect and write about your ideas.

> All thinking is goal-directed, so set controls on your thinking by making those goals as sharp and concise as you can.

⬤ What am I interested in?

Your first concern should be to choose a topic in which you're interested, even one you are passionate about. It must sustain your motivation over the long term as you work alone with no-one around pushing you. What we're interested in we tend to do well at: we show creativity, inventiveness, resourcefulness and, usually, an uncompromising determination to get to the bottom of it. If you're interested in your topic, you will have prepared your mind to notice more things, generate more of your own ideas and see more connections between them.

> Choose a topic you're interested in, even passionate about.

To some extent, of course, the topic may be circumscribed by the subject you're studying and the subject matter this normally involves, whether that's individuals, societies, nature, ideas, or the past. Even so, you've still got a lot of ideas to sort through before you identify the topic that really interests you, so adopt a systematic approach. Work through the following stages in the table below, asking yourself a series of questions. You will end up with three or four possible topics, which you can then explore systematically in more depth to find the best one.

Narrowing down topics
1 Previous courses
2 New data
3 Current developments
4 A case study to replicate
5 Personal experience
6 Previous dissertations
7 Topical subjects
8 Personal interests

Previous courses

First, think back over the units you have studied and the topics you covered in each one, and ask yourself if there are any unresolved issues that really fascinated you at the time; things that intrigued you so much that you thought someday you would like to study this again only in more depth. Finding something that really intrigued you in this way will not only have a better chance of maintaining your motivation, but is also likely to play to your strengths, in that, if you enjoyed it, you probably also did well in it.

Go back over your notes and the reading you did at the time. You may have come across a particular explanation for something, or a theory or hypothesis that stirred your interest in seeing whether or not it is in fact the case. You might wonder just how far it is relevant to the actual experience of a particular community or a country, which you could then use as the subject of a case study.

Look for . . .
1 Intriguing, unresolved issues
2 Theory or explanation to test
3 An interesting book or article
4 A unique and perceptive analysis of something

Is there a book you found really interesting, which you could only skim at the time? If you're studying literature or philosophy, is there a text that has gripped your imagination, which you can analyse and then compare with the analyses of other authors. Perhaps the analysis of one author is so unique and perceptive that you could apply it to other texts. Transferring an analysis from one context to another can open up new ways of looking at a body of material. It also gives you a way of looking at different texts that are not usually associated with each other, so you can bring them together in an original synthesis. Alternatively, you might just test an analysis that you found perceptive.

Example: Literature

If you were interested, say, in the work of George Orwell, you might find that Raymond Williams's analysis of Orwell's work before and after his experiences in the Spanish Civil War is so perceptive that you decide to test it on, say, *Down and Out in Paris and London*, *Homage to Catalonia* and *Nineteen Eighty-Four* to see if it stands up to examination.

If you're studying history you may have come across an article in which the author reinterprets historical records and other primary sources. You may decide to put this to the test or draw out the implications of the findings, particularly if you believe that a number of current studies have overlooked them. Alternatively you may have come across an interpretation of events or concepts in one period that you could apply to another.

Example: The crowd in history

With the rise of totalitarian leaders in the 1930s and 1940s and their mesmeric influence on crowds, some historians began to wonder how significant the crowd and a leader's capacity to manipulate collective sentiment had been in previous periods, with leaders like Napoleon.

New data

You might come across new data in your subject that could provide the focus of your research. Government departments and research groups regularly produce reports full of the latest figures on poverty, social deprivation and crime, broken down into different categories. These may suggest trends and interpretations, which you can test in a case study.

If you're studying history, you might have come across primary material that has simply been overlooked.

> ### Example: First World War
>
> At the Imperial War Museum there are large numbers of diaries, journals and letters of those who fought on the Western Front during the First World War, which have been catalogued, but never closely examined by researchers.

> ### Example: Parish records
>
> There are throughout the country parish records of baptisms, marriages and deaths that are only now being catalogued in a systematic way with access for anyone who wants to explore their family's past. A team at the University of Hull have recently put the Doomsday Book onto the Internet in a form that allows you to process the material in ways previously impossible.

Current developments

There may be developments in your subject that could provide a focus for your research. There may be a new book or article that is particularly significant, or you might have come across in the literature an interesting disagreement or debate. In science and technology a new theory, technique or technology often provides the opportunity to break new ground.

There may be major changes in legislation, the effects of which probably need investigating. How does the new environmental protection legislation affect industries, like the construction industry, which employ large numbers? How will this legislation work in practice for particular sectors of the economy or for certain types of business?

A case study to replicate

Alternatively, you might come across in your reading a particularly interesting case study that you can replicate on a different group. You might come across one that examines the effect of the smoking ban in pubs and restaurants in a particular town, so you decide to do the same in your local town, perhaps even using the same combination of instruments, such as questionnaires and interviews.

Personal experience

If all these sources fail to produce an interesting idea, reflect on your own personal experience. You are, after all, unique in many respects. You have your own personal experiences to draw upon as a student, which may have raised particular interesting concerns that you want to do more with. You might like to know why it is that so many students share the sort of problems you have with study skills, like note-taking, reading and essay writing. You might be a parent struggling with the conflicting demands of also being a student.

> Think about . . .
> . . . your own unique interests and experiences.

You are probably an employee, or you may even be an employer. Perhaps you are a nurse working on a dialysis ward at your local hospital and you'd like to know if the limited medical resources are being used effectively to meet the needs of your patients. You may have campaigned for a cause that you believe is particularly important.

Think about all these things. Don't dismiss them just because they're unique to you. They may possess a germ of an idea that provides a unique and interesting research project.

Example: Literature

Just a simple thing like where you live might provide the idea you're looking for. A student studying at Brighton wanted to write on 'Women in Hardy's Novels', which is probably the most over-visited topic in English literature courses. So her supervisor suggested she think about Brighton in literature. Traditionally portrayed as having a questionable reputation on the fringes of legality, it provided the basis of an interesting dissertation on Brighton in nineteenth- and twentieth-century literature.[1]

Previous dissertations

If you're still struggling to find a topic, have a look at what previous students have done. A couple of hours just going through dissertations will give you ideas which are not only interesting, but practical. They've worked in the past so you'll have a clear idea of how you might go about a similar project of your own.

Topical subjects

Of course, for some subjects, like politics, sociology, economic and social policy, criminology and medical care, you can always find topical issues in newspapers and in the media. New taxes on businesses may give you an idea of how you might examine the effects of fiscal policy on small and medium-sized enterprises. You might find a topic in stories on sub-prime mortgages, money laundering, insider trading, or new evidence of the economic effects of global warming. If you're studying international relations, a crisis might develop in a country whose foreign policy you have been interested in.

Personal interests

But if all this fails and nothing has grabbed your interest, ask yourself a series of questions about the sort of things that interest you when you're not study-ing. The more systematic and exhaustive you can make it the better. Go through the list of questions below and write down your answer to each one. At the end you'll have a list of different interests, a number of which, no doubt, will give you the germ of an idea you can work into a fascinating research project.

Personal interests

1 Is there something you're passionate about doing outside your studies?

2 What sorts of issues most preoccupy your thoughts and discussions?

3 Is there something you like reading about outside college work?

4 Is there something in your family history that has always intrigued you?

5 Is there something interesting about your local community: its history or economy? Does it have particular social problems?

6 When you go on holiday, what interests you most?

7 Are there local or national figures whose lives or work have always interested you?

8 Is there a development in your area – an out-of-town shopping centre, a new factory – about which you have strong opinions?

9 Has there been one incident or figure in your life that has most influenced you? Can you say why this is?

10 List the books, paintings, music and films that you most like.

Summary

1 One of the most difficult problems we have to solve is how to generate our own original ideas.

2 To find the right topic, start by asking yourself what you're interested in, even passionate about.

3 Work through the eight stages, asking yourself the questions involved in each one, to reveal topics you could explore in depth.

 What next?

Now that you've worked through this exercise you will have some very general ideas of what you might like to investigate. The next step is to generate your own ideas about them to see what you've got and how you can develop them.

 Note

1 I owe this example to John Peck, formerly Reader at Cardiff University, who very kindly offered it for me to use.

6 Generating your own ideas

In this chapter you will learn . . .

1 a system you can use routinely to generate your own ideas;
2 the importance of thinking about your topic from the perspective of all those involved and on different levels;
3 how to do an exploratory literature search to see what other researchers have done on similar topics.

The ideas we came up with in the last chapter are very general, so to see how interesting they might be and which way we might prefer to approach them we need to generate our own ideas on them. Then, in the following chapters, we will develop these into workable hypotheses and research questions. In this way we will do what we described in Chapter 3 and ask the ontological questions about the nature of the problem we might investigate: what it's made up of and how each part is interrelated.

● Organising your thinking

The problem is, when anybody tells you to generate your own ideas, they mostly end up just giving you vague, unhelpful advice. They might tell you to, 'Think for yourself' or 'Ask yourself questions', which doesn't tell you exactly what you should do. It's not enough to tell people to think for themselves; it's like telling someone to be clever. In fact we can do this in a much more organised, systematic way. Indeed, this is exactly what most of us do all the time without knowing it. We ask ourselves certain routine trigger questions through which we assemble the ideas and facts we need, to make a decision.

Most of us who have struggled unsuccessfully to start our car know exactly what we mean by this sort of organised thinking. Well-meaning neighbours and passers-by gather around giving you advice as you vainly try to get the car started. Then the mechanic arrives and you know at once that you're in the presence of a thinking, intelligent brain. He quietly goes over the engine asking questions, testing and eliminating hypotheses until he arrives at the solution. It's clear he is using an ordered series of questions as he gathers information and eliminates one hypothesis after another.

> ### Example: Doctors and teachers
>
> In the same way a doctor will systematically work through her questions, gathering evidence of symptoms and matching them to patterns suggesting various causes. A teacher who finds one of his strongest students is suddenly producing poor work, will have a similar set of questions to work through, systematically gathering the evidence before he can come to a solution.

● Routine questions

So, the first thing we must do is look carefully at the series of questions we routinely ask ourselves: a checklist we work through in the same way as the mechanic or doctor or teacher. Most creative thinkers are constantly refining and adapting them, adding new ones they might hear elsewhere. Those whom we describe as geniuses, who solve problems by seeing something no-one else can see, come to their solutions in exactly this way. They ask questions nobody else asks. They approach the problem from a different direction with different classifications.

> Genius: someone who asks questions nobody else asks

Consider, for instance, the unique classifications of human beings invented by creative thinkers in the past. In the nineteenth century William James, an American psychologist and philosopher, classified people as 'tough-minded and tender-minded'. The Swiss psychiatrist Carl Jung invented the now common classification of people as 'introverts and extroverts'. Developments in psychology and behaviourism brought us 'convergent and divergent' thinkers. The point is that such new classifications, and the questions they evoke, can completely change our attitudes and thinking.

Combine them and you get structures for generating all sorts of unexpected, interesting ideas and ways of freeing us from routine, predictable responses. We can now talk about 'divergent introverts', 'divergent extroverts', 'convergent introverts', and 'convergent extroverts'; classifications that can help us explain all sorts of behaviour, which we would otherwise find difficult to explain.

Example: Hotel customers

Recently, researchers at Cornell University examined the attitudes of hotel customers. They broke them down into four research categories by combining four concepts: satisfied stayers; dissatisfied stayers; dissatisfied switchers; and satisfied switchers. Of course it would have been obvious to think about satisfied stayers and dissatisfied switchers, but without combining the concepts in this way it would have been difficult and counter-intuitive to think there may be dissatisfied stayers and, even more, satisfied switchers.

So, ask yourself what questions you routinely ask in your subject: write out a list. And be alert to every new question and classification you think might be useful and add it to your list.

Checklist of routine questions

1 Make a list.

2 Be alert to every new question and classification.

3 Add them to your list.

● Compiling a checklist

So what sort of questions should we expect to find on our checklist? Although the following are not subject-specific you will probably find some of your questions take a similar form.

1 What do we mean by X?
2 Why did that happen?
3 What is the connection between A and B?
4 How do we know that?
5 What evidence have we got for that claim? Is it reliable?
6 If that's the case, what follows?
7 How is it that A is the case when B is or is not the case? Is there an inconsistency?
8 What other examples are there for this sort of thing happening? Are there grounds here for a general rule?
9 What is the history, the background, to this?
10 Is it something unique, or has it developed out of something else?

As you think about your own checklist, it will probably help to keep in mind four useful rules:

1 Generate as many questions as possible.
2 Make them as clear and specific as you can.
3 Then pursue them as far as they will go.
4 If all this comes to nothing, ask another one.

Example: History

If you were studying history, among your routine questions you might have:

1 What was the cause of the event?
2 What was his motive?
3 Is there sufficient evidence to justify that explanation?
4 What were the effects?
  4.1 How large?
  4.2 How significant?
  4.3 Who was most affected: individuals, groups, social classes?
  4.4 What type of effects: economic, social, political, intellectual?
5 Who was involved: social classes, individuals, groups (religious, professional, military)?

Example: Philosophy

If you were studying philosophy, you might have:

1 What do we mean by that concept?
2 Can we deduce that conclusion from those premises?
3 Is there sufficient evidence to support that claim?
4 Does that claim contradict another?
5 Is that a relevant objection to that claim?

If you were studying literature, you would no doubt have questions about the possible influences on a writer's work, comparisons with other writers, and questions on plots, atmosphere and background, common themes, characters, style, dialogue, pace, suspense, humour, tragedy, and so on. The point is that for every subject there is a routine set of trigger questions that we use to generate and marshal our ideas – things we routinely look for.

If you were a history student and, as a result of the questions we asked in the last chapter about your interests, you came up with the general topic, 'The Scientific Revolution of the seventeenth century', you would have to ask yourself, 'What is it that interests me about it?' To answer this you would then work through each of the routine questions above, asking yourself what the causes were, what the motives were and so on. You might discover that it is the motives of those who were involved that most interests you, so you look for commonalities and you find that a very high proportion were Puritans. Now you have something that seems very interesting.

● The power of questions

If you doubt the power of these questions to generate a wealth of ideas to answer your question: 'What is it that most interests me about this?', consider the following. In *The Art of Clear Thinking*,[1] Rudolf Flesch reminds us of the extraordinary power of a popular 1950s TV game to negotiate, through a series of questions, the vast territory of possible answers to a problem and come up with the answer we're looking for.

The programme, known as 'Twenty Questions' or 'Animal, Vegetable, or Mineral', would set four panellists a problem. To find the answer they would be given between them 20 questions, which could only be answered by 'yes' or 'no'. In most cases, in a surprisingly short time, the answer would be found by a series of well-crafted questions. Why is this so extraordinary? Well, as Flesch reminds us, asked by a perfect player these 20 questions would cover a range of 1,048,576 possible solutions. In other words, in the space of five minutes, the time taken to ask and answer 20 questions, you can narrow it down to one answer in a million.

> Using a set of routine questions you can find that 'one in a million' original idea.

Moreover, this is not just the stuff of TV games. Prior to the computer age, police sketch artists would use the 'Identikit' system to help witnesses put together a likeness of a suspect. The face would be divided up into, say, 10 building blocks: the hairline, forehead, eyes, nose and so on down to the chin. Each would be represented on transparent strips with a variety of options to choose from. Let's say there were 10 hairlines, 10 foreheads, 10 eyes and so on, amounting to a total of 100 transparent slips. Using this it would be possible to create 10 billion different faces, out of which the witness could quickly produce a very close likeness of the suspect. So here you have a problem with 10 billion possible solutions, yet using this simple system, composed of a routine set of questions, it is possible to arrive at a solution in no time at all.

● Exploring different perspectives on different levels

Different perspectives

The reason this works is that we routinely remind ourselves to ask questions that we might otherwise forget or assume are irrelevant. As we've said, original thinkers invent new questions to open up new perspectives others have not seen. Likewise, we need a method that gets us to think outside our own limited perspective to ask questions we might otherwise dismiss as irrelevant and unthinkable. In the Cornell research it was counter-intuitive and unthinkable to believe there are actually such people as 'dissatisfied stayers' and 'satisfied switchers', who would do something against their interests. Not until we change perspectives are we likely to think the unthinkable and consider the counter-intuitive.

Different levels

In certain subjects, of course, like history, moral philosophy, social work, nursing, indeed all the caring professions, you learn to do this: you place yourself in someone else's position and vicariously experience their feelings, anxieties, hopes, and so on.

Example: The Industrial Revolution

If you had listed the Industrial Revolution as the subject you're most interested in, you would place yourself imaginatively into the situation faced by those historical agents who were affected by and could affect events: farmers, merchants, industrialists, politicians, labourers, and so on. And then you would consider their situation and responses to events not just on the level of individuals with their particular self-interests, but in terms of how these events affect society (the cultural, political and economic effects) and the physical conditions of life (material needs – food and shelter – transport, climate, and so on).

But no matter what you're studying you, too, can do this routinely. After you've answered all your trigger questions, do two things:

1 Examine your topic from the perspective of all those involved.
2 As you do this, think about each one on different levels:
    2.1   physical (material needs, transport, climate, etc.);
    2.2   individual (biological, psychological, moral, intellectual);
    2.3   social (cultural, political, economic).

Levels	
Physical	1 Material needs
	2 Transport
	3 Climate, etc.
Individual	1 Biological
	2 Psychological
	3 Moral
	4 Intellectual
Social	1 Cultural
	2 Political
	3 Economic

Of course, not all these levels will be relevant for each perspective and for every topic, but a routine that gets us to explore them before we reject an idea makes it less likely that we will miss the sort of idea that the Cornell researchers found so useful. In the case of the Industrial Revolution, the moment you begin to think from the perspective of farmers on the physical level of material needs you might find that what really interests you is how improvements in transport affected market gardeners in your own local area. Now you have a fascinating and original topic to research.

● Exploratory reading

Asking yourself these questions will have helped you narrow the topic down, and the narrower and more specific it is, the better.

Example: The Industrial Revolution

You're no longer just interested in the Industrial Revolution, or the effects of it, or even, say, the effects of agricultural change on it, but the effects of improvements in transport in, say, the 1840s on market gardeners in your area.

Example: Nursing

Similarly, you're no longer just interested in the work of dialysis units, but in how limited medical resources are used to meet the needs of patients.

You should now have three or four of these topics and within each one a number of questions you want to answer; issues you want to explore.

Example: Dialysis units

In the work of dialysis units you want to know:

1 how patients are selected;
2 on what criteria they are chosen;
3 how they are cared for once selected.

The clearer you can make these sub-questions or sub-issues the better. Then you can see how they combine and reinforce each other, or how some are irrelevant to the overall question or issue you want to investigate.

But before you go on in the next chapter to see how these ideas combine and interrelate, you'll find it helpful to do some exploratory reading on the three or four topics that look promising. Do a literature search and skim the contents of the titles you come up with to see if there might be a chapter that deals with your particular topic or a research paper in which the author has done something similar. Some sources will give you direct relevant information on each topic; others will help you generate fresh ideas of your own. You're not reading in any great depth; just seeing what approach has been adopted by other researchers studying similar topics.

Skim for a chapter on your topic or a paper that does something similar.

If you're studying subjects that are likely to call for empirical research, like sociology, criminology and anthropology, it's important to get some familiarity with the evidence that already exists on your topics. If yours are humanities topics, then, similarly, it helps to be clear about what has already been written and what approach has been taken. This will help you refine your topic and give it sharper focus. But don't go too far. At this stage you're only tentatively exploring the feasibility of your idea; how you might organise it to ensure it is meaningful and significant, while at the same time manageable.

Summary

1 Formulate a checklist of routine questions you can use to generate your own original ideas.

2 Think about your ideas from the different perspectives of those involved and on different levels.

3 Do some exploratory reading on your possible topics to see what other ideas and information are out there.

 What next?

In the following chapters, we will structure these ideas into patterns and hierarchies to reveal their interconnections. That way we will have a clearer idea of how our ideas are organised and what is likely to be relevant and worthwhile pursuing. Then, with this structure in front of us, we will design the best question or hypothesis to pursue in our research.

Note

1   Rudolf Flesch, *The Art of Clear Thinking* (New York: Harper & Row, 1951), p. 121.

7 Developing your ideas 1: Causal relations

In this chapter you will learn . . .

1 about the importance of revealing the structure into which your ideas are organised;
2 that the two most effective ways of doing this are through causal and conceptual analysis;
3 the various ways of reproducing this in your notes;
4 how to use these to reveal the hypothesis or research question that will drive your work.

At its simplest, thinking involves memory. Beyond that, it is all about creating relations between ideas. On their own, ideas have little value or significance; it is only when we make connections with other ideas that they become useful. Although the sentence, 'The object in front of me is red', makes sense, it has very limited value or significance. But connect it with other ideas, like 'The object is a person' and 'The red is blood', and it becomes altogether more significant. So it follows that the quality of our thinking is determined by the importance of the relations we find and the connections we make. Now that we've generated our ideas, we must look at their relations, mapping them out in simple patterns or structures.

● The structure of our ideas

Much of our thinking is done in structures. They help us interpret experience, so we can reduce our confusion to manageable levels and predict what is likely to happen if we choose one thing rather than another.

Example: Consumers

As consumers we are presented with such a bewildering range of choices that we cannot hope to evaluate each one before we decide. Instead, we take short-cuts: we form patterns into which we organise information, beliefs, preferences and judgements, which then act as standard operating procedures to guide us routinely as we make these decisions.

But the problem is that the most familiar patterns are not always the most useful. And in most cases we're not likely to be aware of this. Once we've formed them we tend not to second guess them. To do so would be to sabotage them. We choose what we have become used to choosing because it is easier to navigate the immense space of possibilities that way. In the 1950s research into cognitive dissonance found that consumers would continue to read advertisements for a new car after they had bought it, but would avoid information about other brands, fearing post-purchase misgivings.

So, now that we've generated our ideas, we need to bring to the surface the patterns into which we've organised them. We can then test and develop them to create a structure that reflects a more complete and nuanced understanding of the topic. This, in turn, will give us a better working hypothesis or research question.

These structures take familiar forms. The traditional linear notes we all use in note-taking are good at reproducing hierarchies of ideas in which a few main points are broken down into subpoints, and these into sub-subpoints, by steps in the notes from the side of the page to indicate the next level of the hierarchy.

If the structure indicates the analysis of a concept or argument, pattern notes are normally the best way of representing this, as we will see in the next chapter. The concept, or a sentence representing the argument, is placed at the centre of the page and lines are drawn radiating out from it to indicate each part of the analysis. If it indicates causal relationships between the different ideas, you can use one of the many forms of flow chart. Although often used to represent a sequence of operations to be carried out, as in a computer program or in an industrial process, you can adapt it for your own purposes as you can see on page 60.

● The problem's the problem

Whichever method we use to map out the structure, the important thing is to have a detailed understanding of all the ideas and their interrelations that make up the topic. It's often said that the problem's the problem: if we can just sort out our thinking about the actual problem we're interested in, all the rest will fall into place. If we fail to make the structure clear from the start,

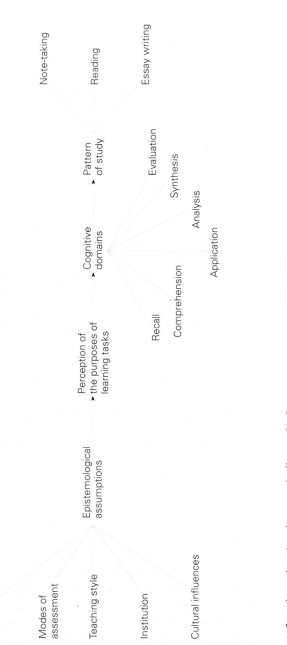

A flowchart showing the causal effects of influences on our perception of the purposes of learning tasks and the consequent impact this has on the way we organise our pattern of study and use our study skills.

either we'll struggle to get started, or we'll make a start only to find we have to rethink it all because there's not enough there, or we haven't seen just how vast it all is.

Equally important, knowing this structure helps us chart the project out: we can visualise it all. It's all there in front of us, so we can then begin to challenge and manipulate it, as we'll see in Chapter 10. By rearranging and reinterpreting the structure, we can pose 'What if' questions until we find the hypothesis or general question we want to explore, which will drive our research.

● Structuring our ideas

Like most of our thinking skills this seems difficult and complex, yet we do it a lot of the time. Structures are not only the scaffolding of our understanding, but they also lie at the heart of wit and humour, and we cannot tackle a cross-word puzzle without recognising, comparing and manipulating them. A typical cryptic clue might be split in two with both parts leading to the same word. As you compare the structure of ideas represented by both words your aim is to find a similarity, which points to the answer. The clue might be 'Savings book (7)' and the answer is, of course, 'Reserve'. Your savings are a reserve and you can book or reserve a table in a restaurant or a seat on a train.[1]

As for wit and humour, Sir Peter Medawar, in his book *Induction and Intuition in Scientific Thought*, gives us this one. He explains:

> The Rev. Sydney Smith, a famous wit, was walking with a friend through the extremely narrow streets of old Edinburgh when they heard a furious altercation between two housewives from high-up windows across the street. 'They can never agree,' said Smith to his companion, 'for they are arguing from different premises.'[2]

As he points out later, in this and similar examples there is a real or apparent structural similarity between two or more schemes of ideas and it is this that makes it witty. We instantly recognise that the word 'premises' can be used in two ways.

More significant, when this similarity is real we experience those wonderfully insightful moments of sudden clarity, when we see for the first time a connection between two structures of ideas. A teacher might give you an analogy, which suddenly makes a difficult subject clear for the first time. This sudden insight and the clarity it brings comes from instantly apprehending the structural similarity between the two sets of ideas: the subject and the analogy.

> Insight is the sudden recognition of the structural similarity between two sets of ideas.

To make sense of isolated facts and ideas, then, we must reveal the connections between them and map out their interrelations. The two most effective means of doing this are by analysing the causal and conceptual relations between ideas.

Structuring ideas
1 Find causal relations
2 Analyse concepts

● Causal relations

Discovering causal relations

Unfortunately, unlike the natural sciences, in many subjects it is not always so easy to identify the pattern of causal relations. In the natural sciences, experiments can be repeated independently by other researchers and, where the results are the same, we can feel confident we've found it. But in subjects, like history, the social sciences and the professions, this is simply not possible.

With social phenomena it is rare to find repeated events that are sufficiently similar and even more difficult to set up experiments as in the natural sciences. Even if we could resolve the many ethical problems involved in experimenting on individuals and social groups, to repeat the experiment it is more difficult to find a suitable fresh supply of subjects who are sufficiently similar in relevant respects to the first. What's more, once we have introduced changes in a social system to see the results, they may be irreversible, making it impossible to repeat the test, because the initial conditions of the second test will be different from those of the first.

Example: Opinion polls
By asking particular questions political pollsters can set the political agenda in the minds of their respondents. These become the burning issues of the day, about which they now have a clear vision.

Moreover, beyond the natural sciences there is a paucity of universal laws, which would provide the predictability necessary for conducting decisive experiments. And even if social scientists had the means of repeating experiments and the universal laws necessary for predictions, they still cannot so easily modify and control all the variables necessary to conduct controlled experiments.

- Subjects are not sufficiently similar.
- Once changes are introduced they may be irreversible.
- Paucity of universal laws.
- Control of the variables.

So, if controlled experiments are not possible or, as in history, we are examining unique historical events that cannot be repeated, like the rise of modern capitalism or of a particular social class, we must turn to alternative strategies to identify the pattern of causal relations.

Lay out a complete account

The first thing to do is lay out as complete an account as you can of the key ideas and facts as you see them. Often we take it for granted that we are aware of everything, so we see no point in doing this. As a result, we not only miss obvious things, but we fail to register the most interesting questions we could ask or hypotheses we could test.

So try to be naïve, take nothing for granted, and set down all you know. Often you will see for the first time interpretations you've never considered. Things will simply jump out at you because they are no longer obscured by the veil of your routine thinking. Along with the ideas and their interrelations, you will see ways in which you could manipulate the structure so you can pose 'What if' questions that might form the basis of interesting and original hypotheses or research questions.

Convergences and divergences

However, if nothing suggests itself as a possible hypothesis or question you want to pursue, you will have to take more deliberate steps to interpret the structure.

Interpreting the structure
1 Convergence
2 Divergence

Say you're interested in the causes of the French Revolution. This may have produced a structure something like the following, although probably a lot more detailed than I can give here.

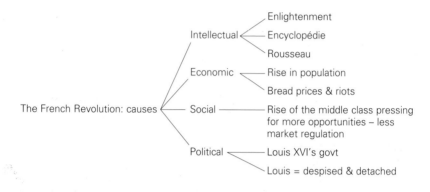

Convergences

The first thing to do is try to identify all those things that converge with each other. Some will *reinforce* each other: they will act in similar ways, perhaps providing the evidence that supports a particular interpretation.

Example: The French Revolution

You will have found that there are a number of different causes – intellectual, economic, social and political – all reinforcing each other in bringing about the Revolution.

Others may *complement* each other: you may find that if *A* is to be true, there must also be *B* – one cannot be present without the other. Alternatively, you may find that in the relationship between two elements one is *supplementary* to another.

Example: The French Revolution

As you generated ideas about the causes you may have listed among the economic causes the pressure exerted on economic resources by the doubling of the population in the 80 years leading up to the Revolution in 1789, and you may also have listed the rise in bread prices as an economic cause. But now, as you develop your structure, you realise that the latter is supplementary to the former: that the increase in bread prices was due in part to the rise in population.

Convergence
1 Reinforcing
2 Complementary
3 Supplementary

Divergences

Even more useful are divergences in suggesting the sort of question you might want to investigate or hypothesis you might want to test.

Example: Study skills

You may be interested in finding a solution to why it is that so many students have problems with study skills. You may have mapped out a structure which suggests a pattern of causes and a likely solution that lies in more study skills courses. But, as part of this process of listing and structuring all you know, you may have already found that many of those who attend such courses still retain the same problems afterwards. This gives you an interesting problem to research.

Summary

1   Much of our thinking is done in structures of interrelated ideas.

2   We need to bring to the surface the structure into which the ideas we have generated are organised.

3   Then we can test and develop them to find a working hypothesis or research question.

4   Mapping out the relations between our ideas is best done by analysing their causal or conceptual relations.

5   One way of mapping out their causal relations is to search for convergences and divergences.

● What next

The alternative way of mapping out the structure of our ideas is by analysing their conceptual relations. In the next chapter we will learn a simple method of doing this.

● Notes

1   This example is from the Guardian Unlimited crossword page, which you can find at www.guardian.co.uk/crossword

2   P. B. Medawar, *Induction and Intuition in Scientific Thought* (London: Methuen, 1969), p. 48.

8 Developing your ideas 2: Conceptual relations

In this chapter you will learn . . .

1 the importance of analysing concepts to original research;
2 a simple three-step technique for analysing concepts;
3 that by analysing them we reveal the subproblems and questions which lie at the heart of our research;
4 how these drive our research by spelling out clearly what these abstract terms mean and how we will recognise them in our research.

The other way of revealing the structure of interrelations between our ideas is conceptual analysis. Indeed, any attempt to map out the organisation of our ideas will almost always involve analysing the concepts we use to express them. Analyse any concept and you will see a structure appearing.

● What is a concept?

A concept is a general classification of particular things. When we conceptualise from our experience we abstract the general concept or principle from the particular concrete experience. Underlying these concepts or general classifications are patterns, through which we group and organise experience, and which allow us to see things in a particular way. The philosopher Bertrand Russell explains: 'Awareness of universals is called *conceiving*, and a universal of which we are aware is called a *concept*.'[1]

● Their effects on our thinking

The important thing about thinking conceptually is that it allows us to think imaginatively about all the possibilities; not just about what is at present a fact, but about how things might or should be. When we think conceptually we abstract the general concept or principle, which applies to all circumstances (past, present and future), and divorce it from the concrete circumstances embedded in the present. By abstracting the universal from the particular we reveal a general pattern through which we can predict the likely effects of doing one thing rather than another. We create patterns that map out the environment, helping us predict what is likely to happen when we act.

Example: Forming a concept

In a chilling scene at the start of Stanley Kubrick's 1968 Oscar-winning film *2001: A Space Odyssey* an ape picks up a bone from the bleached skeleton of an animal and strikes the skull, smashing it into pieces. Then, in the moments that follow, quiet and motionless, with the bone held in both hands high above his head, he forms a concept. This is no longer just a bone to smash this bleached skull before him, but a 'weapon' to strike all the skulls of all his enemies.

But while they liberate us from the tyranny of an uncertain future, concepts can also trap us in the comfortable predictability of routine thinking. They can influence our behaviour quite independently of our rational evaluation by setting off a train of thought which we follow routinely. When we use them they allow us to see things in a particular way. We interpret experience, organise it and advocate a certain type of action as a result. The basis of a concept is a readiness to respond in certain ways rather than others. It is this that makes it so important that we analyse them so that we know, when we use them, which way they are pushing our thinking.

> Make sure . . .
> you analyse the concepts you use, so you control them, rather than the reverse.

● Original research comes from redesigning concepts

Once we've revealed the structure, we can then manipulate it and form new ones, as we saw with humour, wit and the answers in crossword puzzles. Many of the most significant breakthroughs in our understanding have come about not because researchers have new or better data, but because of the quality of their thinking and the type of concepts they create. In many cases, when researchers have been faced with obdurate problems that defy solution, the answers have only finally come as a result of being able to think outside the accepted concepts and methods of their disciplines.

We like to think that most of our solutions come through a straightforward process of logical reasoning. But this is the way the story of discovery is told, rather than how it actually happens. For this we first need the ability to analyse concepts and, out of them, create new patterns, through which we look at the world and organise our information about it.

> Think about this . . .
> Original ideas come from stepping outside our concepts and the routine thinking they dictate.

The problem we all face is that it just seems a rather unnecessary thing to do. It seems obvious: we all know what's meant by words, like 'needs', 'poverty' and 'tragedy'. So we have to learn to ask that characteristically philosophical question, 'Yes, but what do we mean by *X*?', particularly when the meaning seems obvious to everyone. In a probing, self-reflective way we are questioning our own use of these quite ordinary words, which we can no longer take for granted.

● Open and closed concepts

The first step is to realise that words have more than one meaning, depending on the context and purpose for which they are used. They have no meaning in their own right. So, we are concerned about their actual and possible uses. If we were to look up their meaning in a dictionary, we would find just somebody's picture of what they mean in a particular context, or a mere snapshot, a still in the moving reel of images, which records how the concept has changed and is still changing. Our task, therefore, in analysing a concept is to map out all the different ways in which it is used.

Meaning depends on ⟨ Context / Purpose

Closed concept

Even so, with some concepts this task is, indeed, as straightforward as looking up the word in a dictionary. These are what you might describe as 'closed concepts'. They usually have an unchanging, unambiguous meaning. Words like 'bicycle', 'bachelor' and 'triangle' each have a structure to their meaning, which is bound by logical necessity. We all agree to abide by certain conventions that rule the meaning of these words. So, if you were to say, 'This bicycle has one wheel' or 'This triangle has four sides', no-one would be in any doubt that you had made a logical mistake. When we use them according to their conventions we are, in effect, allowing our understanding of the world to be structured in a particular way.

> Closed concept . . .
>   . . . structure is bound by logical necessity

Open concept

But with 'open concepts' it's the reverse: our experience of the world shapes our concepts. Their meaning is not governed by a complex set of formal rules, like closed concepts, so they cannot be pinned down just by looking them up in a dictionary. Their meaning responds to and reflects our changing experience: they change through time and from one culture to another.

Example: Poverty

In some cultures and at some times poverty means having no means of sustenance or permanent shelter from the elements; whereas in Western developed economies today we might argue that it is being without a colour TV, a refrigerator, or even a second car.

● Developing conceptual skills – the three-step technique

So our task is to develop the skills necessary to analyse the open concepts we use. In what follows you'll learn a simple three-step technique, which you can use routinely. As you work through it, think about the concepts you come across in your own subject, concepts like 'bribes', 'authority', 'privacy', 'needs', and 'tragedy', and ask yourself 'What do we mean by this?'

Step 1: Gather your typical examples

First, spend some time gathering the evidence: say, five or six examples of the way you use the concept in your everyday life. Try to make them as different as possible. In this way you'll be able to strip away their differences to reveal more clearly their essential similarities.

Example: Revolution

If you are a historian or social scientist, you may find yourself using the concept 'revolution' in your work. So you will need to know what we mean by this and how it can be distinguished from a revolt, a rebellion or a coup d'état. The first step is to assemble examples of revolutions that are as different as possible from each other, like the French Revolution (1789), the Russian Revolution (1917), the English Revolution (1649), the Portuguese 'Carnation' Revolution (1974), the Hungarian Revolution (1956), the Industrial Revolution, even the Computer Revolution. Then you will need to think about rebellions and revolts, like Jack Cade's Rebellion (1450) and the Peasants' Revolt (1381).

1   How do I use the concept?

If you find it difficult to come up with examples, start by asking yourself three questions. First, 'How do I use the concept – do I use it in more than one way?' If you find you do, then you have a structure emerging: each way needs to be explored and its implications unwrapped. The prepositions we use with concepts are in many cases a very useful indicator of different meanings. For example, we use the concept of 'authority' in two different ways when we say that someone is 'an' authority and when we say they are 'in' authority.

The same can be said about the concept of 'freedom'. We tend to talk about being free *from* things, like repression, constraints, and restrictions of one form or another. I might say with some relief that I am finally free from pain, having taken tablets for pain relief, or that a political prisoner has at last been freed from imprisonment. In both cases we're using the word in a negative way, in that something is being taken away, the pain or the imprisonment.

But we also use the word in what we might describe as a positive way. In this sense the preposition changes from being free *from* something to being free *to do* something. We may say that, because a friend has unexpectedly won a large amount of money, she is now free to do what she has always wanted to do – to go back to college, or to buy her own home. Governments, too, use the concept in this way, arguing that the money they are investing in education will free more people to get better, more satisfying jobs and to fulfil more of their dreams.

2   What sort of thing am I referring to?

If this doesn't help, ask yourself a second question: 'What sort of thing am I referring to when I use the concept?' This means recalling simple everyday situations in which you might find yourself talking about, say, 'authority', even if you don't actually use the word. When you use the word 'bribe', what sort of thing are you referring to?

3　How does it differ from similar things?

To help you with this question it's often useful to ask a third: how does it differ from similar things? When I use the word 'bribe', how does it differ from other things, like commissions, gifts, tips and incentive bonuses? When I use the word 'authority', how does it differ from things like power, force, legitimacy and influence?

Questions
1 How do I use the concept – do I use it in more than one way?
2 What sort of thing am I referring to?
3 How does it differ from similar things?

Step 2: Analyse your examples

Now, using these examples, create your concept: use your conceptual skills to abstract the general from the concrete. In other words, identify the common characteristics in each of your examples, isolating them so that you can then put them together to form the concept. This is one of those things we all know how to do, but most of us would be hard pressed to explain just how we do it.

In effect, it's simple pattern recognition. By recognising the common pattern of characteristics that each example possesses, we visualise what the concept might look like that underlies all the examples. Sometimes you may find you have, say, seven examples, four of which have the same core characteristics, while the other three fail to match them in all respects. That's OK; in these cases you need to corral the four similar examples, using these to create your concept, and then use the remaining three to test it.

Creating your concept – pattern recognition:
1 Identify the common characteristics in your examples.
2 Isolate them and put them together to form the concept.

Example: Revolution

You can see this in the notes on p. 74. In the examples we listed above, the Hungarian, Russian, French and English revolutions all have core characteristics not shared by the others. They involved more than just a change within the leadership or the elite ruling group: they involved deep-seated social change. The scale of each was similar in so far as they involved all of society, geographically and socially. They also involved the concerted use of force and violence to overthrow the established government, unlike the Carnation Revolution and the Industrial and Computer revolutions, which were all largely peaceful.

The pace of change, too, was sudden, a matter of days in some cases, weeks or months in others, unlike the Industrial Revolution, the first phase of which lasted from 1760 to 1850. They also involved ideas, unlike, say, a population revolution or similar economic revolutions, which involve general social and economic trends. Finally they all involved radical change in our values and the way we think about rights, freedom and the way we are governed. So, with these six elements we have a concept: a pattern of ideas, which we can now test.

Step 3: Test your concept

In most cases you will find you have the overall structure right, but there may be details that are wrong or subtle distinctions you haven't seen. So, by testing your concept you will identify those characteristics that are essential, while you ditch those that are only accidental to it. In the process you will sharpen your understanding of the core characteristics.

To test it in this way you need only take some simple, but quite deliberate steps. Our aim is to set up mental experiments to test our concept first against those examples that are borderline cases of it, then against those that are contrasting cases and, finally, against those that are doubtful cases. At each stage we will refine it until we have it right.

1   Borderline cases

First, with your structure in front of you try to think of a borderline case, an example of your concept that doesn't fit comfortably within your structure. It may lack features that are in your structure, or have other features that are absent from it. Then analyse its characteristics to see if, in fact, it does fit after all. You may find there's more to this form of the concept than you first thought and it does, in fact, fit within the structure. Alternatively, after think-ing through all the possibilities, it may become clear that it doesn't fit and you will have to adjust your structure to take account of it.

Revolution

English Rev. 1649/French Rev. 1789

Russian Rev. 1917/Hungarian Rev. 1956

Why 'revolutions' and not just 'revolts' or 'rebellions' like Jack Cade's Rebellion 1450 or Peasants' Revolt 1381?

Radical/novel change
- in ideas/values in the way we think about rights, freedoms and the way we're governed
  - rights
  - idea of freedom

Involves ideas
- Couldn't describe a rapid increase in population as a 'Population Revolution'
  - even though the change in society is thorough and radical

Pace of change
- Sudden change
  - days, weeks, months
  - e.g. Russia 1905
    = just a failed attempt at revolution
    ≠ part of Russian Revolution 1917

Force/violence
- Organisation and gathering of sizeable numbers to overthrow the established government
  - ≠ just a coup d'etat of forces led by different faction of the elite

Scale
- Involves all society
  - Geographically and socially

Not just a change within leadership/elite group
- Different class or elite group
- Different system of government
  - English — Republic for monarchy
  - Russian — Socialist for feudal
  - French — Liberal/capitalist for semi-feudal
  - Hungarian — Capitalist for socialist

Reflects deep-seated social change

Example: Revolution

The Portuguese Revolution seems to match every characteristic except that it didn't involve force and violence. But it did involve the 'threat' of force, so we will have to decide if this is enough to qualify it as an example of a revolution. If it isn't, then we must call it something else. If it is, then we have to decide whether we need to change this core characteristic to read something like 'the actual or threat of force and violence', or just drop this characteristic entirely from the structure of our concept.

2 Contrasting cases

Either way, we will have confirmed important parts of our structure. As a result you will probably feel more confident that you have now got it just about right. So it's time to put this confidence to the sternest test you can find, this time by imagining an example that presents a clear contrast to your concept. Think of the strongest example you can find that clearly doesn't fit within the structure of your concept. The best examples fail to share one or more of the core characteristics of your structure. Again, test your structure against this example to see if you need to make any adjustments to the components and the way they interrelate.

Example: Revolution

The Industrial Revolution doesn't seem to possess two of the six characteristics in our structure: the pace of change and the concerted use of force and violence. However, the more you look at the Industrial Revolution the more you see how force, and sometimes violence, were used to take land, as in the enclosure movement, and rights, like the freedom to belong to a trade union.

If this is enough to satisfy this characteristic, we are then left with just one characteristic that seems not to fit: the pace of change. Here either we have to decide that the Industrial Revolution is simply a case of rapid 'evolution', or we have to modify our structure to take account of the Industrial Revolution by dropping the pace of change from our structure.

Once you have done this you will find that you have sharpened up your concept considerably. You will have identified one or more core characteristics that might not have been sufficiently clear in your original analysis.

3   Doubtful cases

Both of these tests will probably have brought you to a point where you now know the core characteristics of your concept and the structure that defines their interrelations. If you are not this certain, you will have to test it with one or more additional contrasting examples, but it will rarely take more than this. In most cases you will have identified the core characteristics fairly clearly by now.

If this is the case, it's time to move to the next stage and test the consequences of adopting these as your core characteristics. We need to imagine cases in which it would be difficult for you to accept these consequences. Either these are not, after all, examples of the concept, or we have missed something.

Unlike the previous stages, in this one we are neither identifying core characteristics, nor finding others that we need to ditch because they are merely accidental to the concept. We have our core characteristics now, and their interrelations that define the concept. In this stage we are refining the distinctions that were in our original analysis, so we get a clearer, sharper understanding of the core characteristics and their interrelations. As a result we inject more subtle shades of meaning into our distinctions.

Example: Revolution

The clearest example of a doubtful case seems to be the 'Computer Revolution'. It appears to be quite different from all the other examples in that it struggles to make a compelling case in most of our core characteristics. In particular, it appears not to involve any overthrow of government, or the use or threat of force and violence.

Even so, it could be said to elevate a new class of technocrats to positions of greater influence, while bringing systems into government that make it much more certain that information will indeed bring power to those that possess it. And, of course, by disseminating that information more widely through computer technology and the Internet it can be regarded as a powerful agent bringing about more democratic government. You will have to decide whether you think this alone merits the description of it as a 'revolution', or whether we are simply wrong in describing it as such.

As you can see, as we have worked our way through each of these stages we have deliberately asked awkward questions to test and refine the distinctions we made in our original analysis. In the table on page 77 you can see each stage clearly set out, so you can use it step by step.

Structure	The three-step technique
Activity	**Objective**
Step 1: Examples	
List five or six of the most typical examples that are as different as possible.	To get material that will illustrate similarities and differences.
Step 2: Analyse	
Pattern recognition – identify the common characteristics and their interrelations.	To form the hypothesis: the prototype concept.
Step 3: Testing	
1 Borderline cases	
Compare our concept with an example that either lacks features that are in our structure, or has others that are absent from it.	To identify all those features in our structure that are merely accidental.
2 Contrasting cases	
Compare our concept with an example that doesn't share one or more of the core characteristics of our structure.	To identify the core characteristics and their interrelations.
3 Doubtful cases	
Test the core characteristics by examining a case in which it would be difficult to accept their consequences.	To refine the distinctions in our analysis to get a clearer, sharper understanding of the core characteristics and their interrelations.

● Concepts and research

Most research goes from the general to the specific: from the abstract to the concrete. This is the way we develop our explanations of the world: the reverse is the way we come to understand it. Most research questions involve concepts, which we can easily take for granted, even though at the heart of them lie the really interesting issues, questions and insights.

By analysing them, we not only bring structure to our work, enabling us to break it down into manageable tasks and questions, but, more importantly, we give our research that essential layer of subproblems and questions, which are really the interesting heart of the problem. It gives us the mechanism that will drive our research by spelling out clearly what these abstract terms mean, what their implications are and how we will recognise them in our research.

> **Analysing concepts gives our work . . .**
>
> **1** Structure – manageable tasks and questions
>
> **2** A layer of subproblems and questions – the mechanism that will drive our research

In this chapter we have seen how we break abstract concepts down into their component ideas. Later in this book, as we set about our research, we will see how we move from this stage to find answers to these subproblems and questions by using these ideas as indicators of the extent to which we can find actual evidence of these concepts in our research.

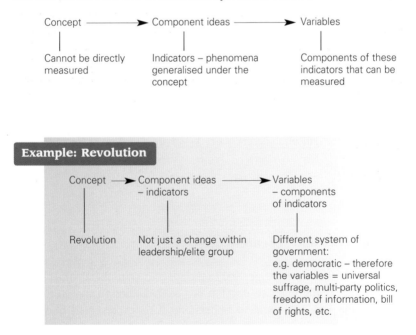

Concept ⟶ Component ideas ⟶ Variables

Cannot be directly measured

Indicators – phenomena generalised under the concept

Components of these indicators that can be measured

Example: Revolution

Concept ⟶ Component ideas – indicators ⟶ Variables – components of indicators

Revolution

Not just a change within leadership/elite group

Different system of government:
e.g. democratic – therefore the variables = universal suffrage, multi-party politics, freedom of information, bill of rights, etc.

Summary

1 Underlying our concepts are structures that organise our thinking.

2 We have to analyse these to ensure *we,* rather than the concepts, control our thinking.

3 Original ideas come from redesigning our concepts.

4 The structure will drive our research by spelling out what the abstract concepts mean, their implications and how we are to recognise them.

● What next?

Now that we have the structure of our ideas clear, we must challenge and manipulate it to generate a series of 'What if' questions, until we find the hypothesis or general question we want to explore in our research. In its conditional form with its antecedent ('What if') and consequent ('then perhaps *B*, *C*, and *D*') it will give us a set of expectations which we can then pursue or test in our research. In the next chapter we will learn a simple, routine method of doing this.

● Note

1 Bertrand Russell, *The Problems of Philosophy* (1912; Oxford: Oxford University Press, 1986), p. 28.

9 Original questions and hypotheses 1: Using analogies

In this chapter you will learn . . .

1 how to become a better thinker;
2 how to conduct mental experiments by empathising with others;
3 how to pose 'What if' questions by detaching yourself from your routine patterns of thought;
4 how to search for analogies and test them for their reliability.

In the Introduction we said that your dissertation may be the first time you've been asked to do some genuine thinking. As you write about your ideas, both you and the examiner can see *how* you think, not just *what* you think. In the process, you will learn to become a genuine thinker, reflecting upon your thinking as you think.

● Good thinkers

Good thinkers can do two things when they approach a problem. First they can detach their minds from routine patterns of thought and apply seemingly unrelated mental frameworks to the problem. In this way they liberate their minds from the narrow grooves in which they might otherwise be trapped, allowing them to scan a wide range of possible mental patterns. Secondly, they can forget about themselves in their thinking. They realise they must forget about what they might wish will be the case in any situation, before they can see what the situation itself requires.

Good thinkers
1 Detach their minds from routine patterns.
2 Forget about themselves.

Both of these transitions in our thinking have resulted in some of the most significant moments in the development of thought, when thinkers actually see for the first time the solutions to problems that have evaded their grasp despite their most determined efforts. Freed from their own routine patterns of thought and from what they might wish to be the answer, they see solutions with the sort of sudden clarity that leaves them wondering why they hadn't seen it before.

As we found in the last chapter, these routine patterns of thought, with which our minds are programmed, may not always be the most useful. We see what we want to see: how we've always seen things and how we think things *should* be, not as they *are*. The mind reshapes and 'corrects' our experience. Read the following passage and see how well you understand it, even though the words in it appear to be largely unrecognisable.

> Aoccdrnig to rseearch at an Elingsh uinervtisy, it deosn't mttaer in waht oredr the ltteers in a wrod are, the olny iprmoatnt tihng is taht the frist and lsat ltteers are in the rghit pclae. The rset can be a toatl mses and you can sitll raed it wouthit porbelm. Tihs is bcuseae we do not raed ervey lteter by itslef but the wrod as a wlohe.

In this case it helps us understand the passage, but it can also limit our capacity to think creatively outside our normal assumptions. Even in science, where you might think new ideas are cherished as the stuff of progress, there is still resistance to theories that challenge the way we are used to thinking. From Semmelweis to Einstein, plate tectonics to quantum theory, the history of modern science is littered with stories of resistance, revolution and the struggle to overthrow theories.

● Learning to become a good thinker

So, how can we learn to do these two things that good thinkers do?

Forgetting about ourselves

First, we need to get into the habit of empathising with others, vicariously experiencing what others in a particular situation might feel, believe or prefer. Conducting this sort of mental experiment must become routine. In Chapter 6 we saw the importance of this in generating our ideas by thinking through a problem from different perspectives on different levels. Now, as we begin to change and work with the structures through which we routinely organise these ideas, it is even more important.

Those who are curious about the lives and experiences of others are more effective at trading places and conducting these mental experiments in which they ask themselves what they would do or feel in similar situations.

They hypothesise more, experience more things, albeit vicariously, and develop the capacity to create more structures through which to process and understand these things.

Good thinking

1 Routinely empathise with others.

2 Suspend judgement and ask 'What if' questions.

Detaching our minds from routine patterns

Second, we need to detach ourselves from our routine patterns of thought and develop the habit of asking 'conditionals': the type of question we all pose when we suspend our judgement and ask, 'What if . . .'. Historians open up areas for investigation by asking counterfactual conditionals, where they ask what would have happened if something that did happen had not in fact happened. They might ask, 'What if the Napoleonic Wars had never happened? Would the Industrial Revolution have developed differently?' From this they might hypothesise, 'If the Napoleonic Wars had not occurred, then the British economy would not have been so dominated by heavy industry.' Scientists, too, in addition to counterfactuals, use subjunctive conditionals to set up experiments: the type of hypothesis that suggests 'If A should occur, then so would B.'

Example: Smoking in public places

Let's say your interest has been aroused by an article you have read about an official report showing a 15 per cent decrease in turnover; for pubs and restaurants since the government's ban on smoking in public places.

What if . . .
. . . you did your own study in your local area and found that there was no decrease in turnover, in fact there was a significant increase? What then? How do you explain it?

Example: Study skills

Despite the customary explanation that students have poor study skills because they haven't been taught how to use them, there may be anecdotal evidence that study skills courses still leave students with the same problems.

What if . . .
. . . students still have problems after taking courses? How do we explain it?

Example: The French Revolution

One explanation for the French Revolution is that it was a bourgeois revolution, driven by middle-class values and a capitalist-orientated middle class. They were increasingly aware that their path to greater social influence and prestige was blocked by a decaying class of parasitic, hereditary, noble landowners and by a monarchy committed to antiquated aristocratic values that denied them opportunities. The resulting conflict and revolution brought about the emergence of a capitalist economy and a class society.

But what if . . .
. . . they weren't this capitalist class with capitalist values? What then?

In each of these cases you have a 'What if' question and an explanation to research.

● Finding 'What if' questions – analogies

If these questions don't jump out at you in this way, you will need to take more deliberate steps, either by searching for an analogy, a similar, though unrelated, structure of thoughts, or by working with and changing your structure.

'What if' questions

1 Analogies

2 Working with and changing our structures

Although breakthroughs in all forms of research might seem logical, even obvious, in hindsight, it is quite different the other way around, from the viewpoint of the original thinkers. To them it seems full of confusion, doubt and uncertainty as they search for alternative patterns of ideas that will give them a different way of explaining things. Like them, we must also develop the art of recognising similarities between unrelated structures to find interesting ways of approaching the topics we're interested in.

One aspect of this involves searching for similarities between patterns gathered through our everyday experience. As the word 'art' suggests, this is not a mechanical process; it calls for a highly selective imagination to identify previously unrelated patterns into which all the pieces fit. Finding them often produces the most surprising rewards. Insight can occur in response to a fact that means nothing to others. To do this we must ask ourselves three simple questions.

Three simple questions:

1 Is there a parallel?

2 Does the pattern fit?

3 Would it solve the problem?

Is there a parallel?

The search for parallel structures is the search for analogies that have a structure the same as or similar to our problem. It involves simple pattern recognition. Miss Marple, the main character in 12 of Agatha Christie's crime novels, often calls upon incidents and characters she has come across in St Mary Mead, the English village in which she lives. Although they are quite unrelated to the problem she is attempting to solve, they usually yield a common pattern of behaviour and human motivation that can be used to explain and solve the problem.

But to do it well we have to prepare our minds thoroughly, immersing ourselves in the ideas. The analogies are there for all of us to see, if we can only prepare ourselves to see them. The problem is that the mind is not naturally creative; therefore it can only see what we have prepared it to see.

Does the pattern fit?

To answer this question we have to concentrate on two things: the quantity and quality of the similarities. Obviously, if one structure is similar to another in many different ways we feel more confident in the conclusions we draw.

But the quality of the similarities is important too: we have to ensure that the analogy establishes credible connections in our experience.

When we search for such connections we are identifying a sufficiently stable pattern in our previous experience, which we think is reliable enough for us to conclude that given one event, the other will follow with high probability. The larger the number of As that have been Cs and the fewer As that have not been Cs, the likelier it is that all As will be Cs, and therefore that the next A will be a C.

> Concentrate on two things:
> Quantity and quality of similarities

If I were to drop my pen and, just a fraction of a second later, we were both to look out of the window to see a car crash in the street below, it would not be convincing for me to argue that the first event caused the second, because we know of no law or uniformity in our experience in which the dropping of pens causes cars to crash. However, if I were to argue that the light reflected off the falling pen, distracting the driver, who then lost control and crashed, it would still not be as convincing as it should be for a satisfactory explanation, but it is on its way.

The reason is that we have had analogous experiences in our own lives when people have been distracted in what they are doing by loud noises or bright lights, and this has led them to make mistakes or have accidents. We have used such patterns of events before; they have a good track record, so we feel confident about using them again in this case.

However, vague associations are the source of almost limitless error and oversimplification. It is the stuff of superstitions, myths and rituals. Seeing a black cat, we are told, is lucky, presumably because someone, at sometime, saw a black cat and subsequently had good luck.

> So make sure . . .
>   . . . you analyse and test the key elements of the identity between the analogy and your problem.

Would it solve the problem?

Once we have established that the resemblance is more than superficial, we have to ask the third question: Would it change our interpretation of the problem, suggesting an alternative way of approaching it – a 'What if' question? Often when this occurs – when the pattern fits the situation – something clicks; suddenly everything makes sense. It is one of those significant moments in the process of genuine thought.

Afterwards, it appears that the key to the problem was a hidden clue that we just didn't see or didn't take notice of because it seemed quite irrelevant. But in fact it wasn't irrelevant at all. It was just that we were using a different pattern to interpret the ideas. Change the pattern and it becomes relevant. The ability to do this can produce moments of genuine originality and real insight.

Summary

1   We must forget about ourselves and conduct mental experiments in which we empathise with others.

2   We must also detach ourselves from our routine patterns of thought and ask 'What if' questions.

3   One way of doing this is through analogies.

4   To do this effectively, ask three questions: Is there a parallel? Does it fit? Would it solve the problem?

● What next?

If analogies fail to produce 'What if' questions, you will have to manipulate and change your structure. In the next chapter we will look at four simple ways of doing this.

10 Original questions and hypotheses 2: Working with your structures

In this chapter you will learn . . .

1 four simple strategies to help you think more creatively about the sort of question or hypothesis you could research;

2 that by manipulating the structures we use to understand the topic, we can see things differently and come up with interesting ways of researching it;

3 how we can use the convergences and divergences in the literature on our topic to find a different way of approaching it.

If we cannot find an analogy to give us a different way of interpreting the topic, and the 'What if' questions that will guide our research, we must experiment with our structure, manipulating and changing it.

We all know that solutions to many difficult problems are often found by looking at them differently. So we shouldn't be surprised to learn that finding an interesting, original problem to research arises in exactly the same way. After all, they are two sides of the same coin. Over the years we've got used to describing this ability to think differently about a problem as 'lateral thinking', although it's probably better described as 'non-linear thinking'. In other words, instead of working through our normal linear steps one by one, we take them in a different order.

● The four strategies

You can learn to do this quite simply by working through the following four strategies. Indeed, all creative work is grounded in the solid foundations of such routine work. Carefully working through them we can place ourselves in the position of being able to think outside the norm and reveal what might otherwise have seemed an inspired way of approaching the problem.

Working with our structures

1 Change the structure.

2 Approach it from a different direction.

3 Start from a different point.

4 Create a new structure.

Changing the structure involves reorganising the elements and their relationships. Working with ideas in this way is the defining characteristic of abstract thought. By contrast, the second and third strategies involve accepting the structure as it is, but looking at it differently. Either we approach it from a different direction, looking at it from different points of view, or we start from a different point. The fourth strategy is perhaps the most radical. This involves creating a new structure, either by combining other structures, or by changing the basic concepts in terms of which the situation is described and interpreted.

Strategy 1: Change the structure
This is what we might describe as a bottom-up strategy in that, starting with the ideas we've gathered, we restructure them. It's the sort of processing we do when we tackle a crossword puzzle. We're given a clue which encourages us to think in one way, when the answer lies in changing this pattern of expectations. The fact that the solution comes through changing the structure and not just one or two parts explains why it always appears like a sudden insight, with the answer revealed as a complete whole. In T. S. Kuhn's *The Structure of Scientific Revolutions*[1] he explains scientific progress using the same terms. The sudden shift between one incompatible paradigm and another comes in the form of a complete revolution; it is not a gradual process.

So the key to this strategy is learning to manipulate and change our normal patterns of expectations. The problem is that the brain allows information to self-organise into patterns, which we then become accustomed to using, so we need to learn simple methods to change the structure to see things from new and more effective perspectives. Try using the following tactics.

Changing the structure

1 Split it up.

2 Rearrange it.

3 Reinterpret it.

1 Split it up

The simplest method is to split up the structure into two or more parts. In many cases this can reduce a bewilderingly difficult problem into two simple problems, whose solution is plain to see. Either we discover that each one can be solved by the application of a structure we have used before, or we realise there is a parallel structure, an analogy, which is the key to the solution. Failing that, once it's split up we can then use one of the other methods and rearrange or reinterpret the problems and come to a solution that way.

Example: Crossword puzzles

The compilers of crossword puzzles often have this strategy in mind when they set their clues. To find the answer to the clue 'Savings book (7)' the compiler expects you to split it in two, with both parts leading to the answer 'Reserve'. The same is true of the clue 'Frequently decimal (5)', which can be split into two and again both parts lead to the answer 'Often'.

2 Rearrange it

Alternatively, with some problems the answer is found by rearranging the structure, which, in most cases, involves identifying a factor that can be moved or changed. The key to this method is seeing each factor as something that will change the situation.

Example: Study skills

If you were to ask why it is that so many students struggle to take notes, read texts and write essays, so they can meet the demands of syllabuses and exams, the normal causal structure would suggest it is most likely to be because they are not given sufficient or effective instruction in how to do these things. But then, if you were to find that with most students this was not the case – that they did in fact get very good instruction, yet still manifested the same problems – you would have to identify a factor that could be moved or changed to reveal the most likely solution.

The normal structure suggests the following causal relationships: study skills instruction shapes the way we use our skills to meet the demands of syllabuses and exams.

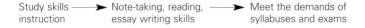

Study skills ———➤ Note-taking, reading, ———➤ Meet the demands of
instruction   essay writing skills   syllabuses and exams

Rearranging this by thinking about the influence of exams and syllabuses gives us an alternative explanation and an interesting hypothesis to guide our research:

Meet the demands of ———➤ Study skills ———➤ Note-taking, reading,
syllabuses and exams   instruction   essay writing skills

It may be that the way we write syllabuses and organise modes of assessment, like essays and exams, so shapes students' perception of the purposes of learning that despite all the instruction in study skills, students still take notes, read and write in the same way, exhibiting exactly the same problems.

If syllabuses encourage students to believe that learning is largely about knowing things and that exams test how many 'right' answers they can recall and trade for marks, despite taking study skills courses, they are likely to continue to read word-for-word and take verbatim, unstructured notes, fearing that if they leave anything out they might be missing a right answer.

3   Reinterpret it

Failing that, we can reinterpret the structure, changing its meaning. The way we make sense of the structure can itself lead us in the wrong direction. So without even changing the structure we can sometimes find the solution by looking at it naïvely, without any preconceptions, as someone who has never seen it before.

Example: The French Revolution

It may be that, in everything you've read, very few writers seem to question the idea of the bourgeoisie in the French Revolution being a capitalist class, whose capitalist values explain why the revolution occurred. But now, say you reinterpret this, perhaps asking 'What if it didn't have these capitalist values at all and in fact was little different from the landed nobility?' Perhaps, like them, the bourgeoisie was also competing for lucrative offices and not striving to be entrepreneurs at all. If this were the case, there would no longer be two mutually antagonistic classes and, therefore, no deep, revolutionary conflict.

Now you have an interesting topic to research, with some fascinating sub-questions: why did non-noble groups take on and defeat noble groups; why did they attack and destroy privilege, thereby destroying the formal organisation of eighteenth-century French society, making way for a more capitalist society?

Strategy 2: Approach it from a different direction

With some problems it's not necessary to change the structure at all, just approach it from a different direction, from a different point of view. In Conan Doyle's story *The Problem of Thor Bridge*, Sherlock Holmes describes one aspect of his theory of detection when he says, 'When once your point of view is changed, the very thing which was so damning becomes a clue to the truth.'[2] The most common strategy we routinely use to approach a problem from a different direction is to reverse the order of things: to turn it upside down, inside out or back to front.

Approach it from a different direction
1 Turn it upside down.
2 Inside out.
3 Back to front.

1   Turn it upside down

In what he described as his 'Copernican Revolution' the eighteenth-century German philosopher Immanuel Kant found a solution to the problem David Hume set by turning Hume's argument upside down, reversing the relationship between our impressions and our intellect. As Copernicus removed the Earth from the centre of creation, so Kant found a solution to Hume's problem by removing the earthly experience of our senses, making it peripheral to the active processing of the mind.

In the same way Karl Marx turned Hegel's argument upside down, arguing that it is not ideas that determine the shape of material forces, but material forces in the form of social and economic factors, like production, that shape society, social relations, the individual and what he believes and values, indeed the whole extent of his freedom.

2   Inside out

As for the second method of turning the problem inside out, this is more difficult to recognise, although it brings the most surprising results. The clearest examples are when we reverse our most intuitive assumptions, turning them inside out, to see what we find when we think the opposite.

Example: Hotel customers

The researchers at Cornell University reversed our assumptions about hotel customers to design four research categories: satisfied stayers; dissatisfied stayers; dissatisfied switchers; and satisfied switchers. While it's obvious to think about satisfied stayers and dissatisfied switchers, it's counter-intuitive to think there may be dissatisfied stayers and satisfied switchers.

Example: Smoking ban

It might be obvious to think of smokers who prefer unclear air and non-smokers who prefer clean air, but it would be counter-intuitive to think there may be smokers who prefer clean air and, even more, non-smokers who prefer unclean air. Nevertheless, you may find this is a source of interesting insights as you investigate why turnover has increased as a result of the smoking ban in pubs and restaurants in your local area.

The asymmetries, the unusual conjunctions and contrasts, created by reversing the way we normally think about things are often the source of the most surprising insights.

3   Back to front

Some of the best examples of the third method can be found in humour. As Sir Peter Medawar's example in Chapter 7 illustrates, it works by manipulating patterns of ideas and the expectations they raise. Our instant realisation that two patterns, united by the same word or phrase, are in fact asymmetrical gives rise to humour and creativity. Although it appears there is a structural similarity between them, we realise that in fact they raise quite different expectations.

Example: Writing across the curriculum

If you were studying for a degree in education, you might think of choosing as the topic of your dissertation, the role of writing across the curriculum. Our normal pattern of expectations encourages us to argue that clear thinking is important because it results in clear writing. But now, if we turn this back to front to suggest that perhaps clear writing makes for clear thinking, then we have an altogether different and interesting hypothesis that you could test.

It suggests that by forcing us to think through our ideas with greater clarity and care, writing could play a more important role across the curriculum, even in the sciences and mathematics. By writing about how they come by their ideas and solve problems, students could begin to understand more about the processes of how they think in these subjects.

Strategy 3: Start from a different point

In contrast to the last strategy, which involved a process of reversing things, this strategy works by starting at a point from which we haven't previously started. We focus our attention on different parts of the structure and start from there. The easiest way of doing this for most of us is to start with the key concepts around which our topic is organised.

As we've seen, at the heart of concepts are structures that organise our ideas. These are made up of organising principle – when we analysed the concept of 'revolution' we found six. One or two of these are likely to dictate the way we generally use the concept. So, those we usually ignore give us different points to start from. They throw different light on the problem and present interesting angles of investigation.

Example: Ideology

In your social science coursework you might generally interpret the concept 'ideology' to mean a system of beliefs characteristic of a particular group or class that promotes and protects their own interests. Now, analysing the concept, you find alternative principles you've tended to neglect, like Lionel Trilling's interpretation of it as a source of 'emotional safety'. This might give you a different way of approaching your topic that may be unique.

Example: Tragedy

In literature you may be interested in a topic that draws upon your understanding of the concept 'tragedy'. Analysing it you find an alternative interpretation of it as something that is self-defeating in that, without meaning to, we destroy the very thing we value most. This may suggest a unique angle of investigation that will give your project an original focus.

But if the key concepts of your topic don't offer you a way of starting from a different point, try something that might seem disarmingly simple: step back from your topic and approach it from a more general standpoint by turning to a sourcebook, like an encyclopaedia. By just browsing it, looking at your topic from this more general perspective, you will almost invariably come up with unusual ways of linking it with other topics that are not usually associated with it. The following example has been offered by a reviewer of this book.

Example: Victorian fiction

> A student wanted to write a dissertation on Victorian fiction and started with an idea of relating it to Florence Nightingale, but at that point could go no further. So his or her supervisor suggested browsing in a sourcebook on Victorian Britain, where the student found references to nursing and a lot of connected material in half-a-dozen novels, which led the student to do a dissertation on 'Nursing in Victorian Fiction'.[3]

Strategy 4: Create a new structure

However, if none of these changes work, you may find your 'What if' questions come from creating a new structure. In contrast to the other strategies, this is a top-down strategy in which a new theory is put in place of the ruling one.

Creating a new structure

1 Combine structures.

2 Change the basic concepts.

1   Combine structures

We can create this new structure either by combining structures or by changing the basic concepts in terms of which the situation is described and interpreted.

Example: Totalitarianism

> Previously we saw how historians were able to combine different structures by borrowing from social science aspects of the theory of totalitarianism after the emergence of totalitarian leaders in the 1930s and 1940s. By combining their understanding of the past with this new theory, historians were able to open up new lines of investigation to see how significant the same mesmeric influence on crowds and the capacity to manipulate collective sentiment had been in previous periods with leaders like Napoleon.

So, ask yourself whether you can import a theory, or just another way of interpreting things, from elsewhere in your subject, from another discipline or even just from your everyday life. It is often possible to synthesise structures from different sources in this way to create new structures. When you search the literature, look out for different bodies of literature that might usefully be synthesised.

It's worth reminding yourself as you search for an original, interesting way of approaching your topic, that creative thinking often means disregarding our own cultural conventions. There may be within your subject an accepted way of approaching your topic, but don't let this trap your thinking. It has been said that genius is the capacity for productive reaction against one's training.

- Can you import a theory or a different way of interpreting things?
- Are there different bodies of literature you can synthesise?
- Don't get trapped by the accepted ways of approaching your topic.

2   Change the basic concepts

Alternatively, think again about changing the basic concepts in which your topic is described.

Example: Medical resources

Part of your research into how we ration limited medical resources to meet the needs of patients, of course, involves the analysis of the concept 'needs'. You may have used it in an absolute sense as something necessary for basic survival. But you realise it also has a relative sense, meaning those things necessary for a certain quality of life, which is the product of living in a particular society. By accepting the possibility that medical care might be this sort of need, an altogether more interesting project emerges.

● **Divergences and convergences**

If all this still comes to nothing, go back to the literature on the topic that you uncovered in your exploratory reading to see if the authors have written something which might throw up an interesting comparison with your own structure of ideas. In particular, see where they diverge and converge.

Divergences

You may find the topic has been reviewed in the past, since when newer work has taken a different contrasting position, which has not been taken onboard by reviewers and may give you an opportunity to see if either position stands up to examination.

Alternatively, consider the different styles of approach to problems, theories and literature of authors from different countries and cultures. Are there differences between them in the literature? Are there inconsistencies in their respective arguments? You might have come across explanations in your coursework from an academic working in another country, and want to see how far these can be applied in your own. This might suggest inadequacies in current ideas, practice or evidence.

* New contrasting positions
* Different styles of approach
* Different explanations

Convergences

Although divergences are the most obvious source of ideas, convergences can be the most exciting. Look at the literature again. Can you find issues, interpretations and points of view that will provide an interesting synthesis of ideas? Look out for ideas that can be brought together to provide a more unusual insight; a different way of looking at a problem or issue.

You may not have come across anyone prepared to argue that a particular author is a romantic, a realist or, say, an existentialist, but you might find ways of arguing this. It might be generally agreed that two philosophers occupy different, contrasting positions, one heavily influenced by German idealism, the other by English empiricism, but you notice that there are issues on which they hold strikingly similar positions or approach problems in similar, largely unexpected ways. You might come across ideas that converge to suggest that a particular social problem, normally regarded as having economic causes, is, in fact, largely a psychological problem.

Summary

1   To produce original questions and hypotheses you don't have to wait for inspiration to strike.

2   Just work through these four simple strategies, deliberately and carefully manipulating your structure.

3   Alternatively, go through the literature to find divergences and convergences.

● **What next?**

As we saw in Chapter 8 with conceptual skills, by using a simple method we can develop our skills and abilities to be creative; to come up with new and interesting ideas and ways of approaching a topic. Like humour, this sort of creativity arises from the asymmetry of the structures we carry around in our minds to understand the world and navigate our way through it. When we manipulate these structures, we suddenly see things differently; we have genuine insights. Armed with these new ideas we can now search through the literature and draw up a shortlist of possible topics, so we can make our final choice.

● **Notes**

1   T. S. Kuhn, *The Structure of Scientific Revolutions* (Chicago: University of Chicago Press, 1970).
2   Sir Arthur Conan Doyle, 'The Problem of Thor Bridge', in *The Casebook of Sherlock Holmes* (1927; London: Penguin, 1951), p. 153.
3   I owe this example to John Peck, formerly Reader at Cardiff University, who very kindly offered it for me to use.

Part Three

Deciding on your project

11 Searching the literature

In this chapter you will learn . . .

1 how to frame your research question to give focus and direction to your reading;

2 how to map out the territory so that you have a full measure of the context in which your research is set;

3 how to avoid getting bogged down and diverted into irrelevant areas;

4 four simple steps to search efficiently and avoid confusion.

You will now have a number of possible topics. Before you can choose you will have to do a more detailed search of the literature to get some idea of how much work has been done on each topic already and whether the project is too large or too small for the time and words available. But first, for each topic we must state the problem clearly, and carefully craft the research question that will guide our work.

● Stating the problem – the research question

Although you will have a clear idea of the topic, within it you must find a question that will give focus and direction to your reading and thinking; that will guide you as you collect, structure and analyse your data and ideas. The clearer you are, the more relevant and usable will be the material you collect. If you allow the question to remain vague, you will run the risk of producing a dissertation that lacks focus and cohesion. So make sure your question forces you to concentrate on something that is specific: a question you want answers to or a comparison that you've drawn between authors, theories or arguments. As you work on your question, keep in mind the following things.

Clarity

The best research questions are hardly ever just found: they are worked on carefully and designed to give clear direction to our work. The time you spend on this will always repay you handsomely. For one thing, you will find it easier to choose the most appropriate research method to ensure the material you collect will be relevant. Otherwise you may find yourself collecting masses of largely irrelevant material which you find yourself processing and analysing in confusing ways, simply because you're not completely sure what you're trying to do. In your literature review alone you are likely to find that much of what you have included will have to be dumped.

So pin down the question clearly, analyse your assumptions to ensure that there are no inherent contradictions and, if it's a complex question, break it down into clear sub-questions. In this form it will chart a clear course through your research.

Interest

In Chapter 5 we said how important it was that the topic should really interest you if you are to maintain your motivation over the long term. Indeed, you should feel passionate about it if you're to catch every idea and insight as they come to you, and create all the connections and contrasts that will make your work original in a very real sense. Equally important, if you're interested in it, you'll make it interesting to your reader. Whether you mean to or not, your enthusiasm will communicate itself.

> If you're interested in it, you'll make it interesting to your reader.

Relevance

This is, perhaps, the most obvious thing to ensure. You may be challenging an accepted interpretation of a theory, a literary text, a historical account, or a certain practice in your profession. You may be comparing authors, interpretations of events, approaches to problems or different theories. Or you may just be finding information that will fill a gap in our knowledge. Whichever it is, make sure you can establish connections with the literature of your subject.

Originality

It doesn't have to push back the frontiers of knowledge in a significant way, but it needs to throw some fresh light on existing knowledge. It can't simply recycle received opinions or reproduce work you've done in previous modules. So make sure that it displays your creativity: your ability to see significant issues and create an effective research strategy that will yield sufficient material from which to develop an interesting dissertation.

Course requirements

Finally, make sure it will meet the course requirements and the demands of the assessment criterion.

The research question
1 Clarity
2 Interest
3 Relevance
4 Originality
5 Course requirement

● The title

Having checked these things, it helps to go one step further and give it a title. You'll now be clearer than at any previous time exactly what your project is about. Giving it a title will seal this clarity, so that each time you read it you will be reminded of this. It could be just a straightforward title that gets to the heart of the problem directly, like the following:

'The effects of the government's smoking ban on pubs and restaurants in Bolton'

'Young people's attitudes to, and experience of, racism'

'The Political Arithmetic of Sir William Petty'

Or you could have a short, general, main title, followed by a subtitle that picks up something specific in the main title – a specific aspect or application:

'The Hudson's Bay Company archives: gender and the fur trade' (University of Swansea)

'Caring for special needs children: a mother's view' (University of Surrey)

'Themes and images in the female gothic novel: Ann Radcliffe, Jane Austen and Charlotte Brontë' (University of Sussex)

Alternatively you could have a main title that is enigmatic, even contradictory, followed by a subtitle that reveals what it's about:

'"Gloomy old sod, aren't I?" An analysis of the poetry of Philip Larkin: Was he a life-affirming writer?' (University of Sussex)

'Rock on Tommy – studying climbers' effects on Yosemite vegetation' (University of Cambridge)

'"We'll show those city bastards how to fight": a social geography of domestic football hooliganism' (University of Cambridge)

Whichever style you choose, make sure it is clear and gives readers as much specific information as possible so they can differentiate it from similar titles and topics. It will help if you avoid all unnecessary words and phrases, like 'A study of', 'An investigation into', 'A comparison of' and 'An examination of'. Unnecessary words will only obscure your meaning.

● Searching the literature

Armed with a clear idea of three or four topics and well crafted titles, you can now turn to the literature to see which of them is the most promising. But be very clear about what you're trying to do, otherwise you could find yourself getting too involved in the material. Without a clearly defined set of aims to guide you through the material, you can spend too much time reading things too deeply at this stage. So, keep at the front of your mind two key objectives.

Objectives
1 Treasure hunting
2 Mapping out the territory

Treasure hunting

Your first concern is to see what's there: you're treasure hunting. You're identifying things that may be useful to you – books, chapters, articles, conference papers, websites, and dissertations, anything that looks like it might be worth reading in more depth later. Systematically explore the literature, listing titles and where they can be found. At this stage just scan the material for ideas, information and the methods the researcher might have used which you, too, could adapt and use. How did she gather the material – questionnaires, interviews, etc.? How did she analyse it? How did she present her findings, set out her arguments and draw her conclusions?

Look for
1 Ideas
2 Information
3 Method – gathering and analysing evidence
4 Presentation of findings
5 Development of arguments
6 How conclusions are drawn

Your aim is not to master the ideas, but just to see how useful each item could be. This is not always an easy thing to do. You're reading extensively, though with a clear sense of proportion, both for the dissertation as a whole, which is, after all, an undergraduate dissertation, not a PhD, and for each aspect of the topic – it makes no sense to read extensively on an issue that is only peripheral to the main issues raised by the topic.

> Make sure . . .
> . . . that you read extensively, though with a sense of proportion.

Mapping out the territory

Your second concern is to map out the territory, all the current issues being debated. Your aim is to get as full a measure as possible of the context in which your research is set. Familiarise yourself with the subject, the research methods employed and how researchers analyse, synthesise and evaluate evidence and ideas to develop their arguments.

For this you will need up-to-date references. Recent volumes of journals will have new articles and reviews of recent books that are relevant to your subject, which you might not find elsewhere. Electronic journals are useful for this, because they can be easily searched. But still, there may be classic texts in your subject that are particularly useful in expounding the theories that underpin your research.

As soon as you're able to, compile a list of sources and decide how crucial each one is. Then, start reading the three or four most crucial texts first. This is the best way to get to the heart of something, even though in the end they may not be as crucial as you first thought.

Mapping
1 Current issues
2 Research methods
3 How researchers analyse, synthesise and evaluate
4 Up-to-date references
5 Classic texts
6 List of sources
7 Start reading crucial texts

The problem is that as soon as we begin to read around the subject in this way we discover all sorts of connections to related issues that show us different ways we can develop our ideas. This can quickly become very complex and confusing – it seems as if you could write a book, not just a dissertation, to cover all this. Therefore,

1 As you read, start mapping out the territory in general terms, using pattern notes (Chapter 17).
2 After you've finished with a source, make brief notes on an index card or in a computer file about why it was useful and how you could use it again. It only has to be two or three sentences.

There should be at the front of your mind three questions that you want answers to.

1 What has been done before?
As you read more, you'll find yourself putting the pieces together, synthesising it all into one complete map. There will be connections between one piece of research and another, and chains will begin to link a number of sources as you navigate your way through them. So, as you are doing it, try to see how your research will follow on from this. What can you add to it?

2   What information is available?

Then, once you've got an idea about how your topic could contribute to this, ask yourself whether there's enough information, or even too much. If you choose a small, largely unexamined topic, it's not difficult to cover it fairly comprehensively, but it's more difficult to come up with relevant sources. Alternatively, if there's an extensive literature on your topic, it's easier to find sufficient sources, but you have more to review.

The same is true in understanding the literature. Where there is limited coverage of a topic, which doesn't go into great depth, it's easier to understand it, but it will be more difficult to find useful and interesting ideas. Whereas in an area that has been well developed, you'll find plenty of ideas, but you'll have more to review and it will probably be more difficult finding just the right niche.

3   What gaps are there in the research?

As for gaps, these should appear as you map out the territory, if you can read critically and inquisitively, asking yourself if the writer has possibly overlooked anything. You may find your topic can fit neatly into a gap, or can be adapted to fit. Someone may have investigated a phenomenon which is sufficiently similar for you to carry out a comparative study. Note the characteristics of the problem or the features of the situation he or she chose to measure. Use the same yourself. Or perhaps the writer has used a research strategy that you could use on a case study of your own? Remember, in your research proposal you will have to justify the relevance of your work. The most persuasive way of doing this is to cite work that has already been done and to identify the gaps your work is filling.

> Make sure . . .
> . . . that you read inquisitively: has the writer overlooked anything?

● How to search

Throughout your project you will undertake a number of searches, some general, some specific, as you hunt something down.

Efficient searching

The key is to be efficient in how you use your time. To avoid the worst mistakes, keep four things in mind.

Efficient searching
1 Don't confuse the search with the review.
2 Be clear about what you're looking for.
3 Don't get bogged down.
4 Don't get diverted into irrelevant areas.

The first one might sound obvious, but as you work with your mind on what you're reading you can easily find yourself producing a thorough review covering every source you read. This will soak up at least half the time you have available to complete the whole project.

The second has almost the same propensity, as anyone who has ever searched the Internet will know. So, be clear about what you're searching for and the keywords you'll use for it, particularly on the Internet. Translate your topic into core search terms and sit down with a blank piece of paper and list all the similar ways you can think of to express the same ideas. Then, think of the best ways of combining them.

The same is true of the third and fourth points. It's easy to get bogged down in too much searching initially, doing a great deal of work you later realise is unnecessary and unusable. You may then find you've left yourself short of time to devote to the other stages. You can always go back and read another source or two later on, which you can then add to your review, but you can't recover the time you have unwisely spent getting bogged down in too much detail too early. In the same way we can find ourselves gathering references that are not strictly relevant, but which we don't want to waste, so we include them whether they're relevant or not, even though they will detract from the clarity of our work.

The steps
To make this a more manageable task, work through the following four simple steps.

1   Search the library catalogues
Your first search will probably produce a great number of hits, so narrow down your keywords. If, however, you don't get many, either your keywords are too narrow, or you're aiming to undertake really ground-breaking research. Although this is to be applauded, it probably won't make the best

undergraduate research project: there simply might not be enough material to analyse, criticise and use as the basis for your project.

2   Check there's enough up-to-date material

Once you've got a list of titles, browse through them, checking that there's enough relevant, up-to-date material available. And look around the catalogue location number on the library shelves. There you will find books on your topic and next to them, filed under adjacent numbers, others that deal with the same topic from a slightly different perspective.

If you have problems, ask your librarians for help. They can usually give you guidance on the range of services they offer and even book a place for you on a training course to improve your searching skills. Subject-specific librarians can direct you to the most relevant databases and help you identify the keywords that will give you access to what you want. But prepare yourself with a list of specific questions to ask them. And give yourself plenty of time to get documents and books that may have to be ordered well in advance.

- Look around catalogue location numbers.
- Ask for help from your librarians.
- Allow plenty of time to order material.

3   Search electronic databases

You'll find a number of electronic databases you can search for material and ideas. Some have a direct link to the full text of the journal article, although most only provide the full bibliographical reference and an abstract. You'll find indexes to journals, official publications and reports: indexes like the Philosopher's Index, the Business Periodicals Index, and the General Science Index. If you search the most recent volumes of journals you'll find new articles and reviews of recent books, which you might not otherwise find. Read the abstracts of journal articles to identify those that you think will be the most relevant to read later in full.

4   Sift for relevance, quality and authority

With the Internet the problems are not just with locating sources, but with reviewing and sifting them for relevance, quality and authority. We can all find sources; the question is, do they come from reputable authorities? The more precise the search parameters, the more manageable the results. Most libraries have Internet guides that will improve your skills in finding just the right parameters. They will probably also have lists devoted to particular subject areas, listing the most useful search engines, sites, databases and Internet gateways and portals. These are collections of reliable academic web resources. Although they have less coverage, they are of a much higher quality. Some are subject- or discipline-specific, like the following:

> Arts Design Architecture and Media Gateway (ADAM)
>> http://adam.ac.uk
>
> Humanities Gateway (HUMBL)   www.humbul.ac.uk/
> Social Science Information Gateway (SOSIG)   www.sosig.ac.uk/

● Recording details

After you've consulted each source, record onto an index card or in a computer file the details you'll need later for citing and, as we suggested earlier, note why it was useful, so you always know how the information might help you and how it relates to the project. This will be useful material for your research proposal and for your dissertation to demonstrate how thoroughly you've researched the background literature.

Try to make sure you handle each source only once, so you only have to use the card each time you want to use the information in your literature review or in the introduction. The following is the sort of information it would be useful for you to record.

1 Citing details:
   1.1   For a book: author, title, place of publication, publisher, and date.
   1.2   For an article: author, title of the article, name of the journal, volume and issue number, date and page numbers.
2 Type of publication (book, journal article, book review, conference paper, etc.).
3 Comments (reason for consulting it, sections, quotations you might use).
4 How you might use it.

Summary

1 Have a clear question and title to give focus and direction to your reading.

2 Map out the territory, asking yourself: what has been done before, what information is available and what gaps are there?

3 Avoid the four worst mistakes: confusing the search with the review; being unclear about what you're looking for; getting bogged down; and getting diverted into irrelevant areas.

● **What next?**

Searching the literature can be a very bewildering exercise, but not if you have a clear question in mind and go about it in an organised way following each step we've described. Now you should be ready to draw up a shortlist and choose your topic.

12 Choosing the topic

In this chapter you will learn . . .

1 how to assess the different factors that will determine the feasibility of each project on your short-list;

2 about the ethical issues you must take into consideration and how to organise your project to take account of them;

3 three ethical principles that will help you identify and avoid any possible problem;

4 how to evaluate and make a realistic comparison between the different projects, and make your final choice.

Now that you've researched the literature and explored the background to each of your potential topics, you should be in a better position to draw up a shortlist of, say, three, maybe four, frontrunners. To do this, talk to your supervisor and ask yourself the following questions:

1 Will the research break new ground?
2 Can the sources (documents, people, literature, etc.) be easily accessed?
3 Are there any practical difficulties involved that I need to consider?
4 Are there any ethical issues I need to deal with before I get started?

● Feasibility

As you can see, one of the most important aspects of this involves assessing just how feasible the project is in the time available. You must be ruthless and assess the likely consequences of certain things going wrong. At this stage it's easier to go back and reconsider than it will be in two months' time.

Scope and scale

First, try to be realistic about the scope and scale of your project. To make it manageable you may have to limit its width and depth. In the time available it simply may not be possible to contact all the people you want to, and gather all the information, statistics and documents you need. So, check early that people are available and they're willing to take part. If you can't get access to people and the equipment you need, you will have to arrange alternatives.

It's important to ensure you're following a strategy that will yield the right quantity of data within the time available. You must be sure that there is sufficient material that you can access to allow you to apply your concepts to the indicators and variables we analysed in Chapter 8. If there are problems, limit the width or depth. You probably won't have time to read all the novels of Thomas Hardy, so limit your choice and be prepared to explain how you came to your decision.

If you're unsure in any way about whether you're taking on too much in the time available, look in the library at previous similar examples of dissertations and check the following:

1   Analysis
How are they broken down? What aspects of the problem have been investigated?

2   Width and depth
Do some cover a wider range of subjects than you plan to, but not in so much depth? How many novels do they use? How long a period in history? Look at the chapter headings – do they suggest a different approach than yours? Could you adopt a similar approach? How much detail do you need to go into? Should it be wider and more superficial or narrower with more depth?

3   Strategy – how was the work done?
3.1   *Empirical research*
What is the balance between primary and secondary sources, and between quantitative and qualitative approaches (Chapter 18)? Does it depend upon collecting quantitative material which is statistically analysed and presented graphically, or does it work by interpreting events and opinions?

3.2   *Theoretical and text-based research*
Does it search out correlations or contrasts? Is it critical and evaluative? If the subject is a novelist, does it analyse just one novel and compare it with the rest, or analyse the whole body of work? Does it relate the novelist's work to his life and experiences, or compare it with the work of a contemporary?

Time
In the same way, be realistic about the time you have available in view of all your other commitments. Work out how much time you can put into the project over the next few months. How much do you already know about the

subject? Try to assess how much time will be needed for each stage: doing the research, collecting and analysing the data or reading the literature and documents, then planning what you will write, writing it up, revising and presenting it. Be generous in your estimate. Some stages will take longer, some shorter.

The one thing you must ensure is that no stage should be compromised because you didn't see at the outset that it was going to take longer than you estimated. So ask yourself really detailed questions.

Example: Empirical study

Do you have time to do all the interviews and transcribe them? You'll need a reasonable sample from your survey if you're going to be able to do a meaningful quantitative analysis and you'll have to allow for the fact that not everyone will respond. Are there sources of secondary data instead that you have access to?

As you can see, your ability to manage your time will be directly tied to your ability to control the boundaries of your study in this way.

Skills and expertise

The last thing to ask yourself, if you're conducting a survey requiring complex quantitative analysis, is whether you have the skills and expertise to analyse the results. If not, can you develop them quickly? There will be research methods tutors who can help and your supervisor may be able to suggest courses you could take, if you have the time. If not, you will have to redesign your approach.

Feasibility checklist

1 Is there a sufficient body of knowledge to support the project? Can I find the necessary literature?

2 Is it possible to complete the project, given the volume of work and the available time?

3 Can I get access to the people, statistics and documents I will need?

4 Do I have, or can I develop rapidly, the skills and expertise to collect and analyse the data?

5 Will this involve costs for travel, etc.? Can I afford this?

6 Are there any ethical problems?

● Ethical issues

The ethical issues of research affect us all, although some projects are affected more than others. They find their way into any project in two ways:

1 the work done by others;
2 the work we do with others.

Work done by others

The work done by others in the research literature, which forms the basis on which our research is built, raises the ethical issues of citing and plagiarism, which we will examine in detail in Chapters 37 and 38. We have an ethical responsibility to draw a clear distinction between our own work and the work of others, which we must acknowledge.

Work done with others

As for the ethical issues involved in working with others, all research participants have moral and legal rights, and in our determination to get the results we can easily ignore or infringe these. The key issues involve:

Privacy
Confidentiality
Consent
Safety
Fairness
Impartiality

Most of these are already covered by certain legal provisions, like the data protection legislation, the system for screening researchers working with vulnerable groups, and the licensing regime that applies to those working with animals or in biomedical research. In addition, there are certain internationally agreed standards, like those in the Declaration of Helsinki, which lay down general principles regarding beneficence (do positive good), non-malfeasance (do no harm), informed consent, and confidentiality (guarantee of anonymity and privacy). There are also likely to be certain university requirements, which means you may have to get approval for your project from your Research Ethics Committee.

Ethical principles

Nevertheless, underscoring all of these are certain non-overridable ethical principles that should guide our actions and decisions irrespective of the law – universalism, the dignity of the individual as an end in him- or herself, and autonomy.

Ethical principles
1 Universalism
2 The dignity of the individual
3 Autonomy

1. Universalism

We believe that to behave morally we must behave consistently: we must be able to universalise our behaviour. I must be able to approve of an action or decision irrespective of the part I play, whether I am the perpetrator or the subject of it. So, in our research we must be able to put ourselves in the position of those we work with and vicariously experience what they are experiencing, and approve of the same thing being done to us. This is the Golden Rule, so familiar to us all regardless of our beliefs or culture: 'Do unto others as you would have them do unto you.'

The eighteenth-century German philosopher Immanuel Kant famously encapsulated this in his 'categorical imperative': 'Act only on that maxim through which you can at the same time will that it should become a universal law.'[1] In other words, I must want all people (including myself) finding themselves in similar circumstances to act in accordance with the same rule. Every action should be judged in the light of how it would appear if it were to be a universal code of behaviour. It should not be based on subjective feelings or inclinations but conform to a law given by reason – a universal law, the categorical imperative.

> We must put ourselves in the position of those we work with and approve of the same thing being done to us.

Therefore, we should not only be able to accept that the questions we ask our subjects, or the way we treat them, are what we ourselves would accept as morally right, but we should accept that everyone should be treated equally. We must ensure not only that the tests and experiments we conduct are fair to everyone, but that they are seen to be so by participants, who will feel they've been cheated if they've been disadvantaged or treated unequally.

2   *The dignity of the individual*

Consequently, we must ask ourselves as we interview, observe or test the subjects of our research, 'Would I like to be treated like this?' In this the two key concerns for us all are:

1   that we should be treated as having intrinsic value in ourselves and not just extrinsic value to serve someone else's ends;
2   and that we should have the freedom to make our own informed choices.

The first of these underscores the importance we attach to the dignity of the individual as an end in him- or herself and not as a mere means of promoting someone else's ends. In particular, our research subjects will want anything they say to remain confidential. In fact, when they're confident that we will respect their anonymity they tend to respond more honestly anyway.

So when you use material make sure you remove anything that may lead to their identification. When you store tapes or notes from interviews, remove identification labels or replace them with false names. Where participants have to be named, because their views lend authority to your conclusions, accurately attribute the material to them and get their agreement that you can use what they say in your dissertation, and in the way you have. The best way of doing this is to send them drafts of the passages in which their opinions are cited so they can check and authorise that they're accurate.

- Remove identification from material.
- Replace with false names.
- Check you have their agreement to use their words.

3   *Autonomy*

Treating somebody with dignity in this way involves allowing them to make their own, fully-informed decisions. So when you seek their consent to ask your questions, let them know why you're asking them and what you're going to do with the results. If you're asking the questions in an interview, tell them before you start. In most cases it helps to have a participant information sheet, which participants read, before they sign the consent form. If you're using a questionnaire, have a brief description of the project at the top explaining these things. Then, completion of the questionnaire implies consent. Similarly, if you're conducting tests or experiments, tell them the reasons and explain your methods clearly.

In all these circumstances give participants the chance to decline, and count refusals as part of the project data. In some cases, where participation is over an extended period, or involves sensitive issues, it is best to draw up a more formal agreement.

- Tell them what you're doing and what you will do with the results.
- Use participant information sheets.
- Give them the chance to decline.
- Count refusals as part of the project.

Observational research

Where you are not intervening in these obvious ways, where you're just observing behaviour, say in a classroom, more subtle considerations come into play. Unless participants are asked for their consent, such observation can only take place where those observed would normally expect to be observed and have, therefore, implicitly given their approval. Nonetheless, keep in mind three considerations:

1 Make sure you're not invading **privacy**;
2 That your presence is not causing any **psychological harm** in the form of stress and anxiety;
3 And that you're aware of the different **cultural conventions** that rule the issues of privacy and public space – in some countries it is not acceptable to take someone's photograph in a public place, even in a crowd, without their permission.

Deliberate deception

However, in some circumstances allowing participants to make fully-informed decisions can compromise the results. If someone knows why you are conducting an interview or getting them to complete a questionnaire, they are likely to want to be good respondents by giving you what they believe you want. In such circumstances deception might be the only recourse. Although the 'acts and omissions' doctrine is used to justify the distinction between deliberately deceiving someone and merely withholding information, they still both amount to deception.

But, where there is no other method and the questions affected are important to the project, there may be no alternative. To compensate for this, debrief participants afterwards and give them the information you've withheld. If necessary, give them contact details so they can talk to you or someone else at the university, even counselling services and help lines. And make it clear from the start that they have the right to withdraw at any time without giving a reason, although in most projects there is a cut-off date to this, usually at the point when you would start your data analysis.

- Debrief the participants.
- Give them contact details.
- Make it clear that they can withdraw.

Keep your readers fully informed

Finally, be equally honest with your readers and allow them also to make fully-informed decisions. You're not a defence lawyer tailoring your evidence to present the strongest case, so let your readers know the full extent and nature of your results, even, indeed especially, where they fail to support the arguments and assumptions you presented in your proposal. In doing so, your readers will learn to trust your integrity. Then, after you've clearly presented all your data, analyse your results and let your readers judge how well you've done it and if your conclusions have been fairly and consistently drawn.

● Choosing from your shortlist

Now you've been through your shortlist and checked each topic to see if there's enough background literature, if it's feasible and if there are no insurmountable ethical problems, it's probably already clear to you which one you should choose. In case it isn't, check each topic against the checklist below, giving marks out of ten for each question. Then compare the totals. This will help you make a realistic comparison. Then, before you decide, talk it over in detail with your supervisor.

Marks out of ten

1 Does the topic have a clear aim?

2 Will it sustain my interest and motivation?

3 Is there sufficient background literature to work with?

4 Is it broad enough to connect with the theoretical background?

5 Is it narrow enough for me to research in depth and do it justice in the time and words available?

6 Is it original?

7 Is it significant and not trivial?

8 Is it consistent with course requirements?

9 Is there a good chance that I'll come up with interesting conclusions, maybe point towards a solution to a problem, or at least clarify the situation to eliminate false answers?

10 Will it add value to my CV?

Summary

1 Assess how much time you have available and how much you'll need for each stage of your project.

2 Make sure the scope and scale of it is manageable in the time.

3 Check that you have the skills and expertise to cope with it.

4 Make sure you have taken account of all the ethical issues involved. Check your project against the three non-overridable principles.

5 Evaluate each of the shortlisted projects against the 10-point checklist.

● What next?

In Part 2 you identified those subjects that most interest you and suit your abilities. You generated your own ideas, developed them and came up with interesting approaches that will make for fascinating topics. In Part 3, you checked to see if each topic on your shortlist is feasible, if it will maintain your interest and motivation over the coming months and if it will produce conclusions that will surprise and impress not just you but those who read your dissertation. Now it's time to organise the practical side of the project before setting about the research.

● Note

1   H. J. Paton (trans.), *The Moral Law: Kant's Groundwork of the Metaphysic of Morals* (London: Hutchinson, 1948), p. 84.

Part Four

Organising your work

13 Planning your research

In this chapter you will learn . . .

1 about the benefits of planning your research in detail before you start;
2 how to assess whether it's practicable, whether it will produce answers relevant to your questions and whether it will meet the official requirements of a dissertation assignment;
3 how to assess your project for its reliability and validity.

We began this book by pointing out that dissertations are important because they allow examiners to see not just *what* you think, but *how* you think. To do both of these things well you need to plan every aspect of your research and your dissertation to take account of every conceivable practicality. So we have reached a significant stage: you must plan your research and put together a provisional outline of the project – a research proposal.

● Research proposal

Your department may insist on this and may have guidelines they want you to follow. But if they don't, it's still an important thing to do. It gives your supervisor the opportunity to cast his or her experienced eye over it, assessing its feasibility: whether it conforms to the university's requirements; whether the results are likely to be significant; whether you've adopted the most appropriate methods; and whether your conclusions and recommendations are likely to be consistent with your aims. Put simply, it places you realistically in the position of actually doing it, so you can see more clearly the likely consequences of your plans.

It's better to do this now rather than later after you've invested so much in it that it's difficult to change what you've done. At that stage, criticism which strikes at the fundamentals of your project can be deeply discouraging. There's not a lot you can do, yet you realise you're set on a course that won't produce your best work. So set your plans down on paper, let your supervisor see them and accept that this is all provisional: you may have to produce a second or third draft until it takes a form that will work. To cope with this you will have to guard against investing too much self-esteem in your plan: it mustn't mean so much to you that it's painful or impossible even to conceive of changing something.

- It places you realistically in the position of actually doing it.
- Better to do this now rather than later when it may be difficult to change things.
- Guard against investing too much self-esteem in your plan.

● What are the benefits to me?

Still, you might ask, 'If my department doesn't insist on one, what are the benefits to me from doing one?' Well, there are a number.

Time
First, it will give you a better idea of whether you can manage it all in the time available. You'll also have a timed map so that each time you're diverted you can remind yourself where you should be. With this by your side, life will be much easier.

Uncertainties
Second, getting ourselves to this stage has involved thinking largely about the big issues: an original idea that interests us and where it sits in the literature of our subject. In our concern for these we tend to overlook the details: uncertainties about our skills and gaps in our knowledge and understanding. So setting out the project in this way will help you identify and eliminate the problems. It might help you find alternative research methods that match your skills or even alter the research questions so you can make your project more practicable.

Confidence
Third, it will develop your confidence to know you have planned the project in detail and chosen the methods and activities you're good at to meet your aims and objectives.

Benefits
1 Time
2 Uncertainties
3 Confidence

● Planning doesn't mean over-theorising

Nevertheless, one word of caution: you can, understandably, spend too much time theorising and searching the literature as you develop your ideas. After all, this is what academic authors seem to do: they develop and set out their theories, and then test them, only to find they were right all along. But remember what we said earlier, this is often the way the story of discovery is told after the event. As Peter Medawar says, it is how we like to appear before the public when the curtain goes up. But it is not how new theories and ideas are discovered.

This is an intensely iterative process. A provisional theory is put forward and tested, then re-worked in line with the results and tested again. This process continues until there is a tight fit between theory and results. So, whether your project is empirical or text-based, don't spend too much time theorising before you start; get down to some substantive research as soon as you can. Of course, you've got to pin your ideas down before you start, but don't get locked into an overdeveloped theoretical position, which may ultimately prove irrelevant and a waste of your time.

● The structure

The aim of your proposal is to make clear three things that will ultimately determine the success of your work:

1 Whether it is practicable, given the time available, your skills and knowledge, and access to people and material.
2 Whether it will be effective in producing answers to the questions posed by your project.
3 Whether it will meet the official requirements of a dissertation assignment.

To answer these, structure your proposal around three key questions:

A What do I want to know?
B How am I going to find out?
C What is likely to be the significance of my answers?

In section A, set out the problem in the context of all the background reading. In section B, describe the sequence of activities and allocate the time needed to gather data and analyse it, or to read and analyse documents or literature. And in section C, give a rough outline of why you think your answers are likely to be significant.

A   What do I want to know?

1   Research problem

The first thing to do is state clearly the research topic or problem we want to investigate. In science-based research this is our thesis, in humanities our general proposition. It will define our purpose in undertaking the research: to evaluate a text, test a claim, develop a theory, monitor a practice, compare and trace similarities between texts, artists, writers, movements in thought, or just to increase our understanding or recommend a change in policy. So we need to be clear about it, otherwise, it might lead to vague results that lack focus. Try more than one way of stating it to see what works best.

For example, our thesis or general proposition might be:

> The French Revolution was not a bourgeois revolution, but a revolt from within the traditional ruling class.

Or,

> Students' study skills problems derive from their perception of the purposes of learning tasks, like essays, and not from the lack of study skills instruction.

2   Hypothesis or question

From the general proposition or thesis we can draw a *hypo*thesis, which, as the name implies, is the conditional form of the thesis, expressed in its characteristic 'If, then' form: 'If *A*, then *B*, *C* and *D*'. This is our 'What if' proposition: 'What if the French Revolution was not a bourgeois revolution?'; 'What if the turnover of pubs and restaurants *increased* after the introduction of the smoking ban?' From each of these we can draw consequences ('. . . then *B*, *C* and *D*'), which we can then test or find evidence for.

In practical terms the hypothesis translates into a general question, which breaks down into sub-questions. Using these we can apply the abstract concepts in the thesis or general proposition to the concrete evidence that we need in order to show whether the claim we've made is true or not. It gives us the mechanism that will drive our research by spelling out clearly the implications of these abstract terms and how we will recognise them in our research.

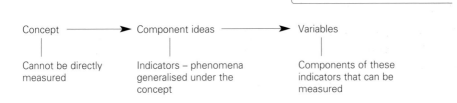

So, from our first thesis or general proposition above, we can derive the following general and sub-questions:

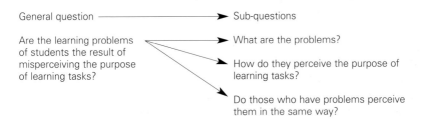

Armed with these, we can go on to decide what variables we're going to use to assess whether the bourgeoisie were 'progressive' and 'capitalist-orientated' or a 'declining aristocratic class of venal office holders'.

We can also do the same with our second thesis above:

General question ──────────────▶ Sub-questions

Are the learning problems of students the result of misperceiving the purpose of learning tasks? ◀──────── What are the problems?

How do they perceive the purpose of learning tasks?

Do those who have problems perceive them in the same way?

Of course, to both of these questions there will be other sub-questions we might want to ask, but you can see how sub-questions are drawn from our general question and how these are the mechanism that drives our research.

Aims and objectives

The distinction between general and sub-questions corresponds to that between 'aims' and 'objectives' respectively. In many outlines that students are asked to complete for their departments there is a section for aims and objectives, which is designed to show how you're going to be able convincingly to confirm or deny your general proposition. While 'aims' are statements of intent expressed in very general terms, 'objectives' are more specific: they clearly spell out the outcomes that we should see if we are to answer our question satisfactorily, or confirm or falsify our hypothesis.

3   Theoretical basis of the research

In this section your main aim is to set your research in the context of the current thinking in your subject and to show how it will make a useful contribution to this. In effect you're arguing that according to the background research there is a problem that needs to be addressed, or a lack of information, or an unanswered question, or a misconception about something, and so on. You're making it clear that you know:

- the background thinking;
- the main issues involved;
- the way opinion divides;
- the gaps in the research;
- and the recent publications on the problem.

You're also showing that you've taken account of all the competing research methods and chosen the most effective tools and techniques.

You need to show how much research you have done, so that you and your supervisor can see if there are any obvious gaps or things you have missed. It's important, therefore, to give the references to your findings, not only to show your supervisor how comprehensive your review has been, but to see if, and where, more work needs to be done.

B   How are you going to find out?

4   Research strategy

A good research design, well chosen, well constructed and relevant to the sort of questions we're asking, is the key to a good project. Once we know our hypothesis or proposal, the main question this raises and the sub-questions this breaks down into, we can set about designing the most appropriate strategy.

In this section we must state clearly what we intend to do and how we intend to do it. So in the first part we might say,

> According to the background literature there is a gap in our understanding . . . a lack of information . . . a problem . . . an unanswered

question about . . . The important aspects to be studied, therefore, are *A*, *B* and *C*.

While in the second part we might say,

In order to investigate these it will be necessary to *X*, *Y* and *Z*.

Remember the way we broke down the relations between these parts in Chapter 3:

Having described the research problem ('the 'aims'), we now have to outline the specific 'objectives' and the activities, procedures and techniques we will use to achieve these. It's important to show clearly how our methods achieve each objective or sub-question. If one of them needs a different method, then we must show that we have catered for this. So be aware of the research methods employed in your discipline and select those most appropriate and apply them thoughtfully. You may want to provide a justification for your choice with perhaps a few references to studies that have used the same or similar methods.

In the humanities you will need to show the kind of ideas you hope to find – contrasts, continuities, correlations, discontinuities, inconsistencies and so on. Then you'll need to show the type of analysis you plan to perform: the way you'll make sense of your findings.

If you choose an empirical study, in which you collect data from primary sources using methods, such as interviews, questionnaires, observations and tests, then reporting these practical elements will affect the content and structure of your dissertation. You will have to have chapters on your research design and on the presentation and discussion of your findings.

Doing this the first time can seem difficult and strange: you're using terms and phrases you're not used to. So go back to the results of your literature search and look at the way academic authors say the same thing when they set out their research:

- How did they describe their methods?
- What terminology did they use?

- What were the key factors studied?
- What methods did they use?

After you've described how you're going to set about your research, give an account of the equipment and costs that may be involved, and any anticipated problems and ethical issues the research might raise. Your aim is to show your supervisor that you've thought of everything. So ask yourself the following questions:

- Does the data I need already exist?
- Have I chosen the right research methods to meet my objectives?
- Would it be best to adopt theoretical or empirical research methods?
- Should I use both quantitative and qualitative methods (see Chapter 18)?
- Are there likely to be obstacles that will slow the research down, or even call for me to rethink the scope of it?

Assess your chosen method: give your reasons for choosing it and the likely advantages and disadvantages. Be prepared to stand back and play devil's advocate. The more problems and weaknesses you try to foresee, the more you will prepare yourself well in advance.

Assessing our research strategy
1 Reliability
2 Validity

Two things are worth considering: reliability and validity. It may seem that both of these are only relevant to research that can genuinely lay claim to being objective, like natural science research. But, although our answers are not likely to be so clear and definitive, we have to find ways of asking the same type of questions in social science and humanities projects.

1   Reliability
In the natural sciences, when we ask whether particular research is reliable, we ask whether the results are repeatable. If we were to use the same methods, equipment and experiments on different subjects, would we get the same result?

In social science and humanities research we ask similar questions. Say, for example, that we have found a certain characteristic of a novelist which, we believe, has been overlooked by reviewers. Before we come to this conclusion, we will have to make sure we can demonstrate it by referring to more than the one novel in which we found it. You might believe that the contradiction you have found at the beginning of chapter 19 of *Adam Bede*, between George Eliot's description of the need for distance and the novel's more general emphasis on novelistic sympathy, runs throughout her work. But if this is to be a reliable conclusion you must demonstrate it in other novels like *Middlemarch* and *Silas Marner*.

2   Validity

The other concern is for validity, that by using the methods we have chosen we are really measuring what we think we are. In our empirical research, above, into the learning problems that students experience when they use their study skills, we must first discover what these problems are. If we decide to use a student questionnaire to discover this, we would have to ask ourselves how reliable this is likely to be; whether we are, in fact, just collecting evidence about what students *think* their problems are and not what they *actually* are.

C   What is likely to be the significance of my answers?

5. Significance – what it might lead to

Although your answer to this is likely to be shorter than the other sections, it calls for just as much thought and deliberation. You must ask yourself what is likely to be the outcome of your research and what value it is likely to have. What will it add to our theoretical understanding and how will it influence future research in this area? Alternatively, who might benefit and what difference will it make to actual practice in the real world?

> * What value will it have?
> * What will it add to our understanding?
> * What influence will it have on future research?
> * What difference will it make?
> * Who will benefit?

● A typical plan

In the table on page 134 you can see each of the components that a typical proposal is likely to include.

Component	Content
Title	Working title – you may have to tighten this up after you've discussed your proposal with your supervisor – keep it short.
Outline of the problem	The proposition or thesis – the gap you want to fill or problem you want to address.
Aim	Statement of intent – general description of the overall purpose – the hypothesis or general question.
Objectives	The sub-questions – the indicators and variables – specific outcomes that will confirm/falsify the hypothesis or answer the question.
Background	A brief summary of the current thinking on the subject – recent publications; main issues involved; the way opinion divides – and the gaps to be filled or new areas to be examined.
Research strategy	Methods you'll use to collect information – relate back to the aim and objectives; how each method deals with each sub-question – costs and equipment; assess your approach: reliability and validity.
Timetable	Breakdown of stages with deadlines built in: a sequence of things to do which charts a course through your work.
Conclusion	What you think is likely to be the outcome – its significance: influence on future research; who might benefit – relate back to aims and objectives.
References	Those cited in the proposal.
Draft plan of dissertation	Proposed sections, chapter headings and subheadings – like the timetable, it gives order and structure to your work.

Summary

1 A research proposal allows you to see whether your project is practicable or needs to be changed.

2 It will also show whether you will produce the answers that are relevant to the questions you pose.

3 It will reveal whether there are any obvious gaps or things you have missed.

4 You will have to show that the activities, procedures and techniques will achieve your objectives.

5 You will assess your research strategy in terms of its reliability and validity.

6 You will also show why the outcome of your research is significant.

● **What next?**

Now that you know in detail what you have to do, you can break it down into stages with time allotted for each one. In the next chapter we will look at how you can manage your time effectively.

14 Managing your time

In this chapter you will learn . . .

1 how to cope with such a large and complex project;
2 how to find more time and use it most effectively;
3 how to design your weekly timetable to get the most out of your time;
4 how to assess how long each task will take and plot it on your research schedule;
5 how to use deadlines and stocktaking to make sure you keep on track and respond promptly to shifts in your thinking.

Completing any large project successfully calls for constant, sustained effort. Therefore, it's important to plot each stage of your work over the weeks and months ahead, giving yourself plenty of time to complete each task without crises or last-minute panics. Planning your time and building in stage deadlines along the way will help you chart a clear course through the work, so you know what you have to do, in what sequence, and when.

● Planning to cope

This is particularly important at this early stage, when you just want to know what you have to do and whether you can cope. Careful planning of your proposal and your time will give you control over your work. It's reassuring to know you can complete the project on time if you stick to the plan.

Of course, you may discover you've been too ambitious, or not ambitious enough. If it's clear you have taken on too much for the time available, it's better to know now that you must narrow your focus, than later when it will be much more difficult to make changes. You may have to reduce,

- the number of sub-questions;
- the amount of data necessary;
- the length of the historical period you want to study;
- the number of novels to be included;
- the groups you had planned to study;
- the time spent processing your data by simplifying your analysis.

● Constant reality checks

But it's not just at the beginning that planning is important: the reality check you get here is just one of a number you'll need along the way. The worst thing is allowing yourself to slip into a false sense of security. By building deadlines into the plan, and the means of regularly taking stock of your progress, you will always know you're on course.

Consequently, you're relieved of the responsibility of constantly nagging yourself to get back to work or interrogating yourself to see if you've forgotten something. We all know how energy-sapping and stressful this can be. You'll have an early warning device to tell you when you've spent more time on a task than you had planned and that you need to make adjustments. As a result, you avoid all those last-minute nail-biting sessions as you rush to get the work done.

● Motivation

Equally important, more than any other aspect of your work, having a plan maintains your motivation and long-term commitment. Your work will never seem aimless as it otherwise can in a large and complex project. Whatever you're doing you'll be able to see that it is a significant part of the project.

● Finding more time

But perhaps the most surprising aspect is that you're likely to find you have more time than you expected. With a clear plan of what you should be doing and how long it should take you're less likely to take a more relaxed approach to your work and allow it to expand to fill the time available (Parkinson's Law[1]). Unchecked, this is like a computer virus: it will invade every aspect of our work without us even knowing.

● Assessing how much time you have available

First you need to know how much time you have available each week, and from there you can calculate the total amount you have over the coming months to complete the dissertation.

Planning your time

1 Constancy of effort.

2 Stage deadlines chart a clear course through your work.

3 Gives you control over your work.

4 Reduces stress.

5 Early warning device.

6 Stimulates and maintains your motivation and long-term commitment.

7 You'll find you have more time than you expected.

A typical week

To get a clear idea of this, use a copy of the weekly timetable on page 139 and, as you go about your normal week, record accurately the way you use each hour. At the end of the week, count up the number of hours you've devoted to studying, relaxation, social activities, sleep, meals and any other activity. This will give you an accurate account of how you use your time. It will make clear to you where the problems are and what you need to do to solve them.

Planning your weekly timetable

To tackle the problems you've identified, take another copy of the weekly timetable and work through the following steps.

Step 1: Regular activities

First enter onto the timetable all the normal routine things you do each week: regular class times, family commitments, meal times, the hours of sleep you normally need, regular social activities, any paid employment, the time you spend travelling each day, and so on.

Step 2: How much study time?

Next, decide how many hours each day you're going to study, and plot them on your timetable. Although this may seem difficult, you need to set yourself boundaries to make sure you use your time efficiently. Otherwise work will just fill up your time, you'll use it wastefully and then experience all the usual frustration and stress.

PERSONAL WEEKLY TIMETABLE

	Monday	Tuesday	Wednesday	Thursday	Friday	Saturday	Sunday
Midnight–1.00							
1.00–2.00							
2.00–3.00							
3.00–4.00							
4.00–5.00							
5.00–6.00							
6.00–7.00							
7.00–8.00							
8.00–9.00							
9.00–10.00							
10.00–11.00							
11.00–12.00							
12.00–13.00							
13.00–14.00							
14.00–15.00							
15.00–16.00							
16.00–17.00							
17.00–18.00							
18.00–19.00							
19.00–20.00							
20.00–21.00							
21.00–22.00							
22.00–23.00							
23.00–24.00							

Step 3: Relaxation

For this reason relaxation needs to be planned just as carefully. You're trying to create the right balance between work and relaxation to give your mind enough time to process your ideas, so that when you return you're clear about what you've done and should be doing. Set aside one day free of work and avoid long unstructured periods of study. Break them up with rest periods.

Step 4: Plotting the times

With all your other activities plotted you can now plot your work, making sure that you plot those activities that call for the highest levels of concentration at those times you work best. For the same reason, try to divide up each study session into manageable periods of, say, two hours, with relaxation in between.

The total time available

Once you've done this, decide how much time you can give your dissertation each week. Then multiply the figure by the number of weeks available, taking out other academic commitments, like assignments and preparation for exams, and holidays.

● **Allocating hours to tasks**

With a clear idea of how many hours you have available, you can begin to allocate them to each task. But, as you do, keep in mind two things:

1 Of all studying, 90 per cent will be undertaken in the last 10 per cent of the time available, so begin early. Start in the summer vacation, or at the latest at the beginning of the autumn term, doing some background reading and assembling your thoughts on possible topics.
2 There's a general rule of research that says you should plan to use only 75 per cent of the time available. This allows for the unexpected and for you to adapt your plans if new opportunities arise. But if this seems too much time to put aside, plan to finish a couple of weeks early to give you a cushion against the unexpected, like delays and illnesses.

List the tasks

List all the tasks and arrange them in a sequence. Be as thorough as you can, listing everything, including bureaucratic jobs and other tasks you think might be good to do if time allows. Until you've been through this exercise you won't know if, in fact, time does allow for them. The project schedule on pages 142–3 will give you an idea of the sort of thing you'll need.

How long will they take?
Once you've compiled this you can begin to assess how long each task will take. It's difficult to be accurate, so give yourself longer than you think. Allow at least 25 per cent of the available time for producing the final draft and two weeks for producing the final product, including binding. The literature review always takes longer than you think and so can the reference list, so play it safe and increase your first estimate, perhaps even double it. The same is true of questionnaires and interview schedules. And you'll be lucky if you're not held up at some point by people, books and other material that suddenly become unavailable.

● **Deadlines**

Now you can begin to enter the start and finish dates for each task onto your project schedule, allowing for all the other commitments we listed above. The more you know about how your time will be spent, the more effective you'll be at managing it and monitoring your progress.

Begin by working back from key dates, when you've got to submit work to your supervisor or fulfil some other requirement, and set yourself interim deadlines to finish each stage. Building in this type of deadline not only breaks up the project into manageable stages marked by them, but helps us avoid Parkinson's Law. Without them we're all inclined to get too involved in one part and lose sight of the overall picture.

● **Stocktaking**

Along with deadlines, another thing you'll find very useful to programme into your schedule a third or half-way through your research, when things are beginning to take shape, is a session with your supervisor to take stock of how things have gone. On the simplest level it's just reassuring for you and your supervisor. You can stand back from your day-to-day work and look back and forward.

Looking back
Looking back, you can both assess how much material you've collected, and its relevance and reliability. If you've experienced problems or you're having

PROJECT SCHEDULE

Stages	Time required	Start date	Finish date	Stocktaking
1 List interests/research preferences				
2 Generate ideas				
3 Shortlist possible hypotheses/research questions				
4 Literature search				
5 Investigate research methods/data collection/analysis				
6 Decide on topic				Supervision
7 Decide on type of investigation/research methods/instruments/techniques				
8 Write this up explaining why you chose them				
9 Write proposal/present to supervisor				Submit to supervisor
10 Plan timetable/deadlines/stocktaking				
11 Organise retrieval system				
12 Plan 1st dissertation outline				

Stages	Time required	Start date	Finish date	Stocktaking
13 Write 1st draft: literature review/ introduction/research methods				Submit to supervisor
14 Gather evidence/data				
15 Sort/analyse results				Supervisor check results
16 Write up results – sort out graphs/ charts etc.				
17 Plan main chapters				
18 Write main chapters				
19 Put 1st draft together – check sequence – co-ordinate intro. conclusions/lit. review				Submit to supervisor
20 Revise structure				
21 Revise content				
22 Reference list/ bibliography				
23 Final presentation Check: contents/ acknowl./title/tables/ pagination				
24 Binding				
25 Submit				

© Bryan Greetham (2009), *How to Write your Undergraduate Dissertation*, Palgrave Macmillan Ltd

difficulties collecting material on one particular aspect of your project, you can take a different route or readjust your project to do without it.

Looking forward

Looking forward, it's reassuring to get a good measure of what you've got left to do. It helps you gain perspective, which might otherwise be buried beneath your day-to-day work. Even more important, you can see how everything fits into the whole with all of their interrelations. If any part is weak or doesn't fit, you have a good chance of seeing it with your supervisor.

Stocktaking
1 Assess relevance and reliability.
2 Make adjustments.
3 Gives you perspective.
4 See how it all fits together.

Of course, it's not unusual to find that either you've got bogged down in one particular area, which has taken on much more significance, or you've been diverted down an unexpected path. This may be a reflection of a shift in your thinking, showing that this is now the really important issue, or that you were interested in this all along and not those you highlighted in your proposal. If so, you will have to work with your supervisor to reconsider and adjust your main question or hypothesis. It may just involve looking again at your sub-questions to realign them with the material you've collected.

> Stocktaking will reveal any significant shift in your thinking.

But it is better to confront these challenging questions now rather than later when the mismatch of questions and evidence will have been written into the structure and content of your first draft. It is much more difficult to deal with it then. So, before you begin to interpret your material or analyse your data in preparation for your first draft, you need to be clear exactly what you want to know and what is driving the way you're processing the material. Stocktaking, after an extending period of working with the material, is your opportunity to deal with this and give your project a clear focus for the final stages of your work.

● Planning more than one thing at a time

If there's not enough time to fit in all the jobs you've listed, you may have to reduce the scope of your project. But, first, ask yourself two things:

1 Can any of the jobs be **compressed** – is every aspect of a job essential?
You may find you're duplicating work by collecting material that you've already got from elsewhere.

2 Can any of the jobs be **done in parallel**? Be clear about those that have to be done in sequence and those that can be done at any time while you're doing something else.

> Think about . . .
> 2.1 Mixing lower, with higher, priority jobs – otherwise you may find the lower priority jobs will never get done.
> 2.2 Mixing longer-term work with shorter-term work.

For example, it's important to start writing early, rather than leave it, intending to write it up at the end. Ideas are organic; they grow and develop the more we work on them. Left to the last minute, not only can they seem rushed, but even naïve and poorly developed.

Nevertheless, be alert to those periods in your schedule when it seems you will be doing too many things at once. If there is no alternative, give yourself sufficient time away from your work to allow your mind to process the ideas and for you to see things in perspective.

● Making your schedule work

Most of us are good at drawing up the most comprehensive plans; the secret is making them work. So get into the habit of regularly reviewing your progress against your schedule. If something goes wrong, let your supervisor know. Beyond that, on a day-to-day basis, try to be constantly aware of what you're doing. You can easily get sidetracked into comfort zones: those familiar, reassuring activities that give us the impression that we're doing real work, particularly when we're tired and under pressure. So, check your schedule every day or two, or at least once a week.

Weekly work schedule

Days	Urgent jobs	Non-urgent jobs
Monday		
Tuesday		
Wednesday		
Thursday		
Friday		
Saturday		
Sunday		

To help you, plot on your weekly timetable a half-hour each day to check the jobs you've got to do the next day, and half an hour at the weekend to check next week's work. You need to have a moment in your week when you check what's been done and what needs to be done.

Check each day and each week what you've got to do.

It helps to have a routine weekly form, like the one on page 146, listing those things that need to be done that week, and then display it prominently where you generally work. You'll also find it useful to list on the same form additional non-urgent things that you might have time for, if one of the urgent items drops out because it can't be done, or because you've completed it sooner than you expected.

● Checklist

The last two chapters have involved a complex process full of difficult decisions and fine judgements. So, before you leave it, check that you have done everything well by going through the checklist below and asking yourself these questions.

Checklist

1 Am I clear about my thesis or general proposition and the research question derived from it?

2 Have I chosen the best sub-questions to produce the evidence to show whether my thesis or proposition is true or false?

3 Have I chosen the best research method to get the data?

4 Have I chosen the most appropriate tools and techniques (e.g. questionnaire, interviews, observations, etc.)?

5 Have I played devil's advocate to check that my project is reliable, valid and significant?

6 Have I made clear the link between my project and the background literature?

7 Is the structure of the project clear?

8 Have I designed a clear, workable weekly timetable?

9 Am I confident that I have allotted the right time to each task and have a well planned project schedule?

10 Have I discussed my proposal and project schedule with my supervisor?

Summary

1 Planning your timetable in detail before you start will allow you to chart a clear course through your work and relieve you of much of the stress.

2 It will also help maintain your motivation as you complete each task.

3 Allow much more time than you think you'll need – there are always unexpected holdups.

4 Plan stocktaking sessions with your supervisor to give you an early warning in case you need to change course.

5 Regularly review your progress each day or two, or at least each week.

● What next?

Now that we know in detail what we have to do and how we're going to use our time to get it done, we have to turn our attention to organising our retrieval system. Otherwise, while we know what we are doing at any time, we will have no guarantee that what we're doing is effective and that we're capturing all the ideas we'll need, to complete our project successfully.

● Note

1   Northcote C. Parkinson, *Parkinson's Law* (London: Helicon, 1958), p. 4.

15 Your retrieval system

In this chapter you will learn . . .

1 how to encourage and catch our own original ideas;
2 how to set up a simple retrieval system using a note-book, journal, card-index system and a project box;
3 how to devise forms we can use routinely in supervisions and as we read to record ideas and things we have to do.

In the 40 years following the invention of printing and the publication of the Gutenberg Bible around 1450, it is thought that anything between 8 million and 24 million books were published. Out of this developed a model of education dependent on a linear exposition of ideas in books and journals, which we read carefully in quiet contemplation as we process and evaluate ideas.

Now, the Internet is changing all that for learners of all ages. According to a recent report by the British Library and researchers at University College London,[1] rather than read in the traditional sense, we 'bounce' 'horizontally' from one site to another in search of quick wins, spending only a few minutes on each. This is likely to have a significant impact on the way we generate and develop our ideas.

● Clearing a space for thought

For those of us engaged in research it presents a real problem. Research is a continuous, unbroken process: our ideas are constantly evolving, suddenly appearing in a new form at unexpected times. Therefore, the quality of our work depends upon whether we can catch our brightest ideas and sharpest insights as and when they occur.

For this we need to de-clutter our minds: in order to lure good thoughts out we need to clear a space for them. But for much of the time our mental space can be full of irrelevant preoccupations that prowl around and hijack our minds. In such a cluttered mind there's no room for serious thought. The thoughts may be there, full of insight and vision, but, if we can't clear a space to think quietly and tap into them, we can easily pass by without even knowing they are there.

● A retrieval system

Then, once we've created space, we need a retrieval system that is sufficiently adaptable to catch the ideas *whenever* and *wherever* they show themselves, and to provide us with a means of accessing them easily. This calls for a thoughtful approach, a little imagination and, above all, flexibility.

> • Clear a space for good ideas to come through.
> • Create a retrieval system to catch ideas whenever and wherever they appear.

It's easy to overlook the importance of this. Its influence is never neutral. Get it right and we can find ourselves with an abundance of insightful ideas that are genuinely our own. Get it wrong and our work struggles to rise above the predictable and imitative.

> Without a good retrieval system we will lose many of our best ideas and our work will be predictable and imitative.

● Notebook

Whether we're aware of it or not, there is a constant internal dialogue going on in our minds as we work at the problems we've set ourselves in our research. But good ideas only come to the prepared mind: one that is alive to this dialogue and ready to record insights whenever they appear. These brilliant flashes emerge briefly, disappearing almost as quickly. So get used to carrying a notebook wherever you go and record them. They may not come again, and even if they do, they may not have the same lustre, the same vividness, that made them suddenly clear to you and will make them just as clear to your reader.

As we said in Chapter 1, dissertations are designed to see how well we think, and writing is a form of thinking, the most effective way of getting inside our ideas. University education is largely concerned with developing the abilities that enable us to do this – our higher cognitive abilities: to analyse arguments and concepts; to synthesise ideas and evidence to create new ways of looking at something; and to evaluate arguments and evidence.

It is not, as it so often seems, just about understanding ideas and using them appropriately.

> The higher cognitive skills:
> - To analyse arguments and concepts
> - To synthesise ideas and evidence to create new ways of looking at something
> - To evaluate arguments and evidence

Our success depends upon whether we can get to the heart of ideas by analysing their parts and their relations with other ideas; by seeing how they correlate, contrast and compare; how they synthesise with others to give us significant, original breakthroughs in what we know. So your notebook is there to catch that sudden insight when you see these relationships. It's the way you record the continual analysis and synthesis of your ideas going on beneath the surface.

And the most remarkable thing is that the process is self-fuelling: the more you invest, the more you are rewarded. If you allow your ideas to come tumbling out onto the page or you write out the problem that's troubling you, the subconscious will go away to sort through your data banks for more ideas and evidence, making connections and analysing your arguments and concepts in ways you just hadn't suspected when you set out to think about the issues. As a result, when you next come to look at your ideas, you'll be surprised by just how far they have developed.

> It's a self-fuelling process: the more you invest, the more you are rewarded.

● Journal

A notebook, then, is the best way of tapping into ideas as they develop. By contrast, a journal gives you a way of being more active; a method of stimulating them. Using either a manual or computer file, work two or three half-hour sessions into your weekly timetable each week to write about your work.

Most of us only very rarely allow ourselves to write freely about our ideas. Usually we write having been set an assignment, or while we work with books or notes, so the ideas that are genuinely ours, untainted by what we're reading or referring to, rarely reach the surface, although they're always there.

And, like the notebook, the process is self-fuelling. The first time may be a struggle, but then on the second and subsequent occasions there are more ideas to develop. You set your mind the task of coming up with the ideas and while you're not consciously thinking about it, it does just that, ready to produce them when you call for them.

> Write freely, untainted by what you read.

Dissertations are about deep, unaided thought: not just showing that you understand an idea and how to use it, or even developing arguments in the way you think your tutors want you to, but allowing your own ideas to come through and developing them for yourself. To do this you need to write freely on a regular basis.

This will give your whole project coherent shape as well as help maintain your motivation and sense of purpose. Recording your continuity of thought will help you avoid the plight of many dissertations that disintegrate into a series of disjointed essays. Remind yourself that research is not a tidy process: your best ideas will not come as if from nothing in those last few weeks you might otherwise give over to writing up your research notes. They only come from a continuous process of coherent thought recorded in notebooks and journals.

> • Dissertations are about genuine thinking; deep, unaided thought.
> • This comes from a continuous process of coherent thought recorded in notebooks and journals.

● Index-card system

Equally important is an index-card system. Divided into sections for each chapter or section of the dissertation, it gives us a unique way of catching things that we would otherwise miss. Whenever we come across an interesting idea, an isolated statistic, or a useful quotation, it's difficult to know exactly what to do with it. Do you write it up on a sheet of paper? But if you do, where are you going to file it? And it's all too easy to lose just one sheet. To catch all these isolated items use a simple, flexible card system. Using just one card for each item – a quotation, an argument, an idea, or a set of figures – you'll have a retrieval system that makes it very easy to find what you want whenever you want it.

It's also a simple way of recording all our sources with a brief note of why they were useful, so we have a clear idea of how we might use them again. This will save you an enormous amount of time, when you begin to compile your reference list and bibliography. There are few things more frustrating than spending hours tracking down a reference that you failed to record at the time. With all the bibliographical details recorded at the top of the card, you have all the information at your fingertips when you need it.

Bibliographical details	
Book	Author – year of publication – title – publisher – place of publication
Journal article	Author – year of publication – title of article – full title of journal – volume and issue numbers – page reference

What's more, with the limited space it forces you to put the ideas into your own words. If the phrase or section in the text is so telling that no summary in your own words will capture the idea, then you're restricted to recording only short quotations of a sentence or two, which must be chosen with much greater care.

The alternative, of course, is to put all the information on a computer file. Although this allows you to record much more than you otherwise might need, it does give you the advantage of being able to search your records using keywords. Of course, this problem is mitigated if you have your card system divided up into the chapters of your dissertation and you have a good idea of the chapter in which you're likely to find what you're looking for.

Index-card system
1 Catches all those isolated items you might otherwise lose.
2 Easy to find what you want whenever you want it.
3 A simple way of recording the bibliographical details of all your sources.

● Project box

Similarly, you might borrow an idea from professional writers, who often use a project box or file, into which they put anything that comes to hand which might be useful for the project. Take a file, or even an actual box – today you can get plastic boxes which you can divide up into chapters using hanging files – and whenever you come across something that might be useful, drop it in. It may be an article taken from a newspaper or magazine; it may be notes taken from a TV programme; it may be anything that just stimulates an idea that you might otherwise forget.

This has all sorts of advantages. On a practical level, the very fact of having a box of this kind will in itself generate material that we would not otherwise notice. Knowing that we have something into which we can throw all sorts of material is all the encouragement most of us need to set about noticing and collecting it wherever we find it. In this way, we learn to view the project as a developing piece of work, on which, consciously and unconsciously, we're always engaged. As a result, we benefit from all the advantages that come from developing our ideas over time and beyond the normal confines of study.

> - Knowing that we have somewhere to put material, we notice and collect more.
> - It prepares the mind to work on the project continuously even when we're not consciously thinking about it.

● Record sheets

Finally, you'll find it helpful to devise a simple routine system of recording important information as it comes in, so that you can access it directly and in a usable form when you need it. For example, a simple A5-size form could be used to record all the vital information that might come from a meeting or a phone conversation. It could include not just the contact details, but the key issues discussed, a summary of the ideas and information that came from it, how this connects with the different sections or aspects of your research, and any follow-up work, like new avenues that need to be pursued and questions that need to be answered.

The same could be said for designing a standard form that you use each time you have a supervision, separate from the normal notes you take. On a

Contact record

Contact details	
Key issues discussed	
Connections	
Follow up	

single sheet you could record the key issues that were raised and the things to follow up as a result. This makes it clear what you have to do. It won't be lost somewhere within the notes you've taken, which often results in over-sights and missed opportunities.

Summary

1   We need a retrieval system which will catch our ideas whenever and wherever they appear.

2   Learning to live with a notebook and journal helps us get inside our ideas and develop our higher cognitive abilities.

3   An index-card system and a project box give us ways of catching material we would otherwise miss.

 What next?

Now that we have a system to catch ideas from our own internal sources, we can begin to read and process the material from our external sources. In the next two chapters we will see what we have to do to become more efficient readers and note-takers.

 Note

1   The study is available from www.tinyurl.com/2eslnr

16 Reading

In this chapter you will learn . . .

1 how to narrow down the sources we have to read by checking their reliability and relevance;
2 how to avoid spending more time than we can spare on our sources;
3 how to read purposefully, skimming, scanning and reading word-for-word;
4 the difference between deep-level and surface-level processing;
5 how to achieve deep-level processing of the ideas and arguments we read.

One of the most time-consuming jobs you will have to do is to place your project in the context of the literature of your subject. This will entail a great deal of reading. It will typically include:

- Standard texts in your subject.
- The most recent research published in books and journal articles.
- Texts on research methods.
- Primary source literature.
- Professional sources.
- Government reports.

A bibliography of an undergraduate dissertation could include anything between 25 and 50 references. So you must make sure,

1 that a particular text is worth reading; and
2 why you're reading it.

Otherwise, it's easy to spend far too much time on the literature, getting involved in what you're reading and forgetting why you're reading it. It has the potential to waste more of your time than you can possibly spare and you'll end up with a vast amount of unusable material. For a typical dissertation the literature search and review could take up to 30–40 per cent of the time, so you must make sure you read only what you have to and in the most efficient way.

● Deciding what's worth reading – reliability

The two questions listed above raise the twin concerns, the two Rs: reliability and relevance. First, reliability: here our job is to assess as far as we can the source and the author of the literature. Each time you pick up a text, ask yourself the questions in the table below. If you can answer satisfactorily more than half, it is probably worth reading, but if you can't, it may not be. And even if it is directly relevant to your topic and indispensable, read the content with these reservations in mind and, perhaps, raise them in your literature review.

The author

Most of these questions raise concerns that are fairly obvious. If no-one is named as the author it may be that no-one is willing to accept responsibility for the views expressed. Their qualifications may be irrelevant to this area of study, so it's worth checking to see if they are well-known authorities, perhaps by entering their name into a search engine. You can also check to see how much they have published in this area before, and perhaps who they work for, whether it's an academic institution or a commercial body.

Reliability of source material	
Authors	Are the authors named?
	Are their qualifications relevant?
	Are they well-known authorities?
	Do they have other publications?
	Who do they work for?
Sources	Has the article been paid for?
	Has it been refereed or edited?
	Is this a primary or a secondary source?
	What references have been cited?
	How does it compare with other sources on the same subject?

Nevertheless, be careful about dismissing a source on this basis alone. An author may not be known, or may not be an authority, but still he or she may have done some quite remarkable, ground-breaking work, which has placed them outside the conventional thinking in their subject.

Example: Modern physics

In 1905, four research papers in physics were published by a lowly, unknown 'Engineer, Second Class' employed in the Patent Office in Bern, who had been rejected by every academic institution and had published nothing before. But now no-one doubts the significance of Einstein's papers and the impact they had on modern physics.

The source

As for the source itself, there are obvious questions that are worth asking. If the article has been paid for, it might be serving other interests than the truth. If it is a secondary source, the authors may have selectively used the primary source in order to support their arguments. Of course it's reassuring to know that the source is supported by other sources on the same subject and that it cites others in support of its case. And if it has appeared in a journal that is refereed by the author's peers, this is usually a good guide to its reliability. Still, this is not always a guarantee of excellence.

Example: Postmodernism

In 1996, Alan Sokal, a physics teacher at New York University, wrote a hoax paper which parodied the arguments of postmodernist thinkers. Despite the fact it made no sense and was just built around quotes from these writers, his paper was published unchanged by a peer-reviewed journal.

● Deciding why you're reading it – relevance

While reliability is an obvious concern, relevance will determine how much of your valuable time you will spend on the literature.

Read purposefully

So, read purposefully: know what you're looking for so you don't waste your time. Now that you've set your ideas down in your proposal you'll know the question and sub-questions you want to answer, so there is less likelihood that you'll be sidetracked. Armed with this you can answer two questions:

1 Is this text/article relevant?
2 If so, what part(s) do I need to read carefully word-for-word?

A search of the literature may throw up as many as 100 different sources, so you need to skim and scan them to decide which you need and what parts of them. Although we all use these different reading strategies, it's useful to know exactly what we mean by them.

Reading strategies

1 We can read carefully **word-for-word** when we're reading a text or a passage we know is of central importance to our work, from which we want to extract in our notes the detailed structure of the main points and subsections.

2 In contrast, when we just want to pick up the general impression of the contents, the key ideas and the broad structure of a text or an article, we would do better to **skim** it.

3 And, if we're just looking for an answer to a specific question, say a date, a name, a set of figures, or what the writer says about a certain subject, we need to **scan** it.

Books

With the books listed in our search, it's unlikely that we'll need to read them from cover to cover. Instead we need to pin down exactly what passages are useful. The usual thing we would do is consult the contents and index pages to locate those pages that deal with the questions and issues we're interested in. But if that doesn't help, read the first paragraph of each chapter, where the authors explain what they will be doing in this chapter, and then the last paragraph, where they explain how they've done it.

Failing this, skim each page, picking up a general impression of the contents of each chapter, taking note of the headings and subheadings of sections, which are likely to give you an overview of the structure of the chapter. Alternatively, you can scan each page swiftly, looking for key concepts. You may find these are highlighted in some way, in bold or in italics. See if you can pick out the sequence of ideas as the authors develop their arguments.

Check:
- the contents page;
- the index;
- chapter headings;
- the first and last chapters;
- summaries at the end of chapters and at the end of the book;
- the first and last paragraphs in each chapter.
- **Skim** the text for a general impression of the contents and structure, taking note of headings and subheadings of sections.
- **Scan** for key concepts.
- Pick out the sequence of ideas.

Journal articles

The same principles apply with journal articles, only here we have a little more help. The most useful aspect is the abstract, in which authors give us the main rationale of the study, the key results and their interpretation of them. So, as you read the abstract, ask yourself:

- Is the article too general or too specific?
- Is its main focus different from the focus of your project?
- Are there restrictions (limited number of years, locations or people involved) that make it less relevant to your project?
- Does it contain useful information about the research methods employed and the practical problems involved?

If this shows it could be useful, skim the summary and conclusions. If there is no summary, skim the discussion section, if that's obvious. The key is to see if it's relevant to the question and sub-questions you analysed in your research proposal.

● Processing the ideas

Now you know why you're reading the sources left on your list and what sections you need to read, you can begin processing the ideas more carefully as you read. Ultimately, the quality of the work we produce depends upon the quality of our internal processing of the ideas.

Surface-level processors

There are 'surface-level processors', who read passively, that is without actively analysing and structuring what they read, and without criticising and evaluating the arguments, evidence and ideas the author presents. In most cases this sort of student will use their lower cognitive skills, just to recall and comprehend what they read, but nothing more. When they produce their

Surface-level processing
1 Reading passively.
2 Without analysing and structuring what they read.
3 Without criticising and evaluating it.
4 Using lower cognitive abilities to recall and comprehend.

own ideas and arguments, these will rely almost exclusively on simple description.

Deep-level processors

To achieve the highest grades we must show examiners that we have developed and can use the higher cognitive skills, to analyse, synthesise and evaluate ideas and arguments. This is 'deep level processing': as we read we discuss the author's ideas; analyse their implications; subject them to our own evaluation; and, as our own ideas begin to form, we synthesise the ideas and arguments into a form that reflects our own way of seeing and understanding the problem. This is the source of our own original ideas and insights so don't ignore it or squander it by not noting it as it occurs.

> ### Deep-level processing
>
> **1** Discuss the author's ideas as you read.
>
> **2** Analyse their implications.
>
> **3** Evaluate them.
>
> **4** Synthesise them into a form that reflects our own way of seeing and understanding the problem.

Reading actively

Get into the habit of allowing yourself to respond to what you read. Get your notebook out and write as the thoughts and ideas come to you. Never put it off. If something comes to you clearly, insisting on your attention, give in to it and write out the ideas, arguments and analyses as clearly as you can. Otherwise the intensity with which you see them will soon fade and you may lose the very thing that marks your work as good and original.

> Write down the ideas as they come to you, otherwise you will lose the intensity in which you first saw them.

● Multiple readings

To ensure 'deep-level processing', in most cases it will be necessary to do two or three readings, particularly if the text is technical and closely argued.

Reading for comprehension

In your first reading you might aim just for the lower ability range, for comprehension, just to understand the author's arguments. It may be a journal article on a subject you've never read about before, or it may include a number of unfamiliar technical terms that you need to think about carefully each time they are used.

Reading for analysis and structure

In the next reading you should be able to analyse the passage into sections and subsections, so that you can see how you're going to organise it in your notes. If the text is not too difficult, you may be able to accomplish both of these tasks (comprehension and analysis) in one reading, but always err on the cautious side, don't rush it. Remember, now that you've narrowed down the sources and the pages you have to read, you can spend more time processing the ideas well.

Reading for criticism and evaluation

The third reading involves criticising and evaluating the authors' arguments. It's clear that in this and the second reading our processing is a lot more active. While in the second we're analysing the passage to take out the structure, in this, the third, we're maintaining our dialogue with the authors, through which we're able to criticise and evaluate their arguments. Later, in Part 7, we will explore in detail how we can improve our own ability to reason. The lessons we learn there can be transferred to our criticism and evaluation of those we read. But for now, as you read, ask yourself the questions in the table on page 164. Take a copy of it and keep it by your side.

Breathing space

One last caution – don't rush into this. You will have to give yourself some breathing space between the second reading and this final evaluative reading. Your mind will need sufficient time to process all the material, preferably overnight, in order for you to see the issues clearly and objectively. If you were to attempt to criticise and evaluate the author's ideas straight after reading them for the structure, your own ideas would be so assimilated into the author's, that you would be left with no room to criticise and assess them. You would probably find very little to disagree with the author about.

Criticism and evaluation

Evaluating arguments
1 What are the key claims made by the author?
2 Does she develop them consistently?
3 Does she leave some parts undeveloped which could lead to alternative conclusions?
4 Have any assumptions been made without acknowledging them?

Evaluating evidence
1 Does she use enough evidence to back up her arguments?
2 What kind of evidence is it and does she describe it accurately?
    • From primary or secondary sources?
    • Statistical – how is it described? Is it accurate?
    • Anecdotal – how reliable/representative is this?
3 Does she draw reasonable inferences from it to develop her arguments?
    • Does she draw conclusions that are too strong?
    • Is the evidence relevant to her arguments?
4 What alternative inferences can be drawn from the evidence?
5 What do other authors have to say about this?

Evaluating language
1 Is she consistent in the way she uses words, or do they mean different things at different times?
2. Is the meaning of her arguments obscured by the use of jargon and abstractions?
3 Do we need to analyse concepts to reveal the hidden implications of her arguments?

Summary

1   Unless you assess carefully the reliability and relevance of texts, a literature search and review could take up more time than you can possibly spare.

2   Read purposefully: know what you're looking for, so you don't waste your time.

3   Choose the best strategy to match your purpose.

4   Read actively, so you process the ideas using your higher cognitive abilities.

● What next?

Having processed what you've read in this way, you now need to record the ideas in your notes, so that you have them in a form you can develop. In the next chapter, we will see the different note-taking strategies we can choose from to suit each type of processing.

17 Note-taking

In this chapter you will
learn . . .

1 of the importance of
   being flexible in using
   different strategies of
   note-taking to record
   the different levels of
   processing;
2 that for the different
   levels of processing
   there are the
   appropriate note-taking
   strategies;
3 how best to use linear
   and pattern notes,
   time lines, and
   matrixes to capture
   and clarify our ideas
   for ourselves.

In the last chapter we saw that reading is a much more complex process than we normally acknowledge. Most of the journal articles you've decided to read you will have to read first carefully word-for-word to understand all the complex issues and arguments, then to analyse the article and extract the structure, followed by another reading so you can criticise and evaluate the arguments.

● Be flexible

Then, different levels of processing will have to be recorded in your notes: first to catch exactly the organisation and structure of the ideas, and second, your reactions to them. For each of these there are appropriate strategies of note-taking that will allow you to capture your ideas: the traditional linear notes for analysis and structure, and pattern notes for criticism and evaluation. So try to be flexible: don't use just one strategy for everything. If you've always used linear notes, experiment with pattern notes until you find a style that captures your ideas perfectly.

● Linear notes

Although you may never have been taught how to analyse concepts, how to synthesise evidence and ideas into new ways of looking at problems, or how to criticise and evaluate arguments, at this level you will still be assessed on how well you can do these things. Nowhere is this more obvious than in researching and writing dissertations. But to use this wider range of abilities effectively requires a much more sophisticated and adaptable strategy that responds well to each new demand. It should promote our abilities, not stunt them by trapping us within a straitjacket.

> A good note-taking strategy should promote our abilities, not stunt them.

Structures

Our first task is to process the ideas we read, into structures. Without clear structures we struggle to use our ideas creatively. We don't have the sort of control over them that we need, so that we can reproduce them, rearrange them, and synthesise them with other structures. In Chapters 7 and 8 we looked at the importance of organising our ideas into structures that we can use and manipulate to create new ideas and solutions to problems. Our aim, then, is to identify and extract the hierarchy of ideas from the passages we read, a process which involves selecting and rejecting material according to its relevance and importance.

Linear notes are particularly good at this sort of analytical task. As you can see in the example on page 168, they are the most common form of note-taking. As we develop the structure, with each step or indentation we indicate a further breakdown of the argument into subsections. These in turn can be broken down into further subsections. In this way we can represent even the most complex argument in a structure that's quite easy to understand.

● Matrixes

Alternatively, if you just want to lay out clearly the relations between facts or people a matrix can often be the best strategy. Once you've done this, finding a solution to a problem can be made much simpler.

● Time lines

Similarly effective are time lines. If you haven't already used them or seen them used, you'll find they are particularly good at making clear a sequence of events or, more usefully, the developing relations between different people, movements in thought, or organisations. Often we just want to see the whole picture: how the different things we have studied separately all interrelate. But this sort of synthesis doesn't lend itself easily to most note-taking strategies that are designed principally for analytical work. So, if you want to piece everything together to see the complete whole, use a time line. In the example on pages 170–1 you can see at a glance the complex

---

A section taken from linear notes on genes and gene therapy

---

3   Gene therapy:
    (a)   Definition: technique for correcting defective genes responsible for disease
    (b)   Methods:
        (i)   Replacements –
                I.   Normal gene replaces non-functional gene
                II.   Abnormal gene replaces normal gene thro homologous recombination
        (ii)   Repairs – abnormal gene repaired – selective reverse mutation
        (iii) Regulation (i.e. degree to which regulation is turned on/off) altered

---

4   Common method = I:
    (a)   Vector = carrier molecule delivers gene to target cells
    (b)   Virus = most common vector:
        (i)   Evolved to infect cells
        (ii)   Replace disease-carrying genes with therapeutic genes
        (iii) Types:
                I.   Retroviruses
                II.   Adenoviruses
                III. Adeno-associated viruses
                IV. Herpes simplex viruses
    (c)   Non-viral delivery systems:
        (i)   Direct intro of therapeutic DNA into target cells
        (ii)   Creation of a lipisome – artificial liquid sphere with aqueous core – to pass DNA thro target cell's membrane
        (iii) Linking therapeutic DNA to a molecule that binds to special cell receptors
        (iv) Introduce 47th (artificial human) chromosome into target cells

interrelations between the different schools of thought in ethical thinking over the last two to three centuries.

● Pattern notes

Pattern notes come in various forms and are known by different names, including spider notes and mind or concept maps (see pages 172–3), but the common element is that they allow us to record and develop our own ideas as quickly as they come to us. They are not to be confused with flow charts and other devices we use to represent our ideas graphically so that our

Arrivals to Caribbean islands 1993 to 1997					
(Figures in 1000s)	*1993*	*1994*	*1995*	*1996*	*1997*
Antigua, Barb	240	255	212	220	232
Aruba	562	582	619	641	650
Bahamas	1489	1516	1598	1633	1592
Barbados	396	426	442	447	472
Bermuda	412	416	387	390	380
Brit Virgin Islands	200	239	219	244	251
Cayman Islands	287	341	361	373	381
Cuba	544	617	742	999	1153
Curaçao	223	238	232	219	209
Dominican Republic	1609	1717	1776	1926	2211
Guadeloupe	453	556	640	625	660
Jamaica	1105	1098	1147	1162	1192
Martinique	366	419	457	477	513
Puerto Rico	2854	3055	3132	3095	3249
Saint Lucia	194	219	231	236	248
Saint Maarten	503	568	445	365	439
Trinidad, Tobago	249	266	260	266	324
US Virgin Islands	550	540	454	373	411

readers can understand them. Pattern notes are a method we devise for *ourselves* of representing and working with our ideas as they form. So the key is to develop a system through which you can quickly record your thinking. The best pattern notes allow you to work as fast as the ideas appear and as you see their connections with other ideas.

Obviously, our ability to discuss and criticise the implications of what we read and to develop our own ideas depends first on the skills needed to lay bare their structure and record it, most probably using linear notes. But after this, as we begin to generate our own ideas on the passage, our criticisms and evaluation, we need a strategy that will respond in a flexible way to capture these as they develop.

Timeline:

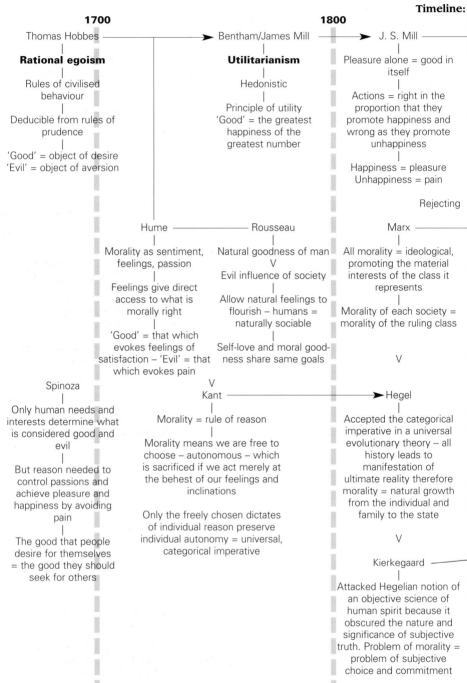

1700

Thomas Hobbes ——→ Bentham/James Mill ——→ J. S. Mill ——

1800

Rational egoism

Rules of civilised behaviour

Deducible from rules of prudence

'Good' = object of desire
'Evil' = object of aversion

Utilitarianism

Hedonistic

Principle of utility
'Good' = the greatest happiness of the greatest number

Pleasure alone = good in itself

Actions = right in the proportion that they promote happiness and wrong as they promote unhappiness

Happiness = pleasure
Unhappiness = pain

Rejecting

Hume ———— Rousseau

Morality as sentiment, feelings, passion

Feelings give direct access to what is morally right

'Good' = that which evokes feelings of satisfaction – 'Evil' = that which evokes pain

Natural goodness of man
V
Evil influence of society

Allow natural feelings to flourish – humans = naturally sociable

Self-love and moral good-ness share same goals
V

Marx ————

All morality = ideological, promoting the material interests of the class it represents

Morality of each society = morality of the ruling class

V

Spinoza

Only human needs and interests determine what is considered good and evil

But reason needed to control passions and achieve pleasure and happiness by avoiding pain

The good that people desire for themselves = the good they should seek for others

Kant ———————→ Hegel

Morality = rule of reason

Morality means we are free to choose – autonomous – which is sacrificed if we act merely at the behest of our feelings and inclinations

Only the freely chosen dictates of individual reason preserve individual autonomy = universal, categorical imperative

Accepted the categorical imperative in a universal evolutionary theory -- all history leads to manifestation of ultimate reality therefore morality = natural growth from the individual and family to the state

V

Kierkegaard ————

Attacked Hegelian notion of an objective science of human spirit because it obscured the nature and significance of subjective truth. Problem of morality = problem of subjective choice and commitment

Ethics

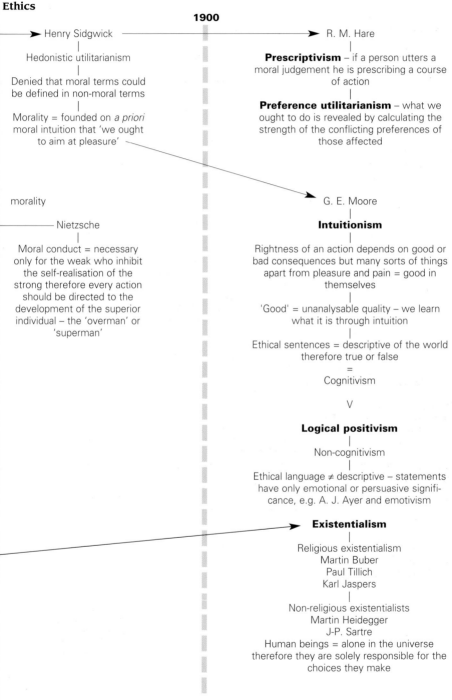

1900

Henry Sidgwick

Hedonistic utilitarianism

Denied that moral terms could
be defined in non-moral terms

Morality = founded on *a priori*
moral intuition that 'we ought
to aim at pleasure'

morality

Nietzsche

Moral conduct = necessary
only for the weak who inhibit
the self-realisation of the
strong therefore every action
should be directed to the
development of the superior
individual – the 'overman' or
'superman'

R. M. Hare

Prescriptivism – if a person utters a
moral judgement he is prescribing a course
of action

Preference utilitarianism – what we
ought to do is revealed by calculating the
strength of the conflicting preferences of
those affected

G. E. Moore

Intuitionism

Rightness of an action depends on good or
bad consequences but many sorts of things
apart from pleasure and pain = good in
themselves

'Good' = unanalysable quality – we learn
what it is through intuition

Ethical sentences = descriptive of the world
therefore true or false
=
Cognitivism

V

Logical positivism

Non-cognitivism

Ethical language ≠ descriptive – statements
have only emotional or persuasive significance, e.g. A. J. Ayer and emotivism

Existentialism

Religious existentialism
Martin Buber
Paul Tillich
Karl Jaspers

Non-religious existentialists
Martin Heidegger
J-P. Sartre
Human beings = alone in the universe
therefore they are solely responsible for the
choices they make

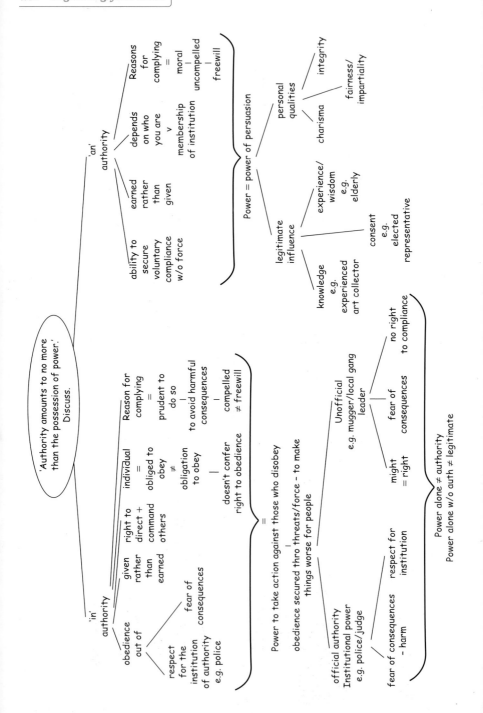

'Authority amounts to no more than the possession of power.' Discuss.

'in' authority

obedience out of
- respect for the institution of authority e.g. police
- fear of consequences

given rather than earned

right to direct + command others

individual = obliged to obey ≠ obligation to obey
- doesn't confer right to obedience

Reason for complying = prudent to do so — to avoid harmful consequences — compelled ≠ freewill

'an' authority

ability to secure voluntary compliance w/o force

earned rather than given

depends on who you are v membership of institution

Reasons for complying = moral — uncompelled — freewill

Power = power of persuasion

legitimate influence
- knowledge e.g. experienced art collector
- experience/wisdom e.g. elderly
- consent e.g. elected representative

personal qualities
- charisma
- integrity
- fairness/impartiality

=
Power to take action against those who disobey — obedience secured thro threats/force – to make things worse for people

Unofficial e.g. mugger/local gang leader
- might = right
- fear of consequences
- no right to compliance

official authority Institutional power e.g. police/judge
- fear of consequences - harm
- respect for institution

Power alone ≠ authority
Power alone w/o auth ≠ legitimate

MIND/CONCEPT MAP

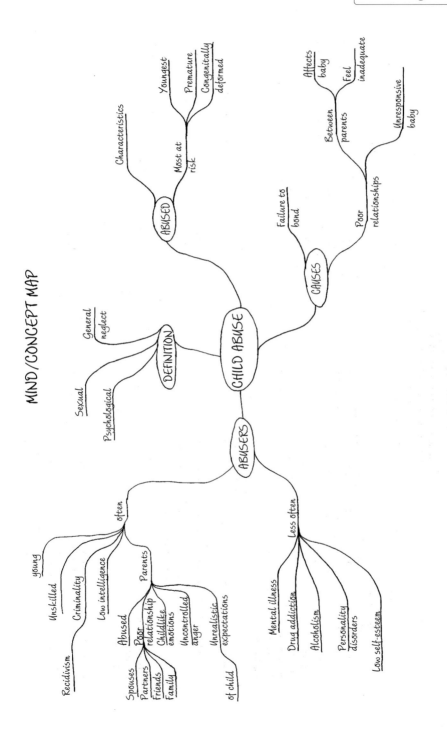

So even if you've already taken one set of linear notes recording the structure, set aside time later to sit down with a blank sheet of paper and tap into your own ideas and criticisms, which will have been self-organising in your mind since you finished reading. It usually takes less than 30 minutes. The ideas will come tumbling out and you will be surprised at just how good they are and how much you have to say about it.

> Set aside time to sit down with a blank piece of paper and write down *your* ideas about what you've just read.

The problem is that in genuinely thinking for ourselves, and not just recycling the received ideas of others, we have to keep up with the ideas as they come at us rapidly from all angles without any apparent predictability. Our minds can simply produce ideas so much faster than we can find the words to write them down. Pattern notes not only allow us to keep up, but also enable us to work on several lines of discussion simultaneously. In the process they give our own ideas much greater prominence, so that when we begin our research we're better prepared to evaluate and select from what we read.

Summary

1 For each level of processing there is the appropriate note-taking strategy.

2 Be flexible: don't just use one strategy for everything.

3 Good note-taking strategies should promote our abilities, not stunt them.

● What next?

We said earlier that the unique importance of dissertations as a mode of assessment is that they allow us to be assessed on not just *what* we think, but *how* we think. Genuine thinking is characterised by the ability to think about our thinking: how we gather evidence, analyse and evaluate it, and use it to create consistent, compelling arguments. As a result, thinking for ourselves and gathering our own ideas and insights take centre stage.

This means we must be flexible in how we organise our retrieval system to catch our own ideas, and in how we read and take notes, so that we can process ideas using our higher cognitive skills. In the last three chapters we've seen different ways in which this can be done. We can now move on to the mechanics of our research to see how we use techniques to gather and analyse evidence; the different skills required for qualitative and quantitative research; and how we can use effectively primary and secondary sources in our research.

Part Five

Doing your research

18 Qualitative and quantitative research

In this chapter you will learn . . .

1 the difference between qualitative and quantitative research and the problems that both present;

2 how to choose the most appropriate methods for gathering and analysing quantitative data for your project;

3 how to triangulate your sources to ensure your conclusions are reliable;

4 three rules for coping with the unique problems of qualitative research;

5 how to pin down exactly what you need and how to find it.

In Chapter 13, as we wrote the research proposal, we found that a key problem at the heart of our research strategy was how to translate the abstract concepts in our thesis or general question into terms that would indicate the concrete evidence we will need in order to show whether our proposition is true or false.

To do this we broke our thesis down into sub-questions, which gave us the variables that we need to measure. We then set this all out in our 'aims' and 'objectives'. If you remember, our aims are statements of intent expressed in very general terms, while our 'objectives' clearly spell out the outcomes that we should see if we are to answer our question satisfactorily, or confirm or falsify our hypothesis.

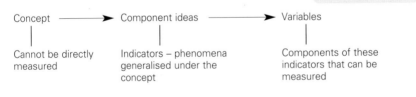

Concept	Component ideas	Variables
Cannot be directly measured	Indicators – phenomena generalised under the concept	Components of these indicators that can be measured

Now we've reached the point where we need to see how we're going to make use of the techniques we've decided to use (quantitative or qualitative) and the tools, if any, we will need to design (questionnaires, interview strategies, case studies and so on). We also need to decide which source or, more likely, combination of sources (primary or secondary) is most likely to meet our needs. In the process we will answer those epistemological questions we mentioned in Chapter 3: what sort of evidence will count as an answer to our problem and how are we to find it?

● Quantitative research

Dissertations can be based on qualitative or quantitative approaches, or a combination of both. What you choose will depend on your abilities and preferences, which we discussed in Chapters 3, 4 and 5, but it has to be suitable to your topic and you must be able to justify your choice.

Modelled on the scientific method, the aim of quantitative research is to be as objective as possible by basing conclusions on statistical findings and other measurable empirical data. The situation or events you are researching must be capable of being expressed in terms of numbers, in an order of magnitude, which can then be analysed mathematically, either simply in terms of percentages, averages and so on, or in more complex ways using statistical tests or mathematical models.

The most obvious examples include population statistics, crime figures, economic and business data and scientific findings. But there are also a surprising number of examples of less obvious subjects and situations that can be converted into numbers, even things like opinions and beliefs – how many people hold a particular opinion and how strongly someone holds a particular belief.

- The situation or event must be capable of being expressed in numbers.
- This can mean all sorts of things, including the strength of people's beliefs and opinions.

Your choice as to how you measure and analyse data will depend on the sophistication of the way you want to use your findings, draw conclusions from them, and then present them in your dissertation. In Chapter 20 we will examine these ways in more detail, but if you explain to your supervisor or research methods tutor what sort of conclusions you would like to draw, he or she will explain the different ways in which data can be analysed and processed. Either that or they can point you to where you can find the statistical help you need or the short courses you could take to develop the necessary skills.

● Qualitative research

In contrast, qualitative research is based on data that cannot be converted into numerical form. Expressed in words describing attitudes, feelings, opinions, ideas, customs and beliefs, it cannot be reduced to averages, maximum and minimum values, or percentages. Still, this sort of material is often rich in subtle insights into human behaviour that are essential to understanding individuals, societies and cultures.

Quantitative	Measurable empirical data expressed in numbers
Qualitative	Expressed in words describing attitudes, feelings, opinions, customs and beliefs

Prising these out often depends upon our analysis of concepts and tracing the complex interrelations between the variables we identify. Although concepts like tragedy, authority and friendship are more difficult to pin down in numerical terms, they are still manifested in detectable ways. We can identify them just as certainly in our daily lives as we read and interpret our observation notes and interview transcripts as well as literary sources, like novels, plays, poems, philosophical texts, historical records, and journals.

Reliability

Nevertheless, as with any source, we have to make a judgement about their reliability. They may be atypical and incomplete, describing just one particular point of view. They may also leave more room for different interpretations and valuations. So we have to develop the habit of 'triangulating' wherever possible: using data from different sources related to the same event or situation to check the completeness and reliability of the account.

Triangulating:	Using different sources related to the same event or situation

An iterative process

Compared with the apparent certainties of quantitative research, with its numerical evidence neatly compiled in charts and computed in percentages, averages and statistics, qualitative research can seem messy and confusing. In many cases our core material is literature and texts, in which are expressed people's ideas, values, beliefs and opinions, all of which we must analyse, interpret, criticise and evaluate. There seems nothing certain in this; just the shifting sands of interpretation. Like the three-step technique that we learnt for analysing concepts, in Chapter 8, an iterative process lies at the heart of all qualitative and text-based work.

The problems are defining precisely what we're looking for and what we should make of it. This is not a simple deductive process in which we start with our thesis or proposition and go in search of material that will support it. As we analyse our material it will reveal new directions to go in as well as dead ends and false leads.

All of this calls for regular re-examination of our original proposition and the questions this gave rise to. Indeed this process of analysis and reinterpretation is the most prominent feature of qualitative research. There is a constant interplay between the material and our interpretation of it. What started off as a simple proposition of what you thought you might find, becomes more developed and nuanced as your understanding deepens and develops.

> The process of analysis and reinterpretation is the most prominent feature of qualitative research.

Start early and keep it focused

Unavoidably, then, this is likely to be both confusing and time consuming. So, start early, don't be too ambitious and try to keep your work fairly focused and limited. There will be a centrifugal force at the heart of your project, urging you to go out further, to pursue ideas to see where they lead just in case they open up new and stunning insights. Although you must allow for this, try to keep it within reason. And remind yourself that whatever your conclusions are, the examiner will want to see that they are based on your materials. If your materials indicate only partial support for your original proposition, then your conclusions and arguments need to reflect this in carefully chosen language that captures precisely the degree of assurance.

- Start early.
- Don't be too ambitious.
- Try to keep your work fairly focused and limited.
- Whatever your conclusions, the examiner will want to see that they are based on your materials.

Your success will depend as much on your capacity to think clearly and argue consistently as it does on your material. You need to have good, convincing arguments to support your interpretation of the material.

Success = sound reasoning + good evidence.

Three rules
To cope with these problems, make sure three simple rules are at the heart of your working practice:

1 Analyse and process material as you go along
Set down your analysis and interpretation of material when it's still fresh in your mind. Research is a time-consuming business. The more time you give your ideas to develop the better they will be. As you record them they will generate new ideas and insights. You'll see gaps and inconsistencies in the material. All of this will throw fresh light on your own assumptions, perhaps revealing your own biases, giving you unexpected ways of developing your project.

So, for example, as soon as possible after the event, process the notes you take during an interview or observation. Otherwise you'll lose those valuable insights, which disappear as quickly as they come. As you're reading a text, ideas will come to you, they will form a pattern. Note it as soon as it takes shape. After a while you'll find yourself looking for material that will support the pattern. But at the same time you'll come across other material that won't fit, so you'll have to adjust the pattern to reflect these nuances and develop a more complete model.

2 Be prepared for change
From your background reading and your analysis of the problem and its concepts in Chapters 7 and 8 you developed a structure composed of a set of concrete components that guides your search for evidence. Be prepared to refine and adapt these as you collect and process material. Test and develop them. You may have to change or even reject them as your understanding develops.

3 Wherever possible, clarify your ideas visually
To help clarify your ideas for yourself, wherever possible illustrate your findings using pattern notes, tables, matrixes, graphs and charts. Processing ideas while we read texts is always difficult. The mind works to create structures out of what it reads, but this is hidden deep in sequential and unstructured text. It's often not easy to see it, hidden by words and complex sentence structures. So make it easier both for you and, ultimately, for your reader by displaying the ideas in visual form.

> **Three rules**
>
> **1** Analyse and process material as you go along.
>
> **2** Be prepared for change.
>
> **3** Wherever possible, clarify your ideas visually.

● **Combining the two**

In practice, outside humanities subjects, few dissertations involve only quantitative or qualitative methods. You may want to balance the quantitative analysis that shows social trends, or reveals the impact of certain government policies, with a qualitative study of people's attitudes, in which you describe what people have told you and quote from interviews you've conducted. This will help you support your findings by triangulating your sources, all of which might, or might not, confirm the effects of the policies.

Even so, in most studies there will be an orientation to one end of the spectrum or the other. So check to see what data you will need, and make a list. Sort them into categories – primary or secondary, and quantitative or qualitative.

Example: Study skills

In our project on the study skills problems of university students, it would be useful to gather quantitative data to show how prevalent are the problems they have with note-taking or reading, perhaps by setting them tests and exercises to see how well they do. But it would also be useful to have qualitative data to show why they think they have these problems and which of them they believe is the most serious, perhaps by interviewing them or observing them in class.

Things to do . . .
1 Make a list of the data you need.
2 Sort them into categories – primary or secondary
                                     – quantitative or qualitative.

● Abstract concepts

Of course in most projects our problem is to make sure that the abstract concepts we've used to describe our proposition or thesis have been analysed into concrete components, for which we can find evidence. For some there will be quantitative sources of evidence, while for others we'll have to rely on qualitative sources.

Example: Study skills

In this project we may have distinguished between 'dependent' and 'autonomous' students, so we need to know exactly what to look for in a student's learning behaviour to decide which category he or she might belong to. An autonomous student, for example, might be someone who is self-motivating, self-reliant and confident about relying upon her own judgement, whereas a dependent student needs clear instructions about what to do and is reluctant to criticise those he regards as authorities.

In Chapter 8 we saw that similar concepts feature in every subject, concepts like 'bribes', 'authority', 'privacy', 'needs', 'tragedy' and 'revolution'. There we looked at the three-step technique of analysing them into their component parts. But whatever the concept, and whatever the subject, you can analyse the concepts in the same way to find the concrete components for which you will need to find evidence – qualitative or quantitative.

To make sure you know exactly what evidence you'll need and how you're going to find it, work through the questions in the checklist on page 186.

Quantitative or qualitative?

---

1 Have I compiled a list of the data I will need?

2 Do I have to gather it all myself or is it already collected, analysed and recorded?

3 How much of it is quantifiable?

4 Will this yield sufficiently meaningful results with enough depth or will my conclusions based on it be superficial, even spurious?

5 Do I have to support it with qualitative evidence?

6 How reliable is the qualitative data I can collect? Are there ways of ensuring it is more reliable?

7 Have I analysed the abstract concepts into concrete components for which I can find evidence?

Summary

1   In practice most dissertations are a combination of both quantitative and qualitative research.

2   There are a surprising number of subjects and situations that can be researched using quantitative research methods.

3   The most prominent feature of qualitative research is the constant process of analysis and reinterpretation.

4   To cope with qualitative research, analyse the material as you go along, be prepared for change and clarify your ideas visually.

● **What next?**

Now that we know the difference between quantitative and qualitative research, and the problems that each presents, we can turn to the other important distinction, between primary and secondary sources.

19 Secondary sources

In this chapter you will learn . . .

1 how to distinguish between primary and secondary sources;
2 how you can do your dissertation, relying entirely on secondary sources, using either quantitative or qualitative methods;
3 how this will affect the structure of your dissertation;
4 the advantages and disadvantages of relying on secondary sources.

For understandable reasons, many students are confused about the difference between primary and secondary sources. So we should start by drawing a clear distinction between them.

● Primary and secondary sources – the distinction

The narrow definition of primary material is anything you have collected yourself through questionnaires, tests, observations, interviews and so on. But this is probably too narrow. It excludes much of what is generally regarded as a primary source, including research papers in academic journals. So it is sometimes said that any material is a secondary source if it has been 'interpreted' or 'evaluated', whereas a primary source is material that's free of anyone's personal values or opinions and comes from the original researcher, who collected the data and presented it.

The problem with this, as you can see, is that the researcher herself will have 'interpreted' and 'evaluated' her findings, which, by definition, involves her processing the material according to her own values. She will select and arrange her findings in a hierarchical structure that reflects the importance of certain elements to her way of making sense of it all. So this will not do either.

Although not as clear cut as we would like, the solution is to argue that a primary source is any record of a situation or event which is as close as we can get to it. Usually this means that the ideas or the data are communicated for the first time: government reports, company accounts, the annual report of crime figures, or the ten-year publication of census figures.

> ### Example: A soldier's journal
>
> The journal of a soldier on the Western Front during the First World War, although just his interpretation, full of his value judgements and opinions, is a primary source, because it is one of those sources that gets us closest to the event and was probably one of the first records to be made of it.

Although it's not the medium through which the data is communicated, but the reinterpretation and recycling that it has undergone, which determines what is primary and what is secondary, still a third criterion is that the data has been published in a refereed journal through which the reliability of the source would have been checked by the author's peers. Nevertheless, as we've seen already with Alan Sokal's hoax paper on postmodernism, this is far from foolproof.

> ### Primary sources – criteria
>
> **1** Material that you have collected yourself.
>
> **2** As close as we can get to the event or situation.
>
> **3** Communicated for the first time.
>
> **4** Published in a refereed journal.

It follows, then, that a secondary source is anything that has been recycled: any source which has taken primary sources and has analysed the material, reinterpreted it, indeed, used and developed it in any way. This, too, can include some journal articles, along with commentaries, book reviews, diaries, journals, records of all kinds, both personal and official, anything that takes data about events or developments and sums up the state of things.

● **Secondary sources**

In the following chapters we will examine in detail primary sources and the tools and techniques, both qualitative and quantitative, that we need, to gather material from them. In this one we will examine the use we can make of secondary sources. Most dissertations, of course, call for both. Even if our project draws exclusively on primary sources, we will still have to explore the literature of our subject to get the background to the problem or question we are researching in terms of the current theories and ideas. Nevertheless, most dissertations are usually orientated to one or the other.

Of course, the problem with relying on secondary sources, as we've just seen, is that this is recycled and reinterpreted data, so we have to be sure that the source is reliable. You may use a professional or trade journal widely known and used in your subject. This is the work of practitioners in the field with a wealth of day-to-day practical experience to draw upon. But you have to assure yourself that the journal itself doesn't have its own perspective, its own axe to grind and interests to protect, which may influence the articles it accepts. Its first priority may be to defend its members' interests and their standards of professionalism, so it might be unwilling to accept articles that threaten this.

> Ask yourself . . .
> . . . Does the journal have its own perspective or interests to protect?

In the humanities, too, there are similar problems, though not so much with journals and their vested interests. If you were to rely on a historian's account of events or developments, your main problem would be to check the reliability of his interpretation and the accuracy of the data on which it is based.

Example: Population figures

The historian may have written an account of the economic development of Britain in the seventeenth century, which uses population figures taken from parish registers of births, deaths and marriages. But you know that prior to the nineteenth century and the first official government census these figures were not always reliable. They depended on the efficiency and attention to detail of local parish priests to keep accurate and complete records. So you will have to assess the reliability of the historian's data and the extent to which he has taken this into account.

Good practice in all these cases, of course, is to compare data from different sources and the different interpretations of those who use the same data. If it's an event or a series of events you're interested in, look at several eyewitness accounts. This way you are likely to identify the differences of interpretation of the same phenomenon and the bias, inaccuracies and simple imagination that may have entered into an interpretation.

> Check . . .
> - Data from different sources
> - Different interpretations
> - Different eyewitness accounts

Secondary sources and qualitative research

A question often asked by students is whether they can do a dissertation that totally relies on secondary sources, and, of course, you can – involving both qualitative and quantitative research.

Example: Humanities

Qualitative research of this kind is common in humanities subjects. In literature you might examine how different critics over the years have reacted to the work of a particular author and how this reflects growing appreciation or otherwise of the author's work. In philosophy you might take as your subject one philosopher's analysis of a particular problem or issue, such as R. M. Hare's account of moral thinking, or Wittgenstein's account of the private language argument, and how others have assessed it. Similarly, in history you might analyse one historian's account of a period, a seminal work that takes a unique approach to history, like Thomas Carlyle's *The French Revolution*, or Ferdinand Braudel's *The Mediterranean and the Mediterranean World in the Age of Philip II*.

Example: Social sciences

In the social sciences, qualitative research of this kind tends to concentrate on theoretical issues. You might undertake a detailed comparison of contrasting theories in terms of how well they can be applied to deal with certain social problems. You could examine the usefulness of certain concepts and theories for understanding particular patterns of behaviour. Or, on a more general level, you could assess the value of key theories and concepts in our understanding of the social world. How relevant is the Marxist class analysis to our understanding of modern societies? How useful is the concept of 'relative deprivation' to our understanding of poverty? Typical of this sort of dissertation is the student from the University of Northampton who decided to examine, 'How challenging are Sociobiology and Evolutionary Psychology to the fundamental premises of Sociology?'

Dissertation structure

One important consequence of choosing this sort of theoretical and textual topic is that the content and structure of your dissertation will be quite different from an empirical study using primary data that you have collected yourself. In a theoretical and textual study the structure will be determined by the content. It will simply depend upon what your analysis of the material throws up.

Example: R. M. Hare's *Moral Thinking*

In your analysis of Hare's *Moral Thinking* you might have chapters with titles, like 'Hare's search for foundations', 'Prescriptions as expressions of preferences', or 'Hare's theory of representation', all of which are important aspects of Hare's theory.

In contrast, the structure of a dissertation on an empirical study, in which you have collected original data from, say, interviews, questionnaires and observations, will be determined by the need for you to report on these practical elements of your research. Among other things, you will need to have chapters on your research design, on the presentation of your findings, and on your discussion of these with any recommendations you feel able to make. All of these things and terms like 'methodology' are a foreign language to those subjects in which dissertations are largely theoretical and textual.

Structure	
Theoretical	Depends on what your analysis of the material throws up.
Empirical	Determined by the need to report on the practical elements of your research.

Secondary sources and quantitative research

As for quantitative research, the fieldwork required by primary sources can give the average undergraduate dissertation real problems. Not only can it be very time-consuming, but it can involve financial costs too. So you may prefer to undertake research that involves secondary sources instead.

This has the added advantage that you can work with much larger datasets than you can possibly collect yourself. If the data has been collected on a random basis you can generalise to the population you are studying. Moreover, given the size of these datasets it means you can confidently discuss trends and social changes. They may even allow you to make comparisons over time, if the dataset is the product of a longitudinal study, as some are.

Advantages
1 Less time-consuming and costly.
2 Larger datasets.
3 Generalise to the population you're studying.
4 Discuss trends and social changes.
5 Comparisons over time.

There are a number of different datasets, all useful for different purposes. Every country has its official censuses, usually undertaken every ten years. Most countries have annual reports on the latest crime figures, with comparisons for previous years, sometimes broken down into different areas, towns and cities. In Britain there is the British Crime Survey and the multi-purpose General Household Survey carried out continuously since 1971, except for a break in 1997–8.

Example: General Household Survey

Organised by the Office for National Statistics, it collects information on people living in private households in Britain covering a range of things. Much of this information can be found on the National Statistics Online website (www.statistics.gov.uk/).

Nevertheless, there are disadvantages to relying on such secondary sources. The most serious is that the data may have been collected for a different purpose from yours. It may not meet your needs exactly. So you will have to use it carefully and find out before you use it about the purpose for collecting the data so that you can justify your use of it.

Summary

1   Your dissertation can rely entirely on secondary sources, using qualitative and quantitative methods.

2   Secondary sources are recycled and reinterpreted data, so we have to be sure of their reliability.

3   Using secondary sources saves you the time and cost of collecting your own primary data.

4   It also gives you the advantage of working with larger datasets.

5   But you have to take into account that they may have been collected for different purposes.

● What next?

Although secondary sources can save you a lot of time collecting your own data, you can't always be sure the data will meet your needs exactly. At least with primary sources *you* design the questions so that you get answers precisely tailored to the needs of your research. In the following chapters, we will look at the practicalities of doing qualitative and quantitative research to gather and analyse material from primary sources, and the simple things we can do to make our research effective.

20 Primary sources 1: Quantitative research

In this chapter you will learn . . .

1 how to assemble the best sample of respondents for your study;
2 the different ways of taking random and non-random samples;
3 how to earn high marks by discussing your choices in your dissertation;
4 the advantages and disadvantages of getting information from your sample through tests and questionnaires.

Gathering the ideas, opinions and feelings of people, recording and measuring activities, and observing people and events, is all very time-consuming. There is so much information out there. So we have to find a way of narrowing it down to make the task manageable in the time available. The normal way of doing this in quantitative research is to take a sample from the population of possible subjects.

As this suggests, the 'population' means the entire group of subjects that might be part of the study – all university students who have study skills problems; all those regular patrons of pubs and restaurants who will be affected by the government ban on smoking in public places. Whereas 'sample' means a subset of this – the 50 students chosen at your university who have study skills problems; the 60 patrons selected from pubs and restaurants in Bolton.

● Sampling

However, sampling presents us with two rather obvious problems. First, while we have to ensure that the sample is small enough for us to manage effectively in terms of time and cost, it must be large enough for us to generalise. The smaller the sample, the less generalisable it is. Second, the sample must be representative of the whole population; it must possess the same qualities. This will obviously affect the reliability of our results: the conclusions, recommendations and generalisations we come to.

- Is it large enough to be generalisable?
- Is it small enough to be manageable?
- Is it representative?

There are two methods of taking a sample: random and non-random. Random sampling is the most reliable, and the larger the sample the better. Non-random sampling, of course, depends upon our judgement about who to select for the study, so it cannot usually be relied upon to make accurate generalisations about the whole population. The key factor influencing our choice of which to use is whether the population is homogeneous or composed of different groups and classes.

Random sampling

If the population is homogeneous, simple random sampling is the best choice, although it's not always as random as we might think. If you go out onto the streets at a certain time of the day to interview people randomly, you may find the population is largely composed of one type of person, most of the rest are at home, at work, at school or at college. Some towns have a high density of retired people, while certain areas are full of office workers.

If the population is not homogeneous, then you may find alternative methods of random sampling more reliable. The population may be composed of distinct and different categories, or strata, of people, in which case you can take a 'stratified sample': equal-sized random samples from each one.

Example: Study skills

You might find that the population of students experiencing study skills problems can be broken down into different categories, one of which is mature students over 25. From this you randomly select a certain number, assuming they possess the same characteristics as all other mature students in the population.

Stratified sample:	Equal-sized random samples from each section

Alternatively you could use 'matched samples' where two groups are selected because they possess qualities that are as alike as possible, or 'cluster samples', where groups within the population are selected in terms of the area in which they live or because they share one or more characteristics (they may all have university degrees), but vary in other respects (in age, nationality, sex and so on). Whichever you choose it must meet the needs of your project, so get advice from your supervisor or your research methods tutor.

Matched samples:	Two groups possessing similar qualities
Cluster samples:	Selected by area or shared characteristics

Non-random sampling

The same advice applies to non-random sampling, where there are an even greater number of strategies from which to choose. When the population is large and there are no known characteristics, non-random sampling is useful, but it provides a weak basis for generalisations. The simplest strategy is just to select names from a list at given intervals, say, every 100th name from the electoral register, or every 50th in the telephone directory.

Random sampling:	Simple random sampling Stratified samples Matched samples Cluster samples
Non-random sampling:	Select names at given intervals

Where the population group is homogeneous you can get away with using a small group, but where it's heterogeneous, to be an accurate reflection of it, you will need to have a larger sample, which, of course, can be costly in terms of time, effort and finance.

Discuss your choice

Whatever your choice you will earn good marks if, in your dissertation, you can show that you've made a well-informed judgement after weighing up all the factors. Discuss your decision and don't hide its weaknesses. Let the examiners know that you have considered all the alternative methods and, although you acknowledge that there are weaknesses to your choice, you've got the best sample possible. Outline all the factors you took into account and then describe how you carried out the sampling. Discuss your choice even if eventually you opt, say, for a project based on case studies.

● Tests

Once you have your sample you've got to decide what you're going to do with it. You can either test your potential respondents in various ways or ask them questions, usually through questionnaires and interviews. Tests can give you a very useful and reliable source of quantitative data.

Example: Study skills

In this project it would be a fairly simple matter to set students comprehension tests to assess their reading efficiency, or give them passages from which to take notes to see how well they select ideas and structure them.

But, as you can see from this example, we have to deal convincingly with three related problems when we design and use tests:

1 We have to be clear about what we're testing;
2 That our tests do actually test that and nothing else that we may have overlooked;
3 And that we evaluate each result according to the same criteria.

Alternatively, if you don't want to design and use your own test, there are professional tests you might use, like personality inventories in psychology. These have been developed, piloted and modified after extensive use over many years, so they have been refined to a level we would be hard pressed to match. So ask you supervisor if there are tests you could usefully apply as part of your research strategy.

● Questionnaires

A key problem that runs throughout our research is how to find sufficient depth and richness of ideas and responses counterbalanced with a good spread of responses over large enough representative samples. In some projects it's simply not possible to get both, at least not in the time available, so we have to settle for one or the other. Nevertheless, wherever possible your results will be so much more convincing if you can balance depth with a good spread of numerical results.

Probably the most effective way of achieving this is to use questionnaires to get a general picture of a situation from a sufficiently large, representative sample and then to support and illustrate this with the richness of ideas and opinions that come from in-depth interviews, observations or case studies.

Advantages

A well written questionnaire used on sufficiently large numbers with the results thoughtfully analysed can be an ideal way of getting a clear overall picture of a situation. In most cases it's relatively cheap in terms of time and cost and it's possible to cover a large number of potential respondents. Indeed you're not even limited to a geographical area, if you distribute them through the post.

What's more, as it's impersonal it's a reliable, objective source of data. The questions are the same for all respondents and they don't change in response to the replies given as they often do in interviews. The questioner is also remote, so respondents are under no pressure one way or another. They can work at their own pace and consider their responses for as long as they like. It also means that if the answers are anonymous, it's possible to cover even the most sensitive question.

Disadvantages

Nonetheless, questionnaires have their limitations. The most obvious is that it's difficult to achieve a high rate of response without spending a lot of time chasing them up. If you collect them yourself, you could achieve a response rate as high as 70 per cent, but if you rely on them being returned through the post it can be as low as 10 per cent.

They also tend to favour the more literate respondents, which may introduce bias into the results, particularly if not all of the sample responds. But perhaps the most serious limitation is that simple questions limit the depth of response. Some issues need probing with follow-up questions.

Questionnaires	
Advantages	*Disadvantages*
1 Cheap in terms of time and cost	1 Low rate of response
2 Possible to cover large number of potential respondents	2 Tend to favour the more literate respondents
3 Not limited to a geographical area	3 Simple questions limit the depth of response
4 Reliable and objective	
5 Questions are the same for all respondents	
6 They can work at their own pace	
7 Can cover the most sensitive question	

Summary

1 The sample must be small enough to manage in the time, but large enough to be generalisable.

2 It must also be representative of the whole population.

3 With questionnaires it's possible to cover a large number of respondents with questions that are the same for everyone.

4 But they can tend to favour the more literate and there's a limit to the depth of response.

● **What next?**

Despite their disadvantages, questionnaires remain the simplest way of covering a sufficiently large and representative sample. In the next chapter we will look at how you design and distribute your own questionnaire.

21 Primary sources 2: Designing and distributing your questionnaire

In this chapter you will learn . . .

1 the four guiding principles to follow as you design your questionnaire;
2 how to write questions to ensure that you get reliable, usable responses;
3 the four simple guidelines for writing questions;
4 the different types of questions you can use and how to avoid the most common mistakes;
5 how to process the results.

The design and distribution of your questionnaire are interdependent factors. If it's a self-completion questionnaire, you can post it or have respondents complete it online. Alternatively, you can deliver it personally and complete it yourself as you ask your respondent the questions.

● **Distribution**

As long as your questions are clear and the whole questionnaire is easy to follow and not too long, self-completion questionnaires can be very effective in collecting data on relatively simple subjects or just for getting a clear overview. There's very little limitation on how many you send out and the geographical area you cover. But it's difficult to predict the rate of response, particularly if there is no follow-up, so you will have to approach more people. In turn, the pattern of non-responses can introduce an element of bias into the data with literate responders and those genuinely interested in the issues predominant. This could leave you with questions about the reliability of your results.

> Ask yourself, will it be . . .
> . . . self-completion – by post or online,
> or delivered personally and completed by you?

Alternatively, questionnaires you deliver personally and complete from your respondents' answers are likely to achieve a much higher completion rate with enough reminders and your skills of persuasion. However, this can take up a lot of your time and cause delays, which you will have to factor into your research schedule. Nevertheless, because you are there recording your respondent's answers, ready to explain the questions when there are problems, you can design a questionnaire that probes in more depth with more complex questions. Of course, the one problem you will have to avoid is not to exert influence over your respondents' answers as you do this.

● Designing a questionnaire

There are four guiding principles that will help you as you begin to think about the design:

1 List your topics.
2 Keep it short with a sharp focus.
3 Ensure a clear, professional presentation.
4 It must have a logical structure.

1 List the topics on which you want information
The first step is to list the topics on which you want information. The primary focus of these will be those variables we identified when we defined our aims and objectives. You will need to make sure that every question is relevant to your hypothesis and research questions. Once you've done this you'll find that many of the questions you first thought of are in fact irrelevant and can be dispensed with.

> **Example: Study skills**
>
> In this project our main concern is to test the hypothesis that it is students' perception of the purposes of learning tasks, like essays, that determines how they use their skills, and not whether they have taken study skills courses. So we want to ask students how they perceive these purposes, how they are related to the way they study and how effective study skills courses are to changing the way they work.

2 Keep it short with a sharp focus
A well designed questionnaire has a fair degree of objectivity and produces a

wealth of information that can be processed without too much difficulty. The key to this is to keep it as short as possible and make sure the focus is as tight as you can get it. This way it will be easier to draw conclusions. They will also be more relevant and meaningful. But to achieve this you will have to know beforehand exactly what you want to know and how you're going to process the results.

3   Clear, professional presentation

Make sure your questionnaire inspires confidence. Let the respondent know that you're clear about the information you want and you know what you're doing. That way you are likely to get a higher rate of response and more thoughtful responses.

Top and tail it carefully

At the beginning, invite people to respond, and at the end, thank them for doing so. Explain the purpose of the questionnaire, the problem you're researching and where the idea came from. Assure them that their identity will not be mentioned in the dissertation and their responses will remain anonymous. If it's a complex and quite extensive questionnaire, write a letter to accompany it explaining the overall purpose, what you're going to do with the results, where the respondent can get access to them and any official contacts they might need at your university, like your supervisor.

- Explain the purpose.
- Assure them of anonymity.
- Thank them.

Simple instructions

Give simple instructions about how to complete the questionnaire, with a rough estimate on how long it should take. Even more important, give simple, clear instructions about how to complete each question. Even if you think it's obvious what needs to be done, be pedantic and explain it clearly. This is particularly important for self-completion questionnaires. For each question, give respondents clear guidelines on how to answer it: do they circle choices or do they tick them; how many answers should they select from those you've listed? In some questionnaires the way respondents answer a question determines which sections they need to complete and those they can skip. You will need to explain this very carefully.

> Explain . . .
> - how they complete the questionnaire;
> - how long it will take;
> - how they complete each question.

4   Structure

As to how to organise the order of the questions, you will find it best to move from the general to the specific. That way there is less chance of an early question influencing the responses to later questions. It's also important to start with questions that establish the details of each respondent – gender, age group and so on. In the dissertation itself you will earn good marks for being able to outline the demographics of the sample group, so think carefully about those characteristics which might be important to your research.

● Writing the questions

As with the design, there are four simple guidelines that will help you as you write each question:

1   Use clear, unambiguous language.
2   Keep questions simple.
3   Don't lead respondents.
4   Pilot it.

1   Clear, unambiguous language

The language you use must be carefully chosen. First, it must be appropriate for those answering the question. It must be simple and direct, free of all specialist jargon. Second, make sure you have identified and removed any possible ambiguity. It's easy to assume that everyone else will make the same assumptions you do and will see clearly what you mean, but more often than not they won't. And third, at all costs avoid vagueness. It will only breed even more vagueness, making your results virtually unusable. Words like 'appropriate', 'generally' and 'usually' are unlikely to mean the same to your respondents as they mean to you.

Complex questions

Look out for two problems in particular. The first is the complex question in which you ask two questions in one, believing that they are just one question. You might ask,

> At elections do you vote for the party with the most experience, who will manage the economy well?

The party that will manage the economy well is not necessarily the same as the most experienced.

Unclear responses
The second comes about as a result of asking for unclear responses. You might ask,

> What is your age? Circle one of the following.
>   0–20, 20–40, 40–60, 60 and over

A 20, 40 or 60 year old would not know which box to circle. The correct set of responses, of course, would be: 0–19, 20–39, 40–59, 60 and over; or 0–20, 21–40, 41–60, over 60.

- Use simple, direct language.
- Remove ambiguity.
- Avoid vagueness.

2   Keep questions simple
Be as consistent as you can in the different styles of response you use. Try to avoid asking respondents to tick options in one question, circle them in the next and write their response in the next. Not only can this be confusing, but it can result in disaffection and a poor response rate. The same is true of the different types of question. If you can, try to standardise throughout the styles of response and the type of question you use.

3   Don't lead the respondent
It's easy to make assumptions, which can lead the respondent to an answer which doesn't reflect their actual opinion. This can be done in the response options you give and in the questions. For example, you might ask your respondent,

> Do you agree with research using human–animal embryos?   Yes/No

Yet these response options fail to reflect the different positions people can hold on the issue and the strength of their assent or dissent. As for a leading question, you might ask,

> A recent report suggests that a growing number of irresponsible parents are allowing their children to drink alcohol from as early as 6 years old. Are you concerned about this trend?

In this case we are conveying our own attitudes and leading the respondent through our choice of words: nobody wants to be thought of as a supporter of 'irresponsible' behaviour. So do an adjective audit – check to see if you have included adjectives that convey your own values and so lead the respondent.

The problem is that few of us write a questionnaire without having some idea of the likely responses and the sort we need to support our hypothesis. So we include leading questions without even knowing it. One solution is to get someone else, who knows little about your research and is unaware of your hypothesis, to read through your questionnaire. See if they can tell from your questions what it is you're after and what you're trying to show.

4   Pilot it
As this suggests, to remove these assumptions and to clear up all ambiguities, pilot the questionnaire. Try it out on a number of people first to see if they have any problems, so that you can iron them out before you use it.

● Types of question

To get useful data on people's beliefs, values and opinions on a range of issues you will have to use different types of question, depending on the nature of the thing you're asking the question about. Very broadly they can be divided into closed and open questions.

Closed questions
The most common type of question we've all seen on questionnaires is the closed question. Carefully chosen and crafted these can yield a wealth of interesting, useful quantitative data. There are six different types of closed question you can choose from.

Closed questions
1 Dichotomous or categorical questions
2 Numerical questions
3 Multiple choice questions
4 Multiple response questions
5 Likert scale questions
6 Ranking questions

1 Dichotomous or categorical questions

Dichotomous questions test different and opposite attitudes to a proposition: like/dislike, agree/disagree, accept/reject, yes/no. You can represent the responses graphically in a bar chart, or a pie chart, or alternatively as percentages of those who chose each option. The problem is that with many opinions there are not clear dichotomous responses, but instead just variations of assent or dissent. So, be clear about this before you choose them.

2 Numerical questions

These ask respondents to give a number: 'What is your age?' or 'How many children do you have?' They are useful for those questions at the beginning of the questionnaire that establish the demographics of your sample.

3 Multiple choice questions

These are familiar to all of us who have taken exams. But in using them, take care to ensure two things. First, make sure that for each question respondents have mutually exclusive options from which to choose. Otherwise the results can be confusing and inconclusive. Second, make sure you've covered as many options as possible, without presenting respondents with an utterly bewildering choice. If you give only a limited choice they will opt for the nearest one, even though it doesn't reflect the facts. It also helps to add the category 'other' with a blank space, so they can add something you may not have thought about. The results can then be presented as bar, and pie, charts or as percentages of respondents choosing each option.

> Make sure . . .
> 1 You offer mutually exclusive options.
> 2 You cover as many options as possible.

4 Multiple response questions

As the name suggests, these allow respondents to choose more than one answer. Then you can present the answers as percentages choosing each option, although, as respondents can choose more than one, the total number of options chosen is likely to be greater than your sample.

Example: Smoking in public places

Assessing the impact on pubs and restaurants, you might want to know more about each respondent's pattern of drinking, so you might ask respondents:

Which of the following outlets have you used in the past month to buy alcohol? (You can tick more than one.)

Public House
Off-licence
Restaurant
Hotel
Supermarket

A useful additional piece of information generated by this type of question, which would be particularly interesting for this project, is the average number of outlets ticked by each respondent.

5 Likert scale questions

Questions of this type are phrased as statements and respondents are asked to ring a number or a response on a scale. You might present the following statement,

> The ban on drinking alcohol in public places is a serious limitation on the freedom of the individual.

Then you might ask:

> Which of the following responses is an accurate reflection of your feelings?

1 Strongly agree
2 Agree
3 Neither agree nor disagree
4 Disagree
5 Strongly disagree

Alternatively, you could represent the different responses numerically and ask respondents to ring the appropriate number:

Strongly agree 1 ...... 2 ...... 3 ...... 4 ...... 5 Strongly disagree

Whichever style you choose, make sure there's a middle value; in other words, use an odd number of total choices available. Still, having said that, some Likert scales use only four categories, omitting the middle value – 'Neither agree nor disagree' – in order to force respondents to express a preference one way or the other. The problem with this, and even the five-point scale, is that it doesn't cover those who are not sure how strongly they agree or disagree, or, in fact, simply don't have an opinion at all. Nonetheless, this is still a very useful type of question. With each option numbered we can use them to find the 'mean response' to the question.

6   Ranking questions
This is the most complex of the different types of question in that it gets respondents to evaluate items and place them in an order of preference, entering 1 to 5 alongside each option. As you're asking respondents to do a complex piece of evaluation, use these questions sparingly. Too many and you can encourage your respondents to plump for choices without seriously considering them. The most useful way of presenting the results is in terms of how many respondents gave a certain item the same evaluation.

Open questions
Open questions allow respondents the freedom to respond as they will without directing them. They are useful when you're unsure of all the possible answers or you don't want to lead your respondent. As a result you can generate some thoughtful responses that provide valuable qualitative material in the form of quotes to support your quantitative data.

What's more, even though you're likely to get a wide range of unpredictable responses, if your sample is large enough, you may be able to categorise them and present them quantitatively in a pie chart showing the proportions that answered in different ways. Still, the likelihood is that it will be difficult for you to draw anything more than broad, tentative generalisations, given the numbers answering one way or another.

The one problem to avoid with open questions, however, is vagueness. If you ask your respondents a vague question in the hope that you'll get an interesting range of responses back, all you're likely to get are vague, unusable answers.

- Qualitative material: use as quotes.
- Quantitative material: use in pie charts.

● Processing your results

As you plan your questionnaire, and later when you come to analyse your results, search out as many connections between questions as possible. This will bring rich and interesting insights into your work. For example, you might find that those who agree strongly with one statement also tend to agree strongly with another or, alternatively, you might find agreement with one statement correlates closely with disagreement with another.[1]

Summary

1 To guarantee a sufficiently high response rate you may have to consider delivering the questionnaire yourself and completing it from your respondents' answers.

2 Keep your questionnaire short, with a sharp focus and clear instructions.

3 Keep your questions simple, using unambiguous language.

4 Try not to lead your respondents.

● What next?

In collecting data we face the problem of ensuring that while our material is objective and reliable, it gives us enough depth and meaning to enrich our work. It's not difficult to gather all sorts of data, but much of it could be trivial and insignificant. Still, this is not an easy balance to maintain: what we sacrifice ensuring we have one element can result in us losing out on the other. For this reason, the solution often lies in using both quantitative and qualitative sources. This way we not only ensure depth and reliability, but we can triangulate our sources to bring added credibility to our conclusions. In the next chapter we will look at the different ways of gathering qualitative material and how to process it reliably.

● Note

1   A useful source full of valuable information about designing, writing and using questionnaires is the Audience Dialogue website, which you can find at www.audiencedialogue.net

22 Primary sources 3: Qualitative research – interviews and focus groups

The most significant advantage of qualitative research is that it can give us deeper responses that are rich in implications for our study. But, of course, there are drawbacks: not only are there questions about the reliability of the responses, how representative they are, but we are left with more difficult problems of how to use them and all their implications.

● Interviews

Interviews illustrate this perfectly. To get the most out of them they need to be thought about carefully beforehand, with questions planned in detail. Then, afterwards, you will need to set time aside to transcribe them, if you've recorded them, and to reflect on the results so that you can draw out their implications and decide how you're going to use them.

Advantages and disadvantages

Nevertheless, the rewards can be significant and fascinating. The most obvious is that they give you the flexibility to probe deeper than questionnaires. You can explore issues that are important to your study, but which you may not have anticipated in your questions or hadn't thought to approach in quite the way that's offered in the interview.

Moreover, unlike questionnaires, you can see when someone doesn't completely understand the question. We tend to communicate as much, if not more, non-verbally through gestures and expressions, than we do through what we say. Facial expression, eye contact, tone of voice and body language are all important ways in which we give expression to the strength of our feelings, emotions and opinions. And, by the same token, they also allow interviewees more control over their responses. They can make clear just how strongly they believe something or redirect the interview towards another aspect they consider more important.

You're left with material that is richer and deeper than that described using numerical data and statistics. It allows you to explore more subtle interpretations of the language used to express the strength of feelings or to describe experiences and attitudes. And even though it is more difficult to compare one person's responses with another's and to generalise, there are still ways of deriving quantitative material for this purpose using structured interviews.

Advantages	Disadvantages
Flexibility to probe deeper	Difficult to make comparisons
Explore unanticipated issues	Difficult to generalise
See when someone doesn't understand	Time needed to transcribe and draw out implications
Non-verbal communication	
Interviewees have more control of their responses	
Richer and deeper material	

Types of interview
Very broadly there are three types of interview:

1 **Structured**
2 **Unstructured**
3 **Semi-structured**

1 Structured
The structured interview is designed to give quantitative evidence for statistical analysis. It has a tight structure with the interviewer asking each interviewee the same questions, answered by selecting from a fixed choice of answers. Of course, the problem with such determinism is that what we perceive as the reality of the situation doesn't always correspond to what our subjects perceive. So, to save a lot of time, it's important to pilot the interview before you use it for real.

2 *Unstructured*

By contrast, the unstructured or open interview is more informal. Designed to explore the interviewee's feelings about the issues raised in the study, it's a useful way of getting information it would be difficult to foresee and plan for. The interview can go into areas you hadn't anticipated.

But the weaker the structure, the greater the skill needed to interpret the material and the greater the danger of bias. In such situations it's easy to commit the fallacy of accent and create misunderstanding by emphasising the wrong word in a sentence. This accounts for much semantic confusion, intentional and otherwise.

3 *Semi-structured*

Between these two lies the semi-structured interview. The interviewer has a schedule of questions, some tightly phrased to elicit clear, simple responses and others open so that some issues can be explored more freely. This way you have the best of both worlds: quantitative evidence that's easier to process, along with the unanticipated responses that might lead the project into new areas.

Organisation

As with every aspect of our research, the more organised we are, the better will be our results. So, make sure you send out letters arranging the interviews well in advance and confirm them nearer the time if necessary. Know exactly what you want to achieve. Write your questions out carefully and plan the sequence in which you're going to ask them. And remind yourself with brief notes why you're asking them – that way you will get the material you're after, and if you don't the first time around you'll know the sort of follow-up questions to ask.

> The better your organisation, the better your results.

Decide how you're going to record the responses. Whatever your choice, it can have an effect on the outcome. Some people are uncomfortable with the idea of being recorded or videoed, while others are unsettled each time you write down their responses. So ask for permission beforehand. If you have to rely exclusively on your notes, help yourself by preparing answer sheets for yourself with every question and response numbered and coded to make it easier to process. This means that you must also be clear in advance what you're going to do with the results and how you're going to process them.

Make sure you . . .
1 write the questions out;
2 plan the sequence;
3 have brief notes about why you're asking them;
4 prepare answer sheets with numbered and coded questions.

Conducting the interview

Telephone interviews
How to conduct the interview, of course, depends on how you've arranged to do it. You may decide to do telephone interviews, which are quick and less costly in time and money. With a short series of questions you can complete it in as little as 20 to 30 minutes. However, there are limitations to what you can do. You can't use visual aids to help explain your questions and there's no non-verbal communication through which you can encourage interviewees and interpret their responses.

Face-to-face interviews
Alternatively, in face-to-face interviews, you have the benefits of this, but you have to ensure that the location is right: that it's quiet, comfortable and you won't be disturbed. If the interview is long, plan for breaks and offer your interviewee refreshments.

Questions and prompts
The key to good interviewing is to be sensitive to your interviewees' feelings, their nervousness, hostility, indeed anything that seems to get in the way of an easy exchange, and about your own responses that you use to prompt your interviewee. Above all, try to phrase your questions and prompts to avoid leading the interviewee one way or the other. You have to avoid giving any indication that there is a response you want.

Be sensitive to your interviewee's feelings and about your own responses

Responses
Interviewees can have a tendency to want to please their interviewer, to be a good interviewee by giving you what they think you want. It's not unnatural to assume, when you're being interviewed, that a good interviewee knows

his or her mind on most issues. Therefore your responses can indicate more conviction than you might have. Where you might normally say you 'suspect' something, under interview conditions you might be willing to declare that you're 'certain'.

So, when you're interviewing, measure your responses carefully, so you don't give the impression that you're pleased and gratified with the response. Be friendly and indicate that you have understood what the interviewee is saying, but avoid expressing too much empathy or support for the interviewee's feelings or opinions. The rule is, be friendly, but formal.

> Make sure you . . .
> 1 avoid expressing too much support for the interviewee's responses;
> 2 are friendly, but formal.

Sequence

But it's not just the questions that can lead an interviewee, so too can the way you sequence your questions. Unless you're careful, it's easy in an early question to place an idea, or to stimulate a judgement about something specific that later affects the way interviewees answer more general questions.

The answer is the same as with questionnaires: arrange the sequence so that you start with the general questions that raise conceptual issues and then move to the more specific questions about which they might have personal experiences and strong opinions.

Guidelines for interviews
1 Arrange questions from the general to the specific.
2 Keep to your schedule of questions.
3 Be sensitive to your interviewees' feelings.
4 Avoid leading the interviewee.
5 Measure your responses carefully.
6 Be friendly, but formal.
7 Be patient, but not patronising.

Assessing the interview

Later, in your dissertation, give details of how the interviews were carried out and assess how well they went. This means acknowledging their weaknesses and how you could have organised them better. Examiners want to see not only that you're a capable researcher, but that you've developed your skills along the way by acknowledging the weaknesses and learning from them.

Discuss the time you allowed and how you structured the interview. Describe the techniques you used to collect the data and assess the influence they may have had on interviewees. How relaxed were they: were they nervous, quiet, perhaps even uncommunicative? Describe the location and the environment in which the interviews were conducted. If each interview were conducted under different circumstances, this would endanger any comparison you might make. Each one would become a unique event in its own right.

Assessing the interviews
1 Time
2 Structure
3 Techniques for collecting data
4 Interviewees' states of mind
5 Location

● Focus groups

The alternative to an interview is a focus group, which allows you to take into account several points of view on a topic at the same time. These are small discussion groups, usually composed of four to six members, who are asked to discuss a tightly defined topic. Your focus is on the interactions between members as well as the content of their discussions. This contrasts with observations where the emphasis is on the behaviour of members, rather than content. The key to successful focus groups is to allow a relatively free rein to the discussion, while you gently keep it on track. For this you will need to have prepared a list of discussion topics and questions related to your project.

Allow a free rein while gently keeping the discussion on track.

If you decide to be part of the group and not just an observer outside looking on, you have to beware of directing the discussion to suit your own needs and opinions and, therefore, introducing bias. The skill is to prompt the discussion to consider new topics or to bring the discussion back from a digression, without giving your own point of view. Digression is one of the constant problems with focus groups, along with the tendency for group members to gravitate towards the consensus, rather than expose themselves to criticism for holding a minority point of view.

Problems

1 Digression

2 Gravitation towards the consensus

Summary

1 Interviews give us access to deeper, richer responses.

2 You can explore further and follow unexpected leads.

3 But each question and their sequence need to be carefully planned.

4 Be careful not to express too much support in your responses.

5 In a focus group, prepare a list of topics to bring it back from digressions.

● What next?

Questionnaires, tests, interviews and focus groups are all methods of sampling that gather data by asking their subjects questions in one form or another. But in some studies it's not possible to do this, or it might be more reliable and interesting to gather evidence by studying a case study or by observing the behaviour of a group. In the next chapter we will examine these alternative strategies.

23 Primary sources 4: Qualitative research – case studies and observations

In this chapter you will learn . . .

1 the secrets of a successful case study;
2 the variety of ways you can use a case study in your research;
3 how to structure a case study dissertation;
4 the different subjects for which you can use observations;
5 the key principles for a successful observation strategy;
6 the five questions you must ask yourself before you begin your research.

One problem runs throughout these chapters on primary sources: how can we get responses from our samples that are rich in meaning and implications, while also being representative of the wider population?

● Case studies

One answer is to choose a case study approach. In a case study your focus might be on a particular community, a group of people, a set of documents or an organisation, even a person, a type of personality, or an event. But, whatever your subject, your rationale is that it is typical of many others, or at least a significant number, therefore the conclusions you draw can be applicable to all those of the same type. Obviously, then, you must make sure that it is, indeed, representative.

Failing that, where there is such a large variation that there is no average or representative case, you might take, say, three cases, one at each end of the spectrum and one in the middle: different diets; different teaching styles on the authoritarian–democratic spectrum; different management styles, top-down, bottom-up and a mix of the two.

What can I use a case study for?
As this suggests, case studies are a means of gathering material on one or more case histories, organising the material, analysing it and coming to carefully judged, well reasoned conclusions about it. You work to find out

what has happened, or who was responsible for what, or what could be done to improve something, and on this basis, from the evidence you've collected, you can offer solutions and explanations.

Example: Action research

One form of this is the sort of 'action research' favoured by many university departments preparing students for careers in professions like social work, nursing and teaching. The research uses the students' own professional work environment, identifies a problem that could be solved, or a practice that could be improved, or just some aspect of the work that could be better understood. Data is collected and observations are carried out. The results are then analysed in the context of prevailing theory and recommendations made.

Still, it doesn't have to have such ambitious intentions, like recommending changes in policy or practices. Most case studies are undertaken for the modest empirical aim of finding out something, often whether a theory, explanation or analysis that you've learnt in your coursework can be applied successfully in your own experience at work or in the area where you live.

Example: Enclosures

In history you may have studied the effects of the enclosure movement at the end of the eighteenth and early nineteenth centuries, so you might choose a case study that looks at the effects of enclosures in your area.

Library-based case studies

As this suggests, there are almost endless possibilities for this type of research. In history, literature and philosophy you might re-analyse primary texts to focus on something that others might have missed, or you might take an analysis developed and applied elsewhere and apply it to another author or text. Like many, these case studies are library-based, involving primary texts, manuscripts and historical documents.

Fieldwork case studies

But others, as we've seen, involve fieldwork at your place of work, conducting surveys in your local area, interviewing local councillors, executives and other policy-makers, or on geography field trips, or archaeological digs.

All of it is likely to produce original material in the sense that it has never been recorded before, although, sadly, this is still no guarantee that it is also significant, or even interesting.

The secrets of successful case studies

This raises the first of two principles for guaranteeing a successful case study. On its own merits a well-organised case study systematically undertaken will reveal something original, but to ensure it is also significant and interesting you must relate it back to the broader theoretical themes and the sort of empirical concerns that dominate the literature. You will need to spell out a clear rationale for the applied work involved, which makes it perfectly clear how it relates to the literature and what it is a case of. This also gives you the opportunity to demonstrate that you understand these theories and can relate them to actual situations and problems.

By extension, this leads to our second principle. A case study cannot just be a descriptive study. You will need to analyse the case you have studied to provide the basis on which you can suggest ways in which the problems you've identified can be solved or explain why a particular action or policy has been successful or unsuccessful. This calls for systematic, meticulous detail thoroughly analysed, otherwise it can degenerate into a series of unstructured descriptions of randomly chosen features.

> **Principles for a successful case study**
>
> **1** Relate it back to the broader theoretical themes and empirical concerns in the literature.
>
> **2** Create the basis for your conclusions from systematic, meticulous detail that is thoroughly analysed.

Structure

Although this sounds on paper an easy thing to do, balancing the two elements – the background theory and the practical empirical findings – can be a nightmare of frustration and lost time. In his book *Studying for a Degree in the Humanities and Social Sciences*,[1] Patrick Dunleavy identifies what he describes as the 'focus-down approach' as the source of much of this.

Focus-down approach

Using this strategy our dissertation starts with a wide-ranging description of the background theory and empirical themes, usually covering much more territory than we need just to demonstrate that we have read widely. Then, in the next chapter, the pace changes as these macro-problems give way to the micro-problems of the case study. So disconnected are these two chapters that we are, in effect, starting the dissertation again on a different track. Then, finally, we assemble our conclusions and recommendations, sometimes without even re-examining the broader issues of the first part to see how the case study connects with them.

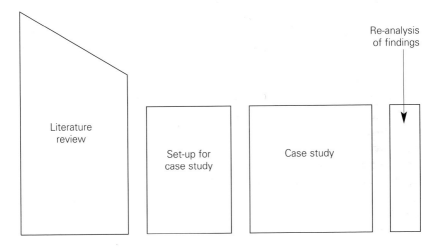

As a result only a small number of the theories that are introduced in the first chapter are ever directly addressed in the case study. It's as if the theoretical background is just tacked on to dignify it, but without having any direct relevance. What's more frustrating is that it's very time-consuming doing this extensive survey of the background theories, leaving us little time for the actual analysis of the results. But perhaps the worst of it lies in the impact it has on our dissertation. As it focuses down, the big concerns drop out and instead of building to an impressive conclusion it goes out with a whimper.

- Much of the theoretical background drops out.
- It's time-consuming.
- The dissertation ends in a whimper.

Opening-out strategy
In contrast, this strategy starts with what Dunleavy describes as a 'scene setter'; not a comprehensive review, just enough to underscore our ratio-

nale. We outline the problems we want to examine and give information about how we selected the materials, the subject, or the location of the case study. After that comes the substantive chapter, in which we outline all our empirical findings without discussing their significance. Then, in the final chapter, we can open out into the analysis that reveals the significance of our findings set against the problems outlined in the opening section and discussed in the context of the wider issues.

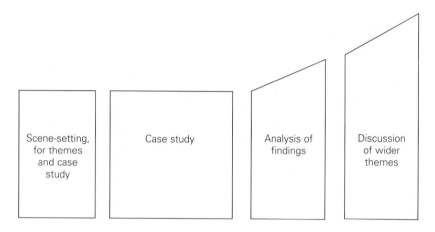

Scene-setting, for themes and case study	Case study	Analysis of findings	Discussion of wider themes

Not only does this mean we concentrate only on those broader themes that are touched by our empirical results, but we only discuss the general theoretical issues once, in the concluding chapter. This results in a more coherent synthesis of the different elements. Both the theoretical and applied elements are integrated into a more coherent piece of work.

- Only involves relevant themes.
- Only discusses them once.
- More coherent synthesis.

⬤ Observations

Observations, too, can involve a range of different subjects, from people, things, artefacts, paintings and buildings to locations, events, conditions and activities. As a research strategy it has particular importance when you suspect that people might be acting in a different way than they say or intend to. Their understanding of the situation is revealed more by their actions than by their explanations.

So, ask yourself . . .
. . . do actions speak louder than words?

Example: Teaching

You might interview a teacher who explains how he plans to conduct a lesson and provides you with a copy of his lesson plan, on which there are long sessions devoted to discussion. But then, when you actually observe the lesson, much of the teacher's activity involves talking to his students and much of theirs involves quietly listening and noting, not discussion and developing their skills. So, while the teacher might plan a lesson believing that at certain times students are doing one thing, in fact they are really doing something quite different. The perception fails to match the facts.

Know what you're looking for

The uniquely valuable thing about observations is that they allow us to assume a detached view, so they can be an important source of objective, reliable data, both quantitative and qualitative. But to gather this we need to organise ourselves well. First we need to have a clear idea of exactly what we're looking for: we must know the variables and record them accurately when we see them.

A simple method of recording observations

This means designing a simple and effective method of recording our observations. It's not difficult to design and test beforehand observation schedules and tally sheets listing those things we should look for and how we should record them. If we can reduce the recording of quantitative data to ticking boxes, entering times and other simple methods, we can leave the rest of our time free to record the more complex, less predictable qualitative data. Our strategy doesn't have to be overly bureaucratic, but it does have to be systematic.

> ### Example: Teaching
>
> If we were observing a lesson we might have an observation schedule to record times when each activity in the lesson began and ended, so that we have a complete record of how each minute was used. We might also have a tally sheet listing different activities, like questioning, answering, discussion, note-taking and reading, which we tick each time it occurs. We might be interested in how much each student engages with the teacher by asking or answering questions, so with a floor plan of the class and students numbered on it we can enter a tick against the number each time he or she engages in a particular type of interaction.

Be as unobtrusive as possible

Of course, you might use recording equipment to create a complete record, although this can, at times, be intrusive, altering the 'normal' situation to such an extent as to invalidate the results. So, make sure it is as unobtrusive as possible. Indeed, this can be the case even with your own presence and activities in taking notes. So, take up a position outside the line of sight, where your activities will be largely unobserved.

Process it promptly

Then, after you've completed your observations, process the material as soon as possible. Don't allow a backlog of transcribing tapes and writing up your notes to develop. Your material will bring to light things you hadn't thought about and other things you may have assumed were less relevant. As you learn from this it will change the way you approach each observation. Leaving it all to cool after the event, you will lose those valuable insights that will make your work unique and original. So for every hour of observation leave another two hours at least to process the material and interpret the ideas to catch these insights.

> ### Strategy
>
> 1 Have a clear idea of exactly what you're looking for.
>
> 2 Design a simple and effective method of recording your observations.
>
> 3 Record your observations as they occur.
>
> 4 Be as unobtrusive as possible.
>
> 5 Process the material as soon as possible.

● Final checks

As you set about your research, work through the following questions checking that you're clear about each one and you've made the right choices.

Am I clear about the information I need?
Do you know what people or phenomena you need to investigate? Are you clear about the variables that you need data on?

Do I know how I am going to go about it?
Usually this means a combination of secondary and primary sources and qualitative and quantitative research. Even if your research seems to involve largely primary sources, you will probably need secondary sources to give you the background from the current literature. It's also likely that you'll need to use two or three research methods to gather your data. It will help to validate your findings if you triangulate information on each aspect of your project.

> **Example: Study skills**
>
> In this project it would be wise to use a questionnaire, interviews, tests and classroom observations to see if students' perceptions of learning tasks correlate with what they do in class and how they use their skills.

Have I decided how I'm going to process the results?
There are a number of methods you can use to unravel the properties of the quantitative data you've collected. Remember, your aim is not just to describe the data, but to discover the relationships between the people, events and materials that are the subject of your research, perhaps even to predict their behaviour. Get advice from your supervisor or your research methods tutor as to the best methods to use and if you need to develop these skills they can usually direct you towards short courses you can take.

> You're not just describing data, but discovering the relationships between people, events and material.

As for qualitative data, you'll have to decide what's relevant and what's not. The key to this is the dialogue you've been having with your own ideas in your notebook and journal as you've responded to the material. As these develop, they will chart your way through the material, making it clear what's important and what's not. Each of your brightest insights will light up the way.

Will my data bear directly on my original research questions?

You must be confident that the data you expect to collect and the provisional conclusions you expect to be able to draw will relate directly back to the research questions you posed at the beginning. So check that what you plan to do will be relevant and your arguments supporting it are sound.

Will I have too much data and too little time to process it?

Before you start, check that you're right in thinking this is all practicable in the time available. After this, you may not have the time to stand back and see it all objectively. You may end up with too much data to process in the time available, or not enough time to collect it all. If this is the case, narrow the research down to make sure it can all be collected and analysed on time.

Ask yourself . . .
1 Am I clear about the information I need?
2 Do I know how I am going to go about it?
3 Have I decided how I'm going to process the results?
4 Will my data bear directly on my original research questions?
5 Will I have too much data and too little time to process it?

Summary

1   To be effective your case study must be related back to the broad theoretical themes and concerns in the literature of your subject.

2   But it cannot be just descriptive: it must be based on systematic analysis of the material.

3   To avoid wasting time and producing an incoherent piece of work, use the 'Opening-out' strategy.

4   In observations, know what you're looking for and organise a simple method to record it unobtrusively.

● What next?

Once you've completed your research you will be ready to enter the writing stage, when you will pull all your material together. For most of us this presents the most formidable of all the challenges we face. As Darwin explained, as long as writing consists of just description it's quite easy, but when reasoning comes into play you must create consistent connections between your ideas and fluency between your arguments. It forces you to think through and clarify your ideas in a way you have not been called upon to do so far. The first step in doing this is to plan each part of your dissertation, as we'll see in the following chapters.

● Note

1   Patrick Dunleavy, *Studying for a Degree in the Humanities and Social Sciences* (Basingstoke: Macmillan, 1986), pp. 117–20.

Part Six

Planning your dissertation

24 The main components and introduction

In this chapter you will learn . . .

1 of the importance of planning not only for producing a coherent piece of work, but for giving you the confidence that you can manage this large project;

2 how to plan the structure of the dissertation and then of individual chapters;

3 the main components of a dissertation and their relative sizes;

4 the importance of an introduction and how to structure it;

5 how to synchronise it with your conclusion.

Now you come to the actual writing of your dissertation. Like any large project, the first thing you must do is plan it. You must know where all the data and ideas are going to go. It must make logical sense to you and to your readers. Planning will not only save time and effort, it will reduce the likelihood of duplicating passages, and your dissertation will be, as a result, more compact and readable.

So, invest a lot of thought in planning your outline in detail, indeed in much more detail than you might think necessary. The last thing you want to be doing is planning while you're writing. The clearer you are about it before you begin, the more confident you'll be about what you're doing. Nevertheless, the outline will change, particularly when you begin to write, but it will make the whole project more manageable, if you know where you're going and what you need to do to get there.

Then, once you've got your structure of chapters, begin to fill out each one with provisional subheadings and, perhaps, even sub-subheadings to give yourself a detailed map. Divide up the final word length, provisionally allocating a certain number of words to each section. This way you will get a better idea of which sections are going to need more space. And, even more important for your confidence, it will make the whole project manageable: it will now be a series of smaller sections and not one daunting 10,000-word project looming ahead of you.

- Plan your outline in detail.
- Structure of chapters.
- Within each chapter provisional subheadings and sub-subheadings.
- Allocate a certain number of words to each section.

● The main components

The structure of chapters will depend on the subject and how you've chosen to deal with it, and on your department's requirements. But, in general, there are usually between five and eight chapters.

In projects that are theoretical and textual the structure will be determined by the content. Your introduction will be followed by a discussion broken up into chapters dictated by your analysis of the documents, papers, and literary or philosophical texts you've used. This is then followed by a conclusion.

The sizes of these chapters are, to put it simply, what seems natural. But, as a general rule, the introduction is usually around 5 to 10 per cent of the word limit; each chapter around 15 to 25 per cent; and the conclusion around 5 per cent. If you find one of your chapters taking up more than 30 per cent, ask yourself whether there is a neat way of splitting it up. If one is less than 10 per cent, can you combine it with another?

Theoretical/textual dissertation
Introduction (5–10 per cent)
Chapters (3 or 4) on each aspect of your analysis of your sources (each one 15–25 per cent)
Conclusion (around 5 per cent)
References and bibliography (5 per cent)
Appendices

In contrast the structure of an empirical study is largely dictated by the methods you have used. You will have to report on these practical elements of your research. You will need to have a chapter explaining your research design, another on the analysis and presentation of your findings, followed by a discussion of them in which you make recommendations.

Empirical dissertation
Introduction (5–10 per cent)
Literature review (15–30 per cent)
Research methods (10 per cent)
Findings (25 per cent)
Discussion (10 per cent)
Conclusion (15 per cent)
References and bibliography (5 per cent)
Appendices

Alternatively, if you want to reduce the dominance of the literature review and introduce more flexibility you might consider the following structure.

Empirical dissertation
Introduction (5–10 per cent)
Background (20 per cent)
Research problem (20 per cent)
Data collection (20 per cent)
Data analysis (15 per cent)
Conclusion (15 per cent)
References/bibliography (5 per cent)
Appendices

● Introduction

The most difficult aspect of writing introductions is explaining what you're going to do in a way that marks it out as an important piece of research, so that you engage the interest of the reader, without revealing the whole plot.

From the general to the specific

You'll find the best way of achieving this is to start with a general description outlining clearly and simply your research problem, the general question and sub-questions that you're going to address. Then, move to the specifics. Explain what you'll be doing to meet these objectives and what you think you might find, without anticipating your conclusions.

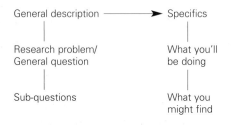

In assessing your work, one measure of your success will be whether you have achieved the objectives you set yourself. Often a project starts out with a set of objectives which then change and evolve along the way. So synchronise your introduction with your conclusion by suggesting what you provisionally expect to be the conclusions. This way you highlight the genuine exploratory nature of your research. It means you won't be able to finish writing your introduction until you know what's going into the conclusion, otherwise you may find that you've raised issues in the conclusion that you hadn't predicted in the introduction.

> Synchronise your introduction with your conclusion.

Nonetheless, it does help to write a provisional draft of your introduction early, particularly if you haven't written a comprehensive proposal. It will point you in the right direction and give you the confidence of having made a good start. As we've said all along, writing is the hardest form of thinking, so it will force you to crystallise your ideas, giving them the sort of shape and clarity they might not otherwise have had, which is essential at this stage as you begin to pull your ideas together.

Significance

Writing the final draft of the introduction last will also give you a better idea of what are the actual contributions of your dissertation and why they are significant. After you've outlined the research problem, the main issues and how you're going to conduct your research, you will need to give a brief outline of what you think are the key reasons for doing this research and why it is significant.

This doesn't have to be in great detail; it will be developed in greater depth in the body of the dissertation. But your aim is to engage the interest of the reader. Explain the background to your research – the work that's already been done. Then explain where your work fits in and what makes it so distinctive. This way you are sure to hook your readers and, with your provisional account of what you expect to find, you will keep them engaged right up to your conclusion.

- Synchronise your introduction with your conclusion.
- This points you in the right direction and gives you the confidence of having made a good start.
- It gives you a better idea of what are the actual contributions of your dissertation and why they are significant.

A map

Finally, you need to tell your readers how you've organised your dissertation. Give them a map they can follow, outlining the structure, the sequence of chapters, so they know at every stage what you will be doing and why. And at this point think about giving each of your chapters a title, other than just 'Literature review', 'Chapter 1' and so on. Otherwise the whole structure can look bland and undistinctive.

Introduction

1 Research problem – general question and sub-questions.

2 How you're going to meet these objectives.

3 What you think you might find.

4 Reasons for doing this research – why it is significant.

5 Structure – the sequence of chapters.

Summary

1 Plan each chapter of your dissertation in detail. That way you'll know what you're doing from the start, your work will be more coherent and you will be more confident.

2 Make sure you synchronise your introduction with your conclusion by leaving the final draft until the end.

3 Outline the significance of your work.

4 Give your readers a map they can follow, outlining the structure of your dissertation.

● What next?

Now you've planned your introduction and know what you're doing, you can outline the background to your research. In the next chapter we will examine how you can cope with the many problems involved in planning and writing your literature review.

25 The literature review

Now that you've written a clear outline of your research problem, the key issues it raises and how you're going to go about it, it should be easier for you to select the relevant literature and write a review that complements your work.

● Why am I writing a literature review?

The problem is knowing exactly why you're writing a literature review. Sometimes we're told we must begin with a synopsis of the literature. But this gets you into the business of summarising all the literature in the area to give some 'background' to your own research, and to impress examiners with how much you've read and understood. Then, when you get down to outlining your own work, the dissertation takes an abrupt change of pace and heads in a substantially different direction, effectively starting again. Indeed, much of what you've mentioned in the literature review is never mentioned again.

This will leave you so confused that you'll simply have no idea where to start. Not only will it be difficult for you to decide what's relevant, but it will encourage you to summarise all the findings of each article you read, when you only need comment on those bits that throw light on what you plan to do.

It will also give you little clue as to how to organise this mass of material and it will take up far too much time and space. Indeed, if you were not to abandon this strategy, you would have little time for anything else. What should take up, say, 20 per cent of the words will, in effect, take up nearer 50 per cent. You'll be left with a mass of material, much of it quite irrelevant, which you will ignore in the rest of your dissertation.

> **Avoid a general synopsis**
>
> **1** It will be difficult to decide what's relevant;
>
> **2** difficult to organise;
>
> **3** take up too much time and space;
>
> **4** leave you with a mass of irrelevant material.

Text-based dissertations

We need to be sure exactly why we're writing a literature review. In some subjects there's more need for them than in others. In text-based dissertations, common in the humanities and in theoretical research in the social sciences, where the subject matter *is* the literature itself in the form of novels, plays, philosophical texts, and theoretical and historical works, a literature review can be quite an alien concept. As you'll be referring to this literature in the body of the dissertation there seems no need to do a lengthy review.

Instead, the most useful thing is to summarise the most important or contentious issues you believe the text raises, or analyse the text so that readers have an interpretative structure they can follow as you work on it. Then, as you begin the critical discussion, you can pick up each of these. Readers will know what you're doing, that it is consistent with your analysis and that you've omitted nothing.

Empirical dissertations

But in empirical research, things are different. Here you will almost always have to do a literature review. However, to avoid the large, time-consuming synopsis that sends you off in a largely irrelevant direction, keep in mind the four main functions of a literature review:

1 to show that you have read widely around your topic: that you've developed a sound understanding of the debates taking place in it and a deep and broad grasp of the issues raised by the topic of your dissertation;

2 to acknowledge the work of others;

3 to lay down a platform for your own research and point you in the right direction;

4 to show that you've got a good critical understanding of the background theories and ideas that may provide the basis for much of the critical evaluation of your findings in the discussion chapter.

Few of us have problems meeting the demands of functions 1 and 2. But this is not a simple exercise in showing how much we know and understand. Genuine thinking lies in what we do with ideas, so we should look more closely at functions 3 and 4.

● Laying down a platform for your research

Scene-setting versus relevance

The dilemma we all face is how to describe and demonstrate our broad understanding of the background of our research and the debates that dominate our subject, while only using sources that bear directly on the specific issues raised by our research. The sort of scene-setting implied by the first function above must not lead us off into areas that are irrelevant to our research.

This means we must check that every source and every quotation we use adds something to our research and answers our questions. So use just those references that relate to your project and be ruthless in only letting in what is centrally relevant. Remember, the main purpose of this is not to impress the examiners with how much you know and understand, but to create a coherent dissertation, in which everything is related and performs a clear, well-conceived role. For this you will need to have a clear idea of the research question that you're researching and the sub-questions that define the sort of evidence you will need to find to settle it one way or the other.

Main purpose:	To create a coherent dissertation in which everything is related and has a clear, well-conceived role

Example: Philosophy

If you're studying whether R. M. Hare in *Moral Thinking* is right in assuming that prescriptions are nothing more than expressions of preferences, you probably won't need to review papers dealing with his concept of rights or whether he was an ethical naturalist.

Example: Smoking in public places

As you're studying the effects of the government's ban on smoking in public places, you probably won't need to review reports and papers on the rise of teenage alcoholism.

New directions

Nevertheless, you may find as the evidence comes in and your ideas develop that you see more things to explore, which are important to your project. This might mean you will have to go back to the literature to re-examine papers and articles you rejected at the time. Still, this is a lot easier to cope with than finding you've devoted an inordinate amount of time that you couldn't afford on something, only 30 per cent of which is relevant. Ruthlessly editing an overweight and irrelevant literature review is not only time-consuming, but dispiriting and frustrating.

Of course, writing your research proposal and your draft introduction will have clarified your ideas, giving you a much clearer idea of what you're looking for and what to include. Nevertheless, it's very easy just to tell someone to be selective; what you need to know is how you go about it. To do it effectively, you need clear criteria to decide whether to use or reject a text. On page 243 are seven questions you can work your way through as you consider each text. Each one contains ideas on how you might use the text. If it's not useful in any of these ways, ditch it.

This will help you process the ideas you read and, in turn, choose what sources you want to use and quote. The key is to be selective and not over-ambitious. The literature may divert you down a different path, or persuade you to adopt a different emphasis in your research. So keep in mind the original insight that first grabbed your attention and which will, similarly, grab that of your reader. Keep it somewhere on a card to remind you whenever you find your focus becoming less sharp.

Of course, the literature review needs to be as comprehensive as possible on your particular project, but if you have clear criteria by which you can select what's relevant, you won't be buried. If you still have hundreds of items from which to quote, you've probably chosen a topic that is too broad, or has been worked on by many people before you and is probably not worth doing because there are not a lot of gaps and areas where you can make an original contribution.

● Critical understanding of the background theories and ideas

A similar dilemma exists because of the need to show you've developed a sound understanding of the literature, while at the same time critically evaluating it. You can get so locked in to showing examiners how much you know that you don't get round to analysing the strengths and weaknesses of your sources. This will provide much of the basis for your critical evaluation

Criteria – How useful is this source?

1 What's in it that gives you **ideas** on which to build your own project?

2 Is there anything in it that reveals the **current debate** on the topic? What are the differences between the contributors? Are there any unsolved problems? Map out the **cross-connections** you find in articles? If there are references to another article, jot down on a card where you saw it and record what the first author said about it.

3 Does it outline different **perceptions** of what the problem is and different ideas about how it should be tackled? Both will be useful in developing your own proposals.

4 Does it indicate how many different **aspects** there are to the problem?
    If so, analyse it. Then, pick up and discuss each aspect in turn, making clear what there is in the literature on each one. Out of this, develop your own contribution.

5 Is there anything in it that reveals the main **theories** and related **concepts** that are used by different contributors?
    Make clear the differences and similarities between them. Then go on to evaluate each one for their internal consistency. Later you'll be able to assess them for their consistency with the data you collect and the observations you make.

6 Are there **omissions** in the article? Has the writer overlooked something?
    Make this clear and justify your conclusion. Then outline what you will be doing that doesn't overlook the same thing.

7 Is the article useful in identifying the different **methodologies**?
    Review the different ones, identifying their key features, before you then indicate the sort of strategy that would best meet the demands of the topic you have chosen. If the writer has used a methodology similar to yours, point it out as justification.

of your own findings in the discussion chapter. Indeed, noting how researchers evaluate each other's work is a useful way of developing your own critical powers.

Synchronising the literature review with your conclusions

This underlines the importance of synchronising the literature review with the discussion chapter or conclusion. When you know what conclusions you're going to draw, you know what your final draft of the introduction will look like, so you will also know what parts of the literature review are no longer relevant. Consequently, you can change your literature review accordingly, editing quotations, deleting others and removing those references that you don't refer to later.

Long quotations

To do this effectively you will have had to process the ideas thoroughly, making them your own. When you've used large sections of the texts, it's almost always a sign that you haven't got to the heart of these ideas. So avoid just quoting or paraphrasing the contents of articles. Weave them into your own arguments, wherever possible using them alongside your own beliefs and opinions. And check that you really need such long quotations. Cut them down now or paraphrase them; it will be much more difficult later.

- Don't just quote or paraphrase, weave them into your own arguments.
- Do you need such long quotations?

Developing your critical skills

In Part 7 we will examine ways of improving our own thinking skills to create consistent arguments and use language and evidence effectively. But the weaknesses in our own arguments are the same as those we find in others, so by learning to improve our own skills we learn how to criticise our sources. But for now, as you read your sources, develop your critical understanding of them by asking yourself the following ten questions (page 245) or use the complete version of this in Chapter 16. In this way you will lay the basis for your critical evaluation of your own findings in the discussion chapter.

● Structure

The most serious problems students have with literature reviews stem from not making explicit their own particular way of approaching the material. This should inform your selection of the material you review. It should run throughout as you present your critical evaluation of each source. Knowing what is likely to be your own contribution, the review should build up naturally to your own specific questions at the heart of your project as you move

---

Criticism – checklist

1 Where does the author get her data/evidence?

2 Is it relevant? Is it sufficient to support her arguments?

3 Has she represented it accurately?

4 Has she drawn the most relevant and consistent inferences from it?

5 Is the argument balanced? Is it fair/biased, objective/subjective?

6 Has she omitted anything?

7 Is the argument consistent?

8 Does she use language accurately? Does she mean different things at different times, when she uses a word?

9 Does she reveal all her assumptions when she uses language, or does she take things for granted?

10 Do her arguments support or contradict what others have said? If so, why?

---

from the general to the specific texts and from the theory to the practice. As we've seen, this means there is no need to review a mass of literature: most of it will be irrelevant to your particular contribution.

From the general to the specific texts

Although it's useful to set your work in the broader context of the sort of work that researchers have done in your area, beware of going into too much detail. All you're doing is showing the scope of your study and how it relates to other areas of study. From here you build naturally to the specific texts that directly touch on the issues that interest you. These, of course, you deal with in more detail. Through them you might indicate the gap in the literature that you're filling. They will provide the platform on which your research will be built. There might be works that you need to evaluate critically from the particular perspective of your own research. Finish with a direct lead that establishes clear contact with your work.

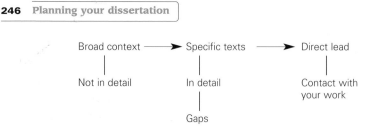

Subsections and subheadings

To help you do this, you will need to plan and structure your review with clear subsections and subheadings. At all costs avoid the review becoming just a mere list of disjointed descriptions of sources – use your sources, don't allow them to use you. Subsections not only help you avoid deviation, keeping you on track as you make your way to your own particular perspective, but they give a sense of proportion to each set of contributions that make up each subsection. So, for example, you might break the review down between the general and specific sources and, within these, break it down further between, say, theoretical and empirical studies.

Summary

1   Avoid the general synopsis in which you summarise the literature to impress examiners with how much you've read.

2   You must create a coherent dissertation in which everything is related with clear, well-defined roles.

3   You can always go back to re-examine papers you rejected at first.

4   Synchronise your literature review with your conclusions.

5   Work from the general to the specific, breaking up each section into subsections.

● What next?

Remind yourself, all the care you invest in choosing the texts and in planning and structuring your review will pay dividends – it is rare for someone to fail a dissertation who has written a good literature review. Now we can move on to the main body of the dissertation: our research methods, findings and conclusions.

26 Research methods, findings, conclusion and appendices

In this chapter you will learn . . .

1 how to integrate each chapter into one coherent piece of work;
2 how to make the best use of your qualitative and quantitative evidence and present it clearly;
3 how to use graphs, pie charts, bar charts and tables effectively;
4 how to plan and write the discussion of your findings;
5 how to write a conclusion that not only establishes the significance of your work, but points towards future research.

One of the most common problems students experience when moving from writing essays to a dissertation is that each chapter can seem quite detached from the rest, so the whole dissertation appears just a series of unconnected essays.

● Research methods

This is, perhaps, more obvious with the chapter on research methods than with any other. So bind it in with the rest by tying the methods you've chosen to your research question and sub-questions, and to the literature review, by using some of the references there to the approaches adopted by other researchers.

Introduction | Literature review | Methods

Research question and sub-questions | References to other researchers' approaches

Methods, techniques and instruments

Your key concerns in this chapter are to show that you have a good grasp of the epistemological issues that underpin your research – that you have a clear idea of what should pass for knowledge in your research – and that you have a sound working knowledge of the methods, techniques and instruments you've used to collect it. You will need to explain the methods you've used (quantitative and qualitative), the sort of study it is (empirical or theoretical) and the sources you've been working with (primary or secondary).

As for the techniques and instruments, you will have to describe the questionnaires, interviews, observations and so on, that you chose to use. If it's a scientific project you will need to explain the equipment you've used, the apparatus and resources, the observations you've made and the experiments you've carried out. In all of this your aim is to present a description detailed enough for someone else to replicate it.

Justification
Then, having described the way you've conducted your research, you need to justify the choices you have made – their relevance to your questions and hypothesis, and why others have been rejected. Nevertheless, don't waste valuable time and space explaining the research methods you haven't chosen. Your paramount concern is to reflect on the research process, so use the references to other methods to outline and discuss the advantages and disadvantages of those you have chosen. It's important to be candid about this, to let readers know about any variations from your original plan and the disadvantages you found with the methods you chose and how you overcame these problems.

- Don't waste time explaining the alternative research methods.
- But be candid about the effectiveness of the one you did choose.

The subject of your research
Finally, describe the important characteristics of the subject of your research: the population you've studied, the sample you chose and the experiments

Research methods

1 Bind it in with the rest.

2 Show that you have a good grasp of the epistemological issues.

3 Show that you have a sound working knowledge of the methods, techniques and instruments.

4 Justify the choices you have made.

5 Describe the important characteristics of your subject .

you've conducted. Readers will need to understand the nature of this and, if any ethical issues have been raised in your study, the way in which you've dealt with them.

● Findings – presentation and analysis

On the face of it this should be the simplest of the chapters, but it's all too easy to slide gently from simple description and analysis of your findings into discussing them. In this chapter all you should be doing is explaining what you did and what you found. To manage this effectively you will need to impose a structure on the data you're presenting. So, divide the chapter up into sections, each one taking up a key problem or question in turn.

> - Just explain what you did and what you found.
> - Impose a clear structure on the data.

Presentation

Within each of these you will be presenting data, so think carefully about how much data you will be collecting and how you're going to analyse it. Large quantities of data will need to be summarised and presented clearly. There are different levels of sophistication in measuring data, so you must make sure you don't leave your readers confused. They shouldn't be forced to re-read any section to get a clear idea of what you've done. Help them visualise the data clearly using charts, tables, graphs, scales, and percentages.

Qualitative evidence

Wherever possible, try to balance the quantitative and qualitative evidence. Verbatim quotations from your participants will engage the reader in your work in a way that figures, charts and graphs simply cannot. Nothing is so effective at generating their empathetic responses. But too much qualitative data can also be a problem. One description followed by another in successive paragraphs can be tedious and confusing, unless you impose a structure on it. And carefully edit and organise your quotations; some may not need to be presented in full.

> Nothing is so effective at generating their empathetic responses.

Quantitative data

As for your quantitative data, you would be wise to get some advice from the specialists in how best to present and analyse it. Your supervisor, your research methods tutor and the statistics department will all have useful advice and may even be able to suggest short courses. The minimum requirement is to make sure that your reader knows exactly the meaning and implications of the scales, tables and keys you're using. Never leave it up to the reader. Label and number them and, if necessary, give a brief explanation. The key principle is that the figures used should be understandable independently of the text.

- Make sure your readers understand your presentation.
- Figures should be understandable independently of the text.

Graphs, pie charts and bar charts

Used well, graphs, pie charts and bar charts can be simple and effective visual aids, particularly in colour. It's easy to extrapolate predicted trends, although you must be careful not to distort either of the two scales to give a false impression. Nevertheless, beware of overkill and make sure they don't obscure the data or give it an importance it doesn't deserve. If it appears you're just trying to be too clever and sophisticated it will defeat your purpose. In your interpretation of them draw attention to the most important features – those that reveal exactly the significance you want your reader to take onboard.

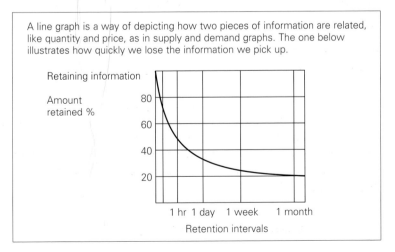

A line graph is a way of depicting how two pieces of information are related, like quantity and price, as in supply and demand graphs. The one below illustrates how quickly we lose the information we pick up.

Retaining information

Amount retained %

This pie chart shows those study skills with which students say they have most problems.

Essay writing   36%
Note-taking   24%
Reading   19%
Organisation   13%
Undecided   8%

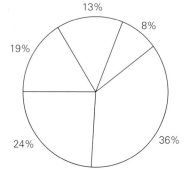

Bar charts are particularly good at showing change over a certain period. This one shows the increases in the Consumer Price Index over four quarters.

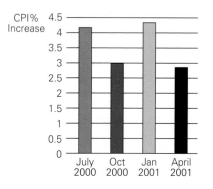

Compound bar charts, like this one, have the added sophistication of showing comparisons of different factors in that period.

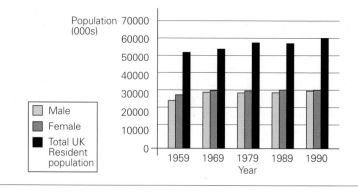

Tables and statistical analysis

Tables, too, can be very effective in presenting simple sets of data, such as survey data. But, as with other methods of presentation, make sure the explanation of them comes directly afterwards. They need careful explanation – what may be obvious to you may not be to the reader, who is less familiar with all this.

Qualifications	Total	Graduate level			Other	
		Post Grad	1st/2nd Hons	Other	HNC	ONC
Languages:						
French	4	–	2	2		
German	1	–	1	–		
Russian	3	1	–	2		
Other						
Social sciences:						
Economics & Political science	9	2	4	3		
Sociology	1	–	–	1		
Humanities	6	1	1	4		
Technical quals:						
Mechanical engineering	29	–	2	2	17	8
Electrical engineering	28	1	2	1	13	11

Table: Part of the inventory of the qualifications of a company's employees

As for more complex statistical analysis, try to avoid pressing it into service to give more rigorous support, where it is clearly inappropriate. Complex analysis that produces only trivial conclusions will weaken your results. It works best with certain types of data, like test, or census, results. The key is to identify clearly the variable you're measuring, and then explain and justify the results carefully.

● Discussion

This is your opportunity to make the most of your hard work; to show how significant your research is and how important it was to do it. Therefore, give yourself plenty of time to plan and write it. In the true sense of the word this is a genuine discussion: you give voice to different contrasting points of view that have a bearing on your research. It's your opportunity to assess your findings in the light of the different perspectives from the literature you've read.

Revisit questions and sub-questions

Above all, start by interpreting your findings in the light of the main problems and questions you outlined in the introduction. Show how your work answers the questions raised there. It's easy to lose sight of the questions and sub-questions, so remind yourself and your readers. Confirm that everything you've done has been relevant. Give your readers that deep sense of satisfaction at being delivered back to the original questions and of having the promises made to them fulfilled.

Give a section to each sub-question so readers can see that you have indeed dealt with them. Highlight all the implications and spell out the main features of your results. Above all, make the most of the key insights you gained from your work.

> • Show how your work answers your questions and sub-questions.
> • Show your readers that you've fulfilled your promises.

Synthesise – bring all the strands together

Then, pull it all together at the end to show how it all answers the main question raised by the dissertation. The important thing is to draw together all the connections you have found. If yours is a theoretical, textual study, in each chapter you may have focused on particular issues raised by the topic. You may have been interested in the way a particular novelist constructs plots or develops characters and in each chapter you may have analysed a different novel. Alternatively, yours may be an empirical study in which each chapter has been devoted to particular aspects of the way you have gone about your research. Whichever it is, now is the time to bring all this together.

Assess your work

Finally, assess your work: how successful was it? You may find it helpful to answer the following questions in this order:

1 What **difficulties** did you encounter and how did these affect your plan of work?
2 What **limitations** were there to your research that might affect the strength of your results? Were there limited responses to your questionnaires, or did the time constraints limit the number of interviews you could conduct? Perhaps you're aware of possible bias that may have entered into the results.
3 What are the **strengths** and **weaknesses** of your data in relation to the questions you set out to answer, or the hypothesis you have tested?
4 To what extent does your data **support** your proposition – is it conclusive, or is there room for doubt?
5 Does it **confirm** or **falsify** your proposition?

If things didn't go according to plan, don't cover up, explain. You will be awarded marks for showing that you have respect for academic integrity and you're not just defending a corner.

● Conclusion

This, too, needs careful planning, otherwise you'll find yourself repeating what you've already written in the discussion, or running out of things to say. Your concern is with higher-order thinking, not with details. So, be concise and ruthless in what you let in. Focus on just two things: the significance of your work and any recommendations for future research. It will help if you use subheadings to maintain your focus.

Significance

Confine yourself to just stating two or three main points. You're not entering into a discussion of these, just drawing conclusions, although you might make reference to relevant chapters in your dissertation, or to the work of other authors for the purpose of comparison.

Pick out those parts of your work that are fundamental, that have important implications for our understanding of the theoretical background, or for the sort of research we might do now to further our understanding. You might suggest that your work has implications for the way we have come to understand these issues and that there may be better ways of understanding them.

Recommendations

Research of any kind is unlikely to answer all the questions it addresses. More often it raises new and more interesting questions. So this is the right place to draw attention to the limitations of small-scale research like yours and indicate possible avenues of research to address similar issues in the future. Indeed, you will be expected to make recommendations about how your work can be improved and about other areas that your research suggests deserve further investigation. In this way you'll show that you have developed an awareness of the importance of your work and its broader implications to related fields.

> ### Conclusion
>
> **1** Significance – two or three of the most important implications.
>
> **2** Recommendations – avenues for further investigation.

● References and bibliography

A reference list with all the books, journal articles and other sources you have cited in your dissertation is obligatory, whereas a bibliography in which you list all those sources you may have referred to, but not necessarily cited, may not be. Although you might impress examiners with the range and relevance of the sources cited, it's best not to pad it out with unnecessary references. In Chapter 38 we will look more closely at reference lists, bibliographies and how to cite your sources.

● Appendices

The best advice on appendices is to try to avoid them. If you do use them, don't include any substantive material, like completed questionnaires and data sheets from observations, or material in which you discuss the issues. Either the material *is* relevant and should be included in the main body of the dissertation, or it *isn't* and shouldn't be included anywhere in the dissertation. Still, it is sometimes useful to include material that would interest a specialist – things that show how you conducted the research:

- Questionnaires (uncompleted).
- Letters and other forms used to gain permission.
- Interview schedule of questions.

- Data sheets from observations (uncompleted).
- Background information about your methods of working that is important to the dissertation, but not central.

The rule is that what goes into an appendix is optional reading, the loss of which will not affect the main themes and conclusions of the dissertation. But it has to be really useful information – every appendix must be referred to in the main text at some point, no matter how briefly.

Summary

1 Bind the research methods chapter in with your research questions and the literature review.

2 Make sure your readers can understand your presentation of data. Don't leave it up to them.

3 In the discussion, show how you have fulfilled your promises and answered all your questions and sub-questions.

4 Assess your work and don't cover up weaknesses and limitations.

5 In the conclusion, explain the significance of your work and make recommendations for future research.

● **What next?**

You are now ready to begin writing your dissertation. However, as we've said throughout this book, writing is a form of thinking. To write clearly we must think clearly. So first, in the following chapters, we will look at how we can improve our thinking.

Part Seven

Organising your thinking

27 Developing consistent arguments 1: The components

We began this book by emphasising that writing is a form of thinking – the most difficult form. As we write we're forced to take a hard look at our thinking to pin our ideas down, organise them rationally and present them clearly. At each point we ask ourselves, 'Is this really what I want to say?' If we can force ourselves to think clearly in this way, we'll write clearly. This explains the importance of setting dissertations as a mode of assessment. They give examiners a window into the minds of students. They can observe you as you reason your way towards a solution, analyse concepts, solve problems, and develop your arguments.

● Thinking: the three elements

So, to do well in our dissertation we must learn how to improve our thinking: not just how to generate our own ideas, but how to develop them. Good thinkers are self-reflective: they think about their thinking while they think. This is 'metacognition'. It means checking that our arguments are consistent as we create them, evaluating our evidence and the way we use it, and analysing our use of concepts and language to reveal their hidden implications. As this makes clear, we need to think routinely about three things.

1 Arguments
  1.1   Are they valid?
  1.2   Do I draw conclusions that are consistent with my assumptions?
  1.3   Are there hidden assumptions in my arguments?

2 **Evidence**

   2.1   Do I have enough evidence to make my points?

   2.2   Do I describe the evidence accurately?

   2.3   Do I draw reliable inferences from it?

3 **Language**

   3.1   Is my meaning clear?

   3.2   Do I use words consistently?

   3.3   Does my language imply more than I acknowledge?

In turn, we will learn how to critically evaluate what we read. We all make the same mistakes; the key is to bring them centre stage in our writing and thinking. In the following chapters you will find handy tables and checklists. Photocopy them, put them up above your desk, or stick them on the edge of your computer screen, so you can remind yourself as you write. You won't catch them all first time around, but you will get better at it. And you always have the revision stages to come.

● Creative and critical thinking

In this and the next chapter we will deal with our first problem above: how to create consistent arguments. As we said earlier, ideas on their own are of little value – they are only significant when we make connections between them. The distinguishing characteristic of intelligence is the ability to identify relevant connections and to put together what ought to be conjoined. This is creative thinking, the sort we saw in Part 2.

In contrast, in the following chapters we will focus on critical thinking. Although this on its own will not generate one new idea, it will show us how to make the connections we want to, so that we develop our ideas rationally and consistently. You may have generated the most revealing insights, synthesising ideas in new and fascinating ways, but unless you can make these connections in a consistent way, you will waste your best work.

● Two kinds of thinking

So, how do we learn to develop our ideas in arguments that move consistently from one point to another? First, we must distinguish between two kinds of thinking: deductive and inductive.

Deductive thinking

In a deductive argument we start with a general or major premise, usually referring to 'All' or 'Some' ('All bachelors are unmarried men'), and then by adding a minor premise, which refers to a specific case ('John is a bachelor'), we draw out the logical conclusion ('Therefore, John is an unmarried man'). As you can see in this simple example, the conclusion follows logically from the premises. Indeed, in a logical or 'valid' deductive argument, if the premises are true, the conclusion must also be true, because the conclusion never states more than is contained in the premises – the assumptions that make up the argument.

> **Example: Valid argument**
>
> If my major premise is,
>
>> All dogs are animals
>
> and I then add the minor premise that refers to just one dog,
>
>> Aldous is a dog,
>
> then I can conclude consistently that
>
>> Aldous is an animal.

Truth and validity

In this case we know that the major premise is true and, if the minor premise is also true, then the conclusion *must* be true, because the argument is valid: in other words the conclusion follows logically from the premises. Note the distinction here between truth and validity.

> Validity: The form of the argument – its consistency
>
> Truth: The substance – whether the premises are true

Validity is a way of ensuring that if we do have true premises then we also guarantee that our conclusion is true. When an argument is valid it is not possible for its premises to be true, while its conclusion is false.

> **Validity**
>
> Validity guarantees that if the premises are true, the conclusion will also be true.

Inductive thinking

In contrast, whereas a deductive argument never states more than is contained in the premises, an inductive argument always goes *beyond* its premises. In an inductive argument we start with singular observation statements that certain events, all similar in some important respect, have occurred, and then we derive a universal generalisation that applies to all events of this type, observed and unobserved, past, present and future. Even though we only possess a finite number of singular observation statements, we come to an infinite, universal conclusion on the basis of them. We have gone beyond what our observation statements will allow.

> Inductive arguments go beyond their premises.

When Blaise Pascal the seventeenth-century French philosopher and physicist set about testing his law of atmospheric pressure he had his brother-in-law, Perier, carry the barometer up the Puy-de-Dôme several times before concluding that the height of the mercury decreases as the altitude increases. So, his justification for his law that barometers fall as the altitude increases was a series of singular observation statements something like the following:

1 The first time the barometer was taken up the mountain (that is, the altitude increased) it fell.
2 The second time the barometer was taken up the mountain it fell.
3 And so on until the nth time the barometer was taken up the mountain it fell.
4 Therefore, all barometers fall when their altitude increases.

To make this a valid argument, we would have to insert another assumption – the principle of induction – after the first three statements, to the effect that,

> All unobserved cases resemble observed cases.

With this in place we can validly argue that 'All barometers fall when their altitude increases.' But unfortunately, as you can see, this assumption suffers from the same problem: it is a universal claim for which we can only have finite evidence. As the Scottish philosopher David Hume pointed out, it's a vicious circle: for the principle of induction to be true we would need to establish that the principle of induction is true.

So, it follows that all inductive arguments must be invalid; in that the premises they are made of can never justify the conclusions we derive from them. Even so, this is the best method we have for reaching general conclusions from empirical evidence. In Chapters 29, 30 and 31 we will examine what we need to do to ensure we avoid the most common problems when we use inductive arguments; in these two chapters we will focus on deductive arguments.

Checking the components – what sort of premises are there?

With deductive thinking there are two simple things we must learn to check in our arguments:

1 the component parts – the premises that contain our ideas; and
2 the connections we make between them – our reasoning.

Facts and values

The first question we should ask is: what sort of premises are there? If we confuse one for another we're likely to make mistakes. Take the most obvious distinction between those that are factual and those that express value judgements. A statement of fact purports to represent the way things *are* and, therefore, can be assessed in terms of its truth or falsehood, whereas a statement of value is about how things *should* or *ought* to be and, therefore, cannot. One is descriptive, the other prescriptive. With many of the value judgements we make it is simply a matter of opinion: there is no objective criterion to which we can appeal to settle the issue.

Fact	Value
A statement about what *is* the case.	A statement about what *ought to* or *should* be the case.
Descriptive	Prescriptive

The problem we have to guard against, therefore, is confusing the two and deducing a conclusion containing a value judgement from purely factual premises. In this way someone can sneak their own opinions in under our radar as if they are just statements of fact. You might find someone argues,

All major engineering projects result in increased taxes.
The new power station is a major engineering project.
Therefore, it should be stopped.

The major and minor premises are both statements of fact, whether or not they are true, but the conclusion is a value judgement. We said earlier that deductive arguments are valid, because they draw out conclusions that are already contained in the premises. The key principle to remember is:

> Nothing can be drawn out by way of a conclusion
> that is not already contained in the premises.

This means that no value judgement can be deduced from any set of premises which do not themselves contain a value judgement. In the argument above, we could only have drawn out this conclusion if the major premise had been instead,

All major engineering works should be stopped because they
increase taxes.

Even though this seems obvious, it's easy to introduce a value into an argument without even knowing it. Some words, like 'honesty', 'heroism' and 'promise', are mixed, both fact and value. Using them in what appears to be a factual argument we can smuggle in a value judgement without realising it.

Example: Promise

The premise 'John promised to pay Sarah £30' is a simple statement of fact. But the word 'promise' means more than just an undertaking to do or to refrain from doing something. It also suggests it's 'good' to keep such an undertaking and 'bad' not to. Consequently, from the statement of fact that 'John promised to pay Sarah £30', we can deduce the value judgement that 'John *should* pay Sarah £30'.

Concepts

The same is true of words representing concepts – they can be mixed too: part concept, part fact or value. The following statements were made about a patient who had his dialysis treatment withdrawn. See if you can identify which are statements of fact, value and concept, and which are mixed. Then decide what these are a mixture of.

1   The patient is rude.
2   He is aggressive.
3   He has poor quality of life.
4   He should be denied treatment.
5   He is unemployed.
6   He lives in a hostel for the homeless.
7   The treatment should be given instead to someone else.
8   He is rootless.
9   He has no family.
10 He makes a mess which the nurses have to clean up.

Answer:
  Mixed: (a) Fact/concept   8, 9, 10
           (b) Fact/value/concept   1, 2
           (c) Value/concept   3
  Unmixed: 4, 5, 6, 7

Fact/concept

In group (a), clearly these are statements of fact, but what is meant by 'rootless', 'mess' and 'family'? One person's mess might be another's everyday disorder; something that it is just not worth getting worked up about. As for 'rootless', the patient might not have a family, but he might have rich personal relations with his friends in the hostel. Even 'family' raises problems. He might not have many close blood relatives, but he might have many close friends he likes to regard as 'family'.

Fact/value/concept

As for group (b), words like 'rude' and 'aggressive' are not just descriptions of a way of behaving, they are also evaluative: we usually don't approve of such behaviour. But then there are also questions of concept raised by these words. What do we mean by 'rude' and 'aggressive'? Do they just convey personal prejudices or is there an objective standard by which we can judge such behaviour?

Value/concept

Similar questions can be raised about the one statement in group (c). Clearly there is a question of value here with the use of the word 'poor', but we can also raise a question of concept about the 'quality of life'. We need to analyse this carefully before we allow ourselves to apply it to this sort of case.

In each case where concepts are used we're asking a unique sort of question: 'Yes, but what do you mean by *X*?' In a probing, self-reflective way we are questioning our own use of these quite ordinary words. We are saying that these can no longer be taken for granted; that there are implications to our argument that are concealed by our use of these words.

In some discussions we have to step back and ask questions like these. In the statements about the dialysis patient we would have to ask: 'What do we mean by "rootlessness", "aggression", or even "family"?' Often our discussions turn on the meaning of such concepts. What seems like a discussion over a difference of fact turns out to be a difference of concept, with both sides using it in different ways.

> The problem . . .
> The precision needed to argue consistently is at odds with the flexibility of language.

One reason we have this problem is the flexibility of language. Words have a capacity for holding many shades of meaning, or even several separate meanings, which compounds our problems in communicating well-reasoned arguments and ideas. While the essence of reasoning is precision, language normally tends toward imprecision. Two opposing forces are at work. The sharpness, clarity and constancy of meaning that are important to consistent reasoning, are at odds with the ambiguity of language, the lack of sharp and stable definitions.

● Suppressed premises – are any missing?

Now that we're sure about what type of premises we're using, we must check that there are none missing. Often in our arguments we make assumptions without making clear that we're doing so: there are unstated premises that we have just suppressed. Our arguments may be valid, but we won't know this until we have revealed the suppressed premise. See if you can identify the suppressed premise in the following argument:

1 Aldous is a dog.
2 Therefore he is very loyal.

Clearly, what would make this argument valid is the suppressed premise that,

> All dogs are loyal.

That's not too difficult, but we often confront simple one-liners, like the following, which can need much more careful thought.

1 The customer can't expect much consideration from a multinational like XXX.
2 Why are you blushing? You have nothing to be ashamed of.
3 You should have no worries about buying this car, the engine's fine.
4 Intolerant? Well yes, of course he is. He's a racist.

● **Checklist**

None of this is too difficult to understand. The most serious problem is organising ourselves to take account of these things routinely as we write and think about our ideas. It helps if you can ask yourself a limited number of short questions as you check your arguments. Photocopy the following checklist and get into the habit of asking yourself the following questions.

The component parts
1 Are my premises purely **factual**?
2 Are there **value judgements** that I haven't revealed?
3 Are there **concepts** about which I should ask, 'But what do I mean by that?'
4 Have I made clear all my premises? Does my argument rely on **suppressed premises**?

Summary

1   You are being assessed on how you think, so check that your arguments are valid.

2   Your arguments will be invalid if you've drawn a value judgement from factual premises.

3   Check to see if your premises are mixed: part concept, part value and fact.

4   You will also lose marks if you have made assumptions that you have not made clear.

● **What next?**

Checking each component of our arguments is the first step in creating consistent arguments. Next we must check the connections we make between them.

28 Developing consistent arguments 2: The connections

In this chapter you will learn . . .

1 how to check that we've made valid connections between our ideas and created consistent arguments;
2 how to avoid the six most common mistakes when we make these connections;
3 a simple routine method of checklists to remind you what to look for;
4 how to use Venn diagrams to detect your mistakes.

Now that you're clear you've got all the components and you know what type they are, you can move on to check the connections between them.

● Qualifiers

First, as you connect your premises to the conclusion, check that the strength of your claims remains the same. If you've claimed in the premises that 'most' people agree about something, you cannot then go on to claim in the conclusion that 'all' people agree about it. Known as 'qualifiers', words like 'some', 'most', 'all', and 'few', indicate the strength of the claim you are making. In the next chapter we will come across this again, when we look at how accurately we describe our evidence, but in this one we're concerned with the connection between our premises and our conclusion.

The problem is that in our normal conversations most of us are not always careful about the qualifiers we use. We might read in a report that a police spokesperson has claimed that older drivers are safer than younger ones. As a result we might argue that because Philip is older than Mark he is a safer driver. But the spokesperson might have meant that it is only true 'as a general rule', whereas we have argued that it is 'always' true and, therefore, it must be true in the cases of Philip and Mark.

Such easy generalisations have a certain beguiling attraction for us. It's easy to slip into a categorical claim ('all', 'every', 'always', etc.) to avoid the effort of weighing up the evidence carefully and selecting just the right qualifier ('almost all', 'almost half', 'few', etc.) that reflects the right strength. They also give us a sense of instant certainty, that we have suddenly uncovered something which makes things so much clearer. We can plan our lives and our thoughts with so much confidence as a result.

> Qualifier – is it accurate and consistent between our premises and conclusion?

● Distributing our terms

Omitting the qualifier gives rise to another very common problem. In many statements, such as 'Businessmen treat their workers badly' or 'Journalists are not concerned with the truth', we've omitted the partial qualifier 'some'. But then, when we include it, the terms of the argument are not 'distributed' in a way which will allow us to draw a conclusion. To distribute a term is to refer to every member of the class of things it represents. If we distributed the term 'businessmen' we might say,

> All businessmen treat their workers badly

which means we can now argue that,

> Malcolm is a businessman
> Therefore Malcolm treats his workers badly.

But if, instead, we only have a partial qualifier, we are left with the argument,

> Some businessmen treat their workers badly.
> Malcolm is a businessman.
> Therefore Malcolm treats his workers badly.

And this, as you can see, is not a valid deduction, because Malcolm may be one of those businessmen who treat their workers well. The best way to detect this mistake is to ask ourselves each time we make a generalisation, 'Is this a universal claim?'

> Distributing our terms – is this a universal claim?

● Processing our terms

If the problems with qualifiers and with distributing our terms are common enough, even more common are the problems that arise from badly processing our terms: that is, assuming they mean either more or less than they actually do and, therefore, using them to assert in the conclusion more, or less, than the premises will allow. Take the following argument,

> All children are innocent.
>
> No grownups are children.
>
> Therefore, no grownups are innocent.

While you might agree with the conclusion, the argument is invalid. The conclusion cannot be deduced from the two premises, because the major premise does not exclude other groups from the category 'innocent', like some grownups, who are ingenuous and unworldly. As you can see in the Venn diagram below, it doesn't follow from the argument 'All children (Cs) are innocent (Is)' that 'All the innocent (Is) are children (Cs).'

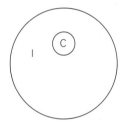

> Processing our terms – have I assumed they mean more, or less, than they do?

● Illicit conversion

This is also a good example of illicit conversion. Conversion is the process of interchanging the subject ('All children', in this case) and the complement ('innocent') of a sentence. In many cases it is quite valid to do this, but not in this. We assume that as long as we can argue 'All As are Bs' we can also argue 'All Bs are As.'

The mistake is not in the premises themselves, but in the way we use them. We assume our premises allow us to do things that in fact we can't. You might assume, quite reasonably, that if a man drinks too much and becomes an alcoholic he's likely to become destitute. He's likely to lose his job, his home and his family, and find himself living on the streets. But from this it's a short step to arguing that if a man is destitute he must be an alcoholic.

The subject and the complement of certain propositions can be interchanged, but only if there is total exclusion between the two classes of things. If I say that no women are members of the football team, I can also say that no members of the football team are women.

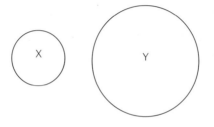

The same is true when there is partial inclusion. If you can argue that 'Some patriots are pacifists', you can also argue that 'Some pacifists are patriots.'

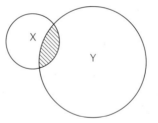

But where there's total inclusion we cannot reverse it. We can't argue that given all statisticians are mathematicians, then all mathematicians are statisticians. This would be a case of illicit conversion.

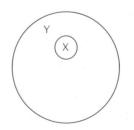

Indeed, most forms of racism and discrimination begin with this mistake. Someone might hear or read about people being mugged in the street and every case appears to have been done by members of a certain ethnic group. So they come to the conclusion that all muggings are carried out by members of that group. Then they convert the generalisation, often without knowing, and argue that all the members of that group are muggers. From arguing that all *X*s are *Y*s, they conclude that all *Y*s are *X*s.

So, there are two principles to remember:

1   Total exclusion is a convertible relation, whereas total inclusion is not.
2   Partial inclusion is convertible too.

> Illicit conversion – have I wrongly interchanged the subject and the complement?

● Illicit obversion

Another common way of misusing premises is illicit obversion. Every proposition can be expressed in both a positive and a negative way. The generalisation 'No golfers are non-competitive', is the same as saying 'All golfers are competitive.'

This form of the original proposition is known as the 'obverse' and the process of changing it is known as 'obversion'. However, in changing from the affirmative to the negative form it is easy to make a fairly common mistake and, as a result, to draw conclusions that are not justified. For example, from the generalisation that,

All golfers are competitive,

someone might conclude that,

All non-golfers are non-competitive.

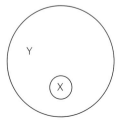

Clearly this is invalid; it's an example of illicit obversion, as you can see from the Venn diagram.

It doesn't necessarily follow that those who are excluded from the *X* class are also excluded from the *Y* class. The fact that someone is not a golfer doesn't mean they are non-competitive. There are many other sports, activities and occupations that call for people to be competitive if they are to be successful.

> Illicit obversion – have I wrongly assumed that not being one thing means you are not another?

Affirming the consequent and denying the antecedent

Finally we come to just about the most common mistake we all make when we bring two ideas together to explain something.

Example: Einstein

> The following argument, presented by a professional scientist to support Einstein's theory of relativity, seems perfectly plausible, but what's wrong with it?
>
> If Einstein's theory is true then light rays passing close to the sun are deflected. Careful experiment reveals that light rays passing close to the sun *are* deflected. Therefore Einstein's theory is true.

As you can see, it is marked by the distinctive 'if/then' structure of a conditional or hypothetical proposition, the type we used when we created our 'What if' questions.

We might agree that people who are found to have taken performance enhancing drugs in sport (one idea) will be disqualified (another idea). So, we might argue,

> If an athlete is found to have taken performance enhancing drugs, then he will be disqualified.

The hypothetical proposition has two parts: the 'if' clause, known as the antecedent, and the 'then' clause, known as the consequent. In this case, if we were to use our hypothetical proposition as the major premise in an argument, we could argue,

1   If an athlete is found to have taken performance enhancing drugs then he will be disqualified.

2   Stephen has been found to have taken performance enhancing drugs.
3   Therefore, he will be disqualified.

Affirming the antecedent

But there are two valid forms of this type of argument. The first, as you can see from this example, is to 'affirm the antecedent', in this case 'If an athlete is found to have taken performance enhancing drugs', which we affirmed in the second premise that 'Stephen has been found to have taken performance enhancing drugs'. Therefore, it was valid to conclude that '. . . he will be disqualified'.

Denying the consequent

The second valid form is to deny the consequent. Using our example again, the consequent of the hypothetical premise was '. . . then he will be disqualified'. So, our argument will be valid if, in the second premise, we deny that Stephen was disqualified, and then conclude that therefore he has not been found to have taken performance enhancing drugs.

Two simple rules

There are, then, quite simple rules to obey. An argument is only valid if you affirm the antecedent or deny the consequent. Keep in mind the following simple table.

	Antecedent	Consequent
Valid	Affirm	Deny
Invalid	Deny	Affirm

As you can see, the fallacies we must avoid are to deny the antecedent and affirm the consequent.

> Invalid forms:
>
> **1** to deny the antecedent
>
> **2** to affirm the consequent

Denying the antecedent

If we deny the antecedent, our argument takes the following invalid form,

1 If an athlete is found to have taken performance enhancing drugs, then he will be disqualified.
2 Stephen has not been found to have taken performance enhancing drugs.
3 Therefore, he will not be disqualified.

Clearly this is invalid. Stephen may not have been found to have taken performance enhancing drugs, but this doesn't mean he will not be disqualified. He may have cheated in other ways.

Affirming the consequent
The other fallacy is to affirm the consequent, which produces equally inconclusive and invalid results:

1 If an athlete is found to have taken performance enhancing drugs, then he will be disqualified.
2 Stephen has been disqualified.
3 Therefore, he has been found to have taken performance enhancing drugs.

Again, Stephen could have been disqualified for many reasons; taking performance enhancing drugs is just one of them.

Necessary and sufficient conditions
One of the reasons many of us make these mistakes is that in the proposition 'If X, then Y' we confuse the claim that X is a sufficient condition for Y with the claim that it is the *only* sufficient and necessary condition: if something is 'sufficient' and 'necessary' for the occurrence of something else, no other alternative reasons need be sought. If we were wrongly to assume this, we would in effect confuse the hypothetical 'If X, then Y' with the proposition 'If, and only if, X, then Y.'

In Stephen's case we would in effect be arguing that 'If, and only if, an athlete is found to have taken performance enhancing drugs, then he will be disqualified.' This means that no other reason will count as justification for his disqualification. So, if he is disqualified, it can only be because he has taken banned drugs.

Hypothetical propositions – have I denied the antecedent or affirmed the consequent?

Example: Einstein

So, what was wrong with the scientist's argument with which we began? By now you'll have realised that the scientist affirmed the consequent:

1 If Einstein's theory is true, then light rays passing close to the sun are deflected.
2 Careful experiment reveals that light rays passing close to the sun *are* deflected.
3 Therefore Einstein's theory is true.

But, like Stephen's disqualification, this may be due to any number of reasons, not just Einstein's theory of relativity. Of course, the argument could be made valid, but only if it was the sufficient and necessary condition for the deflection – that it was the *only* reason for it. However, for this to be the case we would have to argue instead, 'If, and only if, Einstein's theory is true, then light rays passing close to the sun are deflected.'

The connections

1 Qualifiers
Is the strength of my conclusion equal to the strength of my premises?

2 Distributing our terms
Are the terms of my argument distributed in a way that will allow me to draw a conclusion? Is my generalisation a universal or a partial claim?

3 Processing our terms
Do they mean more or less than they actually do? Do I conclude more or less than my premises will allow?

4 Conversion
Do I draw conclusions that are not justified, by interchanging the subject and the complement of a sentence when I shouldn't?

5 Obversion
Do I draw conclusions that are not justified, by making a mistake changing from the affirmative to the negative form?

6 Hypothetical propositions
Have I denied the antecedent, or affirmed the consequent?

Summary

1 It is easy to assume that generalisations without a qualifier are categorical ('all') statements.

2 If the major premise has a partial qualifier, the terms of the argument are not distributed.

3 One of our most common problems is processing our terms: we assume they mean more, or less, than they do.

4 Only total exclusion and partial inclusion are convertible relations.

5 Perhaps our most common mistakes are to affirm the consequent and deny the antecedent in hypothetical propositions.

● What next?

We began the last chapter by arguing that the distinguishing characteristic of intelligence is not what you know, but what you do with it: the ability to identify relevant connections and put together what ought to be conjoined. Neither logic nor critical thinking can help us in this. Between them they cannot help us generate a single new idea. But they can help us decide which are worth retaining. In the next chapter we will learn what's worth retaining as we use evidence in our inductive arguments, and the problems we must avoid.

29 Using evidence 1: Describing it

Now that we know how to avoid the problems in developing our arguments deductively, we can turn our attention to our inductive thinking. Here our concern is to draw sound conclusions from our evidence, otherwise we can invalidate our most persuasive and consistent arguments. To avoid this we must make sure of two things: that our descriptions of the evidence we're using are accurate, and then that we draw the right inferences from them.

Unfortunately, all too often, well constructed arguments are rendered ineffective by the way we describe our evidence. Unless we're careful it's easy to exaggerate or underestimate it, or generalise on the basis of untypical examples, or on insufficient or weighted evidence.

● Untypical examples and insufficient or weighted evidence

This last problem is, perhaps, the most common. It occurs frequently as a result of three fairly common errors: we generalise from single or isolated instances, or from selected instances, or just rely on unexamined assumptions or prejudices about what we think something should be like. We can easily avoid these errors by just asking ourselves three simple questions:

> ### Three questions
>
> 1 Is my generalisation based on a sufficient number of observed instances?
>
> 2 Do these instances represent a fair sample?
>   2.1 Are they typical?
>   2.2 Are there special conditions prevailing?
>   2.3 Are there any exceptions?
>
> 3 What is the probability of such a generalisation being true? Does this make it reasonable to believe it *is* true?

Even when we've met the first two questions, we then have to consider how probable it is that such a generalisation could be true. We might claim that 'All heavier-than-air objects fall to the ground when unsupported', but we only have finite evidence for what is an infinite, universal claim. Every observed instance supports this, but we can never claim to have observed 'all' instances of it. A universal claim covers not just those instances in the past and present, but, of course, those in the future too.

So our claim must rest on our confidence that we have observed sufficient cases and that such a law being true seems highly probable. And, of course, in subjects like history, anthropology, social sciences and in some natural sciences, where experiments cannot be done to demonstrate the reliability of such generalisations, we must take extra care to ensure this confidence is well-placed. The appearance of comets, supernovas and the decline and fall of civilisations are, after all, relatively rare events.

● **Exaggerating or underestimating evidence**

As for exaggerating or underestimating our evidence in our descriptions of it, the most common mistake is to claim more than the evidence will allow.

All/some
Consciously or unconsciously we don't make enough effort to match the strength of our words to the strength of the evidence. We might claim something is 'always' the case when in fact it is only 'usually' so. We might argue, 'The bad weather always comes from the west', when in fact the most we can claim is that it 'usually' comes from the west. Qualifiers like 'usually', 'almost', 'seldom', 'hardly ever' and so on, are replaced by simple absolutes,

like 'all', 'always', 'never' and 'none', even though there is rarely sufficient evidence to support such claims.

- Matching our words to the strength of the evidence
- Using simple absolutes carefully

Once we've avoided exaggerating our evidence through simple absolutes, we then have to choose carefully from the range of well-qualified words and phrases available to us.

Examples

If we claim that 'Usually bad weather comes from the west', we need to ask ourselves whether the evidence only supports the claim that 'some of the time' it does. If we argue that 'Very few people believe the public should not know that convicted paedophiles are living among them', does the evidence really support this or is the proportion just less than 50 per cent? If we use adjectives like 'probably' or 'likely', is the balance more like 50/50?

'Some' statements lose significance

There are very obvious reasons why we would much prefer to use the simple absolute 'all' in a statement. In the previous chapter we saw that, because categorical ('all') statements distribute their terms, we can draw conclusions from our premises. Equally important, once we use the word 'some', unless we establish how great this proportion is, the statement has at least lost a lot of its significance, if it hasn't actually become meaningless. 'All' statements are easily disproved: all we have to do is find one counter-example. But 'some' statements are almost impossible to disprove.

Example

If we argue that 'Some businessmen treat their workers badly' there is little point in arguing about it. All we have to do is find two businessmen that treat their workers badly to have proved the statement to be true. But then it says very little, unless we can establish precisely how great the proportion.

'Typical', 'normal', 'average'

As this suggests, the way to avoid these problems is to present the evidence on which the claim is based and describe it carefully, with as much precision as it allows. One way the media attempts to inject this sort of precision into its claims is to use adjectives like 'typical', 'normal' and 'average', but, before you use them yourself, make sure what you mean by the 'typical home-owner', the 'normal family' or the 'average worker'.

Example: Journalists

Journalists are fond of summing up whole cultures in an imaginary individual. They talk about the 'British worker', the 'American taxpayer' and the 'Australian farmer' as if they represent simple homogeneous groups whose values, aspirations, interests and needs are instantly known to us all.

But what are they typical of and how many don't conform to this stereotype? We may know someone is British and that he or she works, but we may not know any more than that. So to use this to identify a certain sample of evidence, we must carefully qualify it.

Averages

Even the more precise 'average' creates almost as much confusion. We have to be clear what we have in mind: mean, median or mode? In most cases it's mean or mode averages. But the mean average may be misleading, because it doesn't give us information as to how the results are distributed. They may be clustered around the centre, or evenly distributed from the lowest mark to the highest, or an unrepresentative few at the top may pull up the mean average or a few at the bottom pull it down. If we were to use this to calculate the average income of inhabitants of many industrialised countries, we would be liable to get a very false impression, because wealth is unevenly distributed.

Mean average:	No information about the distribution

For this the mode average is more useful. When the range of distribution is considerable it represents the group better, because, as it identifies the item that occurs most frequently, it indicates the largest sub-group in the whole series. For this reason it is often regarded as the 'typical' representative of the series. In our everyday speech, the average usually means mode:

the thing you are most likely to run into; the 'mode' or 'model person'. It's not affected by being pulled up or down by the extremes on one side or the other like the mean average.

Statistics

One way of avoiding these problems should be to use the precision of statistics. But we all know how misleading statistics can be. As the Scottish poet Andrew Lang once said, at times they are used as a drunken man uses a lamppost – for support rather than illumination. Any of three common errors can be the cause of this: hidden qualifications, the lack of uniformity between different sets of statistics used for comparison, and confusion between absolute and comparative figures.

Statistics – three common errors
1 Hidden qualifications.
2 Lack of uniformity between different sets.
3 Absolute versus comparative figures.

Hidden qualifications

Perhaps the most common error, which can make an argument compelling when it least deserves to be, is the failure to reveal hidden qualifications.

Example: Breakfast cereal

In a recent advertising campaign the makers of a popular breakfast cereal made the claim that 'Research shows that when they eat a cereal like ours kids are 9 per cent more alert.' To assess the reliability of this claim we need to know at least two things: the number of children involved in the study, and any hidden assumption. In particular we need to know whether this just means that if children eat a breakfast *at all*, of any sort, then they will not be falling asleep at their desks. Having eaten something, their energy levels will be maintained so they can concentrate and perform better.

Lack of uniformity

We also need to know what was meant by 'alert' and how it was measured. For long periods as we do our research our attention is consumed by the multitude of small things that must be done. It's easy, then, just to take things for granted and accept that we all share the same assumptions about those things we're measuring. We might assume we all mean the same thing when we use words like 'stress' and 'depression', or that our perception of a problem matches everybody else's.

Example: Stress and breast cancer

Recently it was reported in the *British Medical Journal* that an 18-year study involving over 6,500 women found that those with high levels of stress were 40 per cent less likely to develop breast cancer than those who described their stress as low. But another study, this one over 24 years, published in 2003, found that women who endured high levels of stress ran twice the risk.

Comparing the two studies, there seems no uniformity between what each describes as stress. It means different things to different people. It is also difficult to disentangle stress from other factors that may have a significant influence, like lifestyle, diet and family history of the disease. Even more, in the first study it may be that those who were better at reporting their stress levels were also better at noting other things that might lead to cancer and thus do something to lesson the danger. To evaluate both of these findings we must be able to compare them on the same basis.

Absolute and comparative figures

Our third problem, it would seem, is the most obvious and easy to avoid. But still, it's surprising how often we read reports in which simple totals are given to indicate trends over a certain period.

Example: Crime figures

Official figures might show what appears to be an alarming annual increase in crime, but unless we are also told how fast it has been growing in previous years and how fast the country's population is increasing we have no way of knowing how significant this is. A more reliable indicator is the number of crimes per 100,000 people.

Figures like these, showing ratios, are safer indications of trends, although even these can be manipulated to suit the purposes of an advocate who needs statistics for support rather than illumination.

Evidence – descriptions and generalisations

1 Are my generalisations based on a sufficient number?

2 Are they a fair sample?

3 Is there a reasonable probability that they are true?

4 Have I used simple absolutes, like 'all', where other qualifiers, like 'some', would be more accurate?

5 Have I presented my evidence with enough precision?

6 Is it clear what I mean by 'typical', 'normal' and 'average'?

7 Have I chosen the right average to use: mean, median or mode?

8 Have I checked in the statistics I've used that . . .

    8.1   there are no hidden qualifications;
    8.2   there is uniformity between the comparisons I make;
    8.3   I have not confused absolute and comparative figures?

Summary

1   To use our evidence well, we must describe it accurately and draw the right inferences.

2   We must avoid the two key problems: exaggerating or underestimating evidence; and generalising on the basis of untypical examples, or insufficient or weighted evidence.

3   This means matching the strength of our words to the strength of our evidence and using simple absolutes carefully.

4   We must be careful in using adjectives like 'typical', 'normal' and 'average'.

5   We must also avoid the three common errors in using statistics.

● **What next?**

Accurate descriptions of our evidence place us on firm foundations. Now we must learn to draw the right inferences from them.

30 Using evidence 2: Drawing inferences

Now that we've described our evidence accurately we can begin to draw inferences from it. There are all sorts of inferences we can draw about all manner of things. Some are worthwhile, others not. The question is: how do we decide which are worthwhile?

● Using analogies

The most natural thing to do is search for a close analogy. We assume that because things resemble each other in some respects they will continue to resemble each other in a further respect and this gives us our inference. So the key to understanding the implications of our evidence lies in the way we understand something familiar that is similar. Indeed, we learn to reason by such analogies long before we learn to reason using abstract concepts.

Example: Parables

From an early age we're impressed by the power of parables to convey a moral message. They depend for their effectiveness upon our ability to see that one story or situation is similar in important respects to another.

In this way analogies give us the means of extending our knowledge by using what we already know we can rely upon. They can also have remarkable persuasive power, helping us clarify, simplify and make more vivid a complex idea.

However, not all analogies are so reliable: not all things alike in some way are alike in others. Analogies can only be a guide. Although we use them to *suggest* a conclusion, they are incapable of *establishing* one. We still need to test them against the evidence to find the causal connection. The principle, therefore, is that we can only safely argue from the possession of one set of characteristics to another when there is a causal connection between them and not just a vivid similarity.

> Analogies can only *suggest*, not *establish*, a conclusion.

Therefore, if you use an analogy to draw your inferences, check the following three key points: the nature of the connection between the analogy and the explanation; the number of similarities involved; and the reliability of the relation between the analogy and the conclusion derived from it.

Analogies – check:

1 Connection:
   1.1 Causal connection.
   1.2 When does it break down?

2 Numbers:
   2.1 The number of samples used.
   2.2 The number and variety of characteristics thought to be similar.

3 Relation to the conclusion:
   3.1 Is it the right strength?
   3.2 How significant are the differences and similarities?

Connection

The first thing to check is whether the analogy establishes a causal connection and is not just a vivid way of presenting an idea. In Chapter 9 we found that, if I were to argue that the car crashed because I had dropped my pen, this wouldn't be convincing because there is simply nothing analogous between these two events: we know of no law or uniformity in our experience in which the dropping of pens causes cars to crash. For the analogy to work there must be a credible causal connection. It could only have some chance of working if I could argue that light flashing off my falling pen somehow distracted the driver, because we do know of uniformities in our experience in which people have accidents when they are distracted.

But the second thing we need to ask is: When does the analogy break down? They all have a tendency to at some point.

Example: Light

Sir Isaac Newton used the analogy of billiard balls to explain the behaviour of light as molecules or particles. Although useful, it reached a point when it became clear that light behaves in ways the analogy cannot help us explain. Along with other electromagnetic radiation it behaves like a wave motion when being propagated and like particles when interacting with matter.

Numbers

Up to a point, the more samples we can find between which the analogy is thought to hold, the more confidence we are likely to have in it. The same is true of the number and variety of characteristics shared by the analogy and the actual situation. But problems arise when we ignore differences and push similarities beyond what is reasonable – the 'fallacy of false analogy'.

Example: The economy

In the 1980s, in an effort to persuade us that cuts in government expenditure were unavoidable, some governments seized upon what seemed like a useful analogy, telling us that 'The economy is like a household budget' and we were simply spending beyond our means and getting into debt. But, despite their similarities, there were significant differences between the two. For one thing, what you spend in a household budget doesn't usually generate more income and jobs in the household, whereas in the national economy such investment not only can improve productivity, but can have significant multiplier effects, lifting economic activity, increasing revenue from direct and indirect taxes and reducing welfare costs by taking more people into jobs.

Relation to the conclusion

Lastly, we have to be sure that the conclusion drawn from the analogy is of the right strength and takes into account all the significant similarities and differences between the analogy and the situation it helps to explain. We have to decide how significant these similarities and differences are and whether we've overlooked other conditions, which need to be considered to make the analogy safe.

Example: Life on other planets

You might argue that there must be life on other planets in our solar system – after all, they are similar to Earth in so many ways: they revolve around the sun, their sole source of light; all are subject to gravitation; some revolve around their axis, giving them day and night like the Earth; and some have moons. With all these similarities, by analogy, it is reasonable to assume they must be inhabited too. But these are not the most relevant conditions we would look for in a planet that could sustain life. Among others, we would want to see a plentiful supply of water and for this we need the so-called 'Goldilocks zone': an orbit that is not too far from the sun, which would make it so cold that water would remain frozen, and not too close, where water would boil, but just right. And, of course, we need a breathable atmosphere.

● Objectivity and subjectivity

Checking the reliability of analogies in this way we are better able to exert control over the inferences we and others make. But there are still likely to be judgements in our inferences that cannot be justified by appealing to anything like an objective criterion in the same way.

Value judgements cannot be avoided. Not everything is objective, so evidence has to be weighed and value judgements taken about its strength. Even though some generalisations are supported by a substantial body of evidence, that evidence is capable of being interpreted in different ways depending on who does the interpreting and their background, tastes, experiences, values and so on. We all see what our minds prepare us to see.

> Value judgements are unavoidable – evidence has to be weighed and judgements taken about its strength.

Misconceptions

But, while we can't exclude value judgements from our work, we can avoid using them in such a way that they will weaken our arguments. So, how do we do this? First, let's clear up some common misconceptions, like those below:

1 'A statement is **objective** if it is a balanced view of all the facts.'

It all depends on what you mean by 'balanced': it's a matter of opinion. One person's balanced account is another's biased spin. It also has the potential of being contradictory. Once we have 'all the facts', it may be clear that the situation is seriously unbalanced, with the weight of evidence tipped heavily in favour of one view rather than another.

2 'Something is **true**, and therefore not a value judgement, if everyone agrees.'

Although everyone agrees, it may still be false. A jury may unanimously convict an innocent defendant.

3 'Something is **subjective** if it is just one person's opinion.'

This is an extension of 2: an individual may still be right, while everyone else is wrong. In 1633 Galileo was forced to retract his opinion that the Earth revolved around the sun, because the weight of opinion was against him, but he was still right.

Using value judgements
So, how should we use value judgements so that we don't weaken our arguments?

Verifiable value judgements
First, there are some that *are* ultimately verifiable by reference to an objective criterion. If we were both to look out of my study window and I were to judge that the tree opposite was 30 yards away and you were to judge that it was more like 50 yards, the difference in our judgements could ultimately be settled by using a standard measuring tape. There is, in other words, an objective standard that we both accept, to which we can appeal.

No objective criteria
Other judgements, however, for which there is no objective standard, cannot be settled so easily. We might not be able to agree over whether it was right for Jane to lie to her boyfriend to protect his feelings or whether Verdi's *Requiem* is a great piece of music.

> ### Example: Music
>
> To settle the latter we would have to agree on three value judgements. First, we would have to draw up a commonly accepted definition and standard of 'greatness'. Then we would have to agree whether the *Requiem* possesses the qualities that make up this standard and, thirdly, whether it possesses them in sufficient quantity to be described as a 'great' piece of music.

Solution: Be open!

This may sound complex, but in it lies the solution. When you make a value judgement for which there are no objective criteria, make clear the basis on which you've made it. Unlike the standard of measurement we used above, the standard used for our evaluation of whether the *Requiem* is or is not a great piece of music isn't obvious. So come clean and let your readers see how reasonable and well thought out your criteria are. In your work and in the work of others check that no material has been withheld to support the conclusions reached. Reveal all the evidence you think is relevant. This, in itself, contains a value judgement, so justify it – be open.

> - Make clear the basis of your judgement.
> - Show reasonable, well thought out criteria.

● Irrelevant inferences

Nevertheless, as you get more deeply involved in your research, such openness is often replaced by an eagerness to defend a point of view to which you've become increasingly committed. As a result, all sorts of irrelevant inferences and arguments are pressed into service to support your case. The technical name for this fallacy is *ignoratio elenchi* (ignoring the issue): we appear to strengthen our argument by proving another that is irrelevant to the issue. Instead of keeping to the point, we shift attention to a different question on which we feel a lot more confident. There are four forms you should look out for, as you can see in the table on page 295.

Irrelevant inferences

The person   (*ad hominem* – to the man)

Popularity   (*ad populum* – to the people)

Authority   (*ad verecundiam* – to awe or reverence)

The compromise

The person

Often this takes the form of appeals to prejudices and emotions. In the argument *ad hominem* (to the man) the argument is sidestepped by discrediting the person who proposed it. Presenting supposedly damaging evidence against someone's motives, character or private life diverts attention from the argument to a subject which is more likely to stir prejudices.

Example: Dissertations in art, music and literature

In this type of dissertation it's tempting to focus on the artist, rather than his or her work. The fact that a writer may have been cruel and ruthless, a womaniser who deceived his wife and left his children to fend for themselves, has nothing to do with judgements about the quality of his work.

Popularity

The argument *ad populum* (to the people) is similar in that it deals with a difficult argument by appealing to the sentiments of popular opinion. It sidesteps or supports the argument by appealing to mass emotion, assuming that whatever the crowd thinks must be right. Rhetorical questions are a common way of making such appeals: 'Don't you agree that Mr X should be elected to the post?' They are designed to appeal to our like-minded attitudes and opinions.

They have built into them the expected answer. When they're successful they compel agreement on the grounds that failure to agree would place us on the other side of a vast body of opinion that thinks otherwise. So, whenever you begin a sentence with words, like 'surely', 'plainly', 'clearly', which often introduce such appeals, ask yourself if you're really developing the argument, or just appealing to the like-mindedness of the reader.

Authority

The argument *ad verecundiam* (to awe or reverence) is a similar method of diverting attention, but this makes an appeal not to popular opinion, but to a prestigious or authoritative name or figure, a revered authority, even conventional propriety.

Of course, there's nothing wrong with appealing to legitimate authorities. The problem begins when we appeal to an authority that is not really an authority, or is not a relevant authority in the field that the argument is about. We should beware of giving or taking advice from someone who is being paid to give it and we should remind ourselves that competence in one field doesn't necessarily transfer to another. Get into the habit of asking yourself the following simple questions about the so-called authority.

Assessing authorities

1 Does he know what he's talking about?

2 Are her views based on careful study or extensive experience?

3 Does her position offer her greater authority than others?

4 Has he shown himself to be a better observer and a shrewder judge than the rest of us?

5 What are his motives? Is he promoting his own self-interest?

Even when we're citing relevant authorities we need to ask who they are and whether they have sufficient experience and a good reputation in this area.

The compromise

Finally, beware of the argument which is presented as a compromise between two undesirable extremes, so that anyone who refuses to accept it comes across as unreasonable. This exerts strong pressure on readers to agree. And yet almost any argument can be presented as a compromise between two others, so this alone doesn't mean there is good reason to accept it. The truth is just as likely to lie on one of the extremes as in the middle. Using this device, attention is diverted away from the strength of your argument and trained, instead, on its appearance as the most 'reasonable' compromise.

Drawing inferences

1 Have I checked that my analogies stand up according to the three key points?

2 Have I thought through clear criteria for my value judgements?

3 Have I made clear the basis of them?

4 Have I avoided arguing my case by using irrelevant inferences to support them?

Summary

1 The most common way of drawing inferences from evidence is to use analogies, but we must make sure they are safe and reliable.

2 They can only *suggest*, not *establish*, a conclusion.

3 Value judgements are unavoidable.

4 With those that cannot be verified, be open about the criteria you've used.

5 Avoid using irrelevant inferences to give your arguments support.

● **What next?**

Earlier in this chapter, we saw that to show an analogy is reliable we have to find a causal connection. In the next chapter we will see how we do this and the most common problems we must avoid.

31 Using evidence 3: Creating causal connections

In this chapter you will learn . . .

1 how to avoid oversimplifying, or drawing invalid causal connections in your arguments;
2 the four most common forms of oversimplification and what you can do to avoid them;
3 the five most common ways in which we create invalid causal connections from our evidence;
4 the questions we need to ask ourselves routinely to avoid these problems.

No matter what the subject of the dissertation, as we draw inferences from our evidence, we must make sure the causal connections we make are sound – that they are neither oversimplified, nor invalid.

● Oversimplifying

Stereotypes

Perhaps the most common way of oversimplifying is by using stereotypes. In some circumstances, of course, stereotypes are justified, particularly if we're targeting an advertising campaign or using police resources effectively to target a certain type of crime. Those that aren't are most often racial and social. It's easier to find a causal connection between two things, if we restrict the factors involved to someone's membership of a particular group, about which we've made a few glib assumptions to help us understand the diversity of it. But such connections are very rarely reliable.

The straw man

Equally familiar is the fallacy of the straw man, committed when we oversimplify a causal explanation, either deliberately or accidentally, so that we can dismiss it as false.

To guard against this, ask yourself if you have accepted without analysis or justification any preconceptions. You might find the defence of these is now distorting your selection and interpretation of evidence.

Example: Miracles

Someone might argue, 'It's absurd to claim that miracles never happen, after all we live in an age of miracles: the existence of the TV, computers, space travel, and medical treatment that can now save people from what would have been certain death just fifty years ago.' The person developing this argument has reinterpreted the claim that miracles never happen to mean that extraordinary inventions cannot take place. And, of course, it's not difficult to prove this claim to be false.

Special pleading

The fallacy of special pleading is similar and just as easy to fall into when we are so convinced of our side of the argument that we're tempted to present just the evidence that supports our view, ignoring all that contradicts it. Alternatively, we can find ourselves doing this when we use an argument in one context, but refuse to use it in another where it would lead to an opposite conclusion.

Special pleading

1 Present just the evidence that supports our view, ignoring all that contradicts it.

2 Use an argument in one context, but refuse to use it in another, where it leads to an opposite conclusion.

In practice, be aware of doing this, particularly when you use generalisations in your arguments. This can take two forms:

1 We argue from a **specially qualified** case to a **generalised conclusion** that ignores the qualifications. In this way we can avoid having to consider all the characteristics of a particular case.
2 The converse: we argue from the **unqualified statement** to a statement about a **special case**. In this form the fallacy consists in arguing that the circumstances are relevantly different when in fact they are not at all.

Example: Trickle-down economics

In the 1980s the supporters of the theory of 'Trickle-down economics' – those in government, CEOs and heads of industry – criticised the high wage demands of workers on the grounds that they were over the rate of inflation, while they awarded themselves increases many times higher. Justification was sought by arguing that they were a special case, although, in fact, there appeared to be no relevant differences. They argued that as they spent their increased incomes this would trickle down into the economy and generate jobs, even though workers could argue the same and in even greater numbers.

Special pleading: generalisations

1 Qualified $\longrightarrow$ unqualified.

2 Unqualified $\longrightarrow$ qualified.

As you come across the different forms of special pleading in your own and other people's work, do one of three things. First, **compare** what is said by the same person at different times. Second, try to evaluate the **credentials** of those who make the claim – does it come from an interested party? And, third, for those arguments that omit relevant points and gloss over the omission using general, unspecific language with wide implications, get into the habit of asking those who make the claims to **specify** what they mean—ask them who, what, why and how?

Example: Breakfast cereal

In the case of the advertisement for the breakfast cereal that we referred to earlier, we need to know:

1 **Who** did the research?
2 **What** numbers were involved?
3 **Why** should the same effect not be found with a breakfast of any type?
4 **How** was the children's alertness measured?

Remedies
1 Compare what is said by the same person at different times.
2 Credentials – does it come from an interested party?
3 Omitting relevant points – specify! Who? What? Why? How?

Fallacy of false dilemma

In the 'all-or-nothing' fallacy, or the fallacy of false dilemma, we assume that the problem we're dealing with has an either/or solution; that there are just two alternatives, when in fact there may be several. In political, religious and moral controversies attempts are often made to convince us that there are only black and white choices available, although most of the decisions we make are not of this type. So, when you find yourself presenting a case in these terms, ask yourself whether there are in fact more than these choices available.

Oversimplifying causal connections
1 Stereotypes.
2 The straw man.
3 Special pleading.
4 Fallacy of false dilemma.

● Invalid causal connections

Creating invalid causal connections from our evidence, like oversimplifying, will seriously weaken our arguments. It can undermine the causal explanations at the heart of our thesis or proposition.

The *post hoc* fallacy

Probably one of the most tempting is the *post hoc* fallacy (in fact, the *post hoc ergo propter hoc* fallacy – 'After this, therefore because of this'). This is the mistake of assuming that just because an event follows another, it must be caused by it. When we see two things regularly occur together, one after the other, we're inclined to associate them as cause and effect. In fact, so common is this mistake that, like analogies, it's the source of many of our most enduring superstitions. No doubt someone noticed often enough that walking under a ladder was followed by bad luck, so the superstition got started that the former was responsible for the latter.

> So, ask yourself . . .
> . . . is this a coincidence or a cause?

Cause/correlation

A similar mistake occurs when we confuse a cause with a correlation.

Example: Crime

In our attempt to explain the rise in violence in Western societies we might find that 80 per cent of all those convicted of violent offences regularly watch violent programmes on TV. Such a correlation is very persuasive, but is it any more than this? Is it just a correlation or is it also the cause? We might find that 80 per cent of those convicted also chew gum, but we're less likely to believe that this is the cause.

So, prior to identifying such regularities, we must have something analogous between the two events, something that allows us to conclude that one might be the cause of the other. We know of no causal link between violence and chewing gum, so we probably wouldn't have looked for any correlation between the two, but we do have an idea how there might exist a causal link between violent programmes and violent behaviour.

> So ask yourself . . .
> . . . is there something analogous between them that would suggest a causal link?

Multiple causes

As this suggests, situations are often more complex than we imagine. It's a warning that for most events there are almost certainly many interrelated causes and not just one: the causes of the outbreak of the Second World War; the reasons why many students struggle with their study skills; or why house-martins are arriving three weeks earlier that they were 10 years ago. A single cause is confirmed only if it *alone* can produce the effect, which is, in fact, much rarer than we like to believe.

> **Example: A doctor's diagnosis**
>
> A doctor will ask a battery of questions to get at the causes of someone's heart attack. They will be carefully devised to search out evidence of the long-term causes (diet, lifestyle and genetic history), medium-term causes (controls over diet and cholesterol) and short-term causes (recent levels of stress, overwork and poor sleep patterns).

To assume that there is only one cause often oversimplifies the explanation, which frequently leads to the *post hoc* fallacy.

> So ask yourself . . .
> . . . is it more complex than I assume?

Underlying causes

Nevertheless, in some circumstances, where there appear to be multiple factors operating, there may either be an underlying cause explaining them all, or they may not be causally related at all. Take the first case: you may come across a situation where you find two conditions side by side, say, poverty and gambling. The obvious causal explanation is to argue that gambling causes poverty, but the person involved may be in a poorly paid, boring job, so he turns to gambling to inject a sense of excitement into his life. So gambling has not caused his poverty: they are, in fact, both the effect of the underlying problem of his poorly paid, boring job.

> So ask yourself . . .
> . . . is there an underlying cause that explains these effects?

Fallacy of false cause

Alternatively, two or more factors may not be causally related at all: the fallacy of false cause (*non-sequitur* – 'does not follow'). Strictly speaking, we commit this fallacy when we draw a conclusion that doesn't follow logically from the premises. More loosely, it is basing a conclusion on insufficient, incorrect or irrelevant reasons.

Example: Stress and breast cancer

In the study which found that women with high levels of stress were 40 per cent less likely to develop breast cancer than those who described their stress as low, it could be that both stress and breast cancer are linked non-causally. It might be that the women who are better at reporting stress are also better at monitoring their health and responding promptly to lessen the danger of other unstated factors.

So ask yourself . . .
   . . . are there insufficient reasons for assuming that these factors are causally related?

Invalid causal connections

1 The *post hoc* fallacy.

2 Cause/correlation.

3 Multiple causes.

4 Underlying causes.

5 The fallacy of false cause (*non-sequitur*).

Summary

1   Oversimplifying the causal connections we make will seriously weaken our arguments.

2   The most common ways we do this are by using stereotypes, special pleading, the straw man and false dilemma fallacies.

3   Drawing invalid causal connections can undermine the explanations at the heart of our dissertation.

4   By routinely asking ourselves certain questions we can guard against the five most common forms of this.

● What next?

The way we describe our evidence and draw inferences from it will determine the conclusions we draw and whether they stand up to scrutiny. Now we turn our attention to the most common problems we must learn to avoid as we use language to develop our arguments.

32 Using language 1: Clarity

The effort of giving our ideas form in words and sentences is indispensable to clear thinking. It crystallises our ideas, giving them the sort of clarity and consistency they might not otherwise have had. The problem, as we said earlier, is that the flexibility of language, the capacity of words to hold many shades of meaning, even different meanings altogether, is at odds with the logical consistency we need for clear thinking, which calls for sharp, clear and constant meanings. In these two chapters we will learn how to settle this conflict and meet the needs of both clarity and consistency in our thinking.

● Clarity

The clarity of our ideas owes much to the way we use them. As we communicate with others we give the ideas clearer shape and form. Unfortunately, many of us at universities are inducted into ways of expressing our ideas that lead to obscurity, rather than clarity. As students we are encouraged to read turgid, polysyllabic, badly written prose that drowns us in the mire of convoluted sentences and misleading jargon. The next time you're sitting in the library poring over a journal article which you have read three times already and still struggle to understand, try to summon up the confidence to question whether it's not your fault but the writer's.

One reason for such academic obscurity, it seems, is the assumption that a simple style is a sign of a simple mind, whereas in fact it is the result of harder thinking and harder work. Much academic writing lacks clarity because it's insulated from everyday human reality and the concrete details of ordinary speech by a plethora of passive verbs, long generalised nouns and unnecessary jargon. As Sir Peter Medawar argues, if the text is hard to follow, because of a general determination to keep such vulgar sensibilities at bay, then we'll have great difficulty finding out what the author intends us to understand: 'We shall have to reason it out . . . much as we reasoned out a passage in some language we didn't fully understand.'[1]

- A simple style is the result of harder thinking.
- Passages that are insulated from concrete details of everyday life will be difficult to understand.
- There is no subject so complex that it cannot be expressed simply.

We should, instead, learn to write unpretentious prose that carries our ideas clearly, grounding them in the concrete reality of our lives. No matter how complex the subject, it can be expressed simply: there is no subject that cannot be made accessible in good, clear English. If you doubt this, just read any passage from Einstein's *Relativity: The Special and General Theory*, or Bertrand Russell's *The Problems of Philosophy*, or G. M. Trevelyan's *British History in the Nineteenth Century and After*. Each of them explains the most esoteric and difficult subjects, yet in a simple, elegant language that makes the most complex idea accessible to all.

Clear, unpretentious prose

1 Short words

2 Active verbs

3 Concrete details of ordinary speech

Jargon

There is no better way of exposing the gaps in our thinking than writing our ideas down. It's the most effective way of revealing what we don't know or understand, and where our thinking has broken down. But, equally, the most common and effective way of concealing this is to resort to jargon and abstractions.

As students this presents us with a difficult dilemma. A large part of learning any subject is learning its language, but then we should also be developing our ideas with absolute clarity and precision. So, how are we to distinguish between using a legitimate concept and jargon?

Concept

A simple way of answering this is to say that a legitimate concept can always be analysed with clarity and precision into its parts, each of which can be expressed in language grounded in our everyday lives.

Jargon

Jargon is the language of specialists who have convinced themselves that their ideas cannot be expressed in any other way. A word that is merely jargon makes its users feel like insiders, but, in fact, is quite meaningless.

Jargon immunises ideas from criticism and evaluation

At times jargon seems like deliberate obfuscation in the hope that this will pass for depth and meaning.

Example: English

> In her account of her time studying English at a top US university, Helena Echlin describes the long sentences, received with awe and thoughtful silence, which sounded like English, but lacked all meaning:
>
> The ode must traverse the problem of solipsism before it can approach participating in the unity which is no longer accessible.[2]
>
> As she says, 'How can one "traverse" a problem, or "participate" in a unity?' Indeed, how can you participate in something which is no longer accessible? Words are adorned with suffixes for no other reason than to make them seem more obscure and arcane: 'inert' becomes 'inertial', 'relation' becomes 'relationality' and 'technology' is substituted for 'method', as in the sentence,
>
> Let's talk about the technology for the production of interiority.

Such obfuscation immunises the sense of what's being said from all evaluation and criticism. As Echlin says, 'Where there is no paraphrasable meaning, dissent is impossible, because there is no threshold for attack.'

But as writers we have an obligation to make sure our readers are comfortable with the words we use, not to use words to impress them or make them feel excluded. We are not the gatekeepers to an exclusive club, in which only an esoteric language is spoken. In his book *Writing to Learn*, William Zinsser cites a 'famous sociologist', whose entire book is written in the style below:

The third major component of modeling phenomena involves the utilization of symbolic representations of modeled patterns in the form of imaginal and verbal contents to guide overt performances. It is assumed that reinstatement of representational schemes provides a basis for self-instruction on how component responses must be combined and sequenced to produce new patterns of behavior.[3]

Cleaning up our language

This may, of course, be excused as just one sociologist talking to another, but still we all have an obligation to clean up our language wherever we can to make it simple, elegant and accessible to all. One way of doing this is to reduce what you want to say to a logical sequence of clearly thought-out sentences. In this way you will reveal the gaps in your knowledge and reasoning. Where you don't understand something, except in terms of a sequence of jargon, break the jargon down into concrete words that ground your ideas in everyday reality. Rather than describe an educational initiative as

a communication facilitation skills development intervention,

a description in which no human activity has been allowed to intrude, translate it using concrete language of everyday reality, so that it reads

a programme to help people communicate better.

- Reduce what you want to say to a logical sequence of clearly thought-out sentences.
- Break the jargon down into concrete words that ground your ideas in everyday reality.

● Abstractions

Nevertheless, we use words in many different ways and not all of them have their meaning fixed by tying them to concrete things, so that we all know what we're referring to. From numerous, largely different, situations we take a common set of characteristics to form an abstract general concept. As the process continues there are different levels of abstraction. When we describe an object as white we ignore all its other attributes, but then when we use the concept of whiteness we take one further step into abstraction, omitting consideration of concrete objects altogether.

We use them as if they are real in themselves

These are powerful tools for thinking, enabling us to create significant relations between ideas that can generate the most revealing insights, advancing our understanding of ourselves and the world around us. But at times we trade in abstractions as if they are real things in themselves and, because there is no object to which we can relate them, we allow ourselves to give them the meaning we want them to have. It's tempting to believe that because we see them in a dictionary there are concrete referents by virtue of which they can be defined. But in many cases there are no such referents; they are just high abstractions.

> With no concrete referents we give them the meaning we want them to have.

We assume other people share the same meaning

And from there it's easy to take the next step and assume that when we use them other people share the same meaning, even though the referents of a word (if there are any) may be different from one person to another and for one person in different situations. To talk of 'liberty' or 'equality' is to know how having either will affect our lives in actual terms in the society in which we live.

The two steps

1 We give them the meaning we want them to have.

2 We assume other people share the same meaning.

These two simple steps can result in meaningless, though very persuasive, nonsense. Remember Helena Echlin's example, 'The ode must traverse the problem of solipsism before it can approach participating in the unity which is no longer accessible', and Alan Sokal's hoax paper which parodied the worst of the postmodernist arguments and was so persuasive it was published unchanged by a peer-reviewed journal. He considered his biggest challenge was to write sufficiently incomprehensibly. He explained, 'I had to revise and revise to achieve the desired level of unclarity.'[4]

Our writing becomes heavy and difficult to understand

What's more, passages with only abstract concepts in them – no people, no human agency – are heavy and ponderous. They're drained of all their vigour. Nouns denoting abstract concepts, like 'liberty', 'justice' and 'humanity', mean little until applied to concrete cases set in a particular cultural context. Good, clear, vigorous writing is specific and concrete. It's vivid, grounded in details we recognise from our own experience. In this way it makes contact with the humanity of the reader. Given a familiar picture readers instantly recognise, they know the meaning we want to convey.

- Good, clear, vigorous writing is specific and concrete.
- It makes contact through a familiar picture we all recognise.

What can we do?

Nevertheless, the answer is not to refuse to use abstractions, or to be suspicious of any argument that does. Isolated concrete facts are meaningless on their own without abstractions, generalisations and theories to make sense of them.

So, as you write, keep to the following three guidelines:

1   Balance

Get the balance right between abstractions and the concrete details of everyday life that grounds them in our experience.

2   Distance

Become more conscious as you use them of the distance they are from their concrete referents and the implications this may have for the reliability of the way you use them.

3 Move back and forth

Get into the habit of moving back and forth between the abstractions and the things they represent. In this way you can assess whether you can use them reliably in all different contexts or whether there are limitations on their use which you should acknowledge.

It's easy to deceive ourselves into thinking that because we're familiar with a word and frequently use it, we're also familiar with the idea it represents and its implications. It's also easy to believe we're thinking when we're only stringing together words that have a warm familiarity. If, in fact, these words stand for nothing, then the passage makes no sense.

> So ask yourself . . .
> . . . what is the cash value of what I'm saying?
> . . . what do these words stand for?
> . . . what is their objective meaning?

Analyse abstractions and translate them into everyday language. We have to ask what difference they make to our lives: how will our readers come to understand the way they work in their experience? Above all, be constantly vigilant against the tendency to view abstractions as something in their own right.

Using abstractions:

1 Get the balance right.

2 Be aware of the distance between them and their concrete referents.

3 How does this affect their reliability?

4 Ask yourself 'What do these words stand for?' 'What is their objective meaning?

5 Try not to view them as something in their own right.

● **Loaded language**

The problem we all have with writing and thinking is controlling the language so that we develop our ideas in the direction we want to them to go. Unfortunately, instead of us controlling the language, often it controls us. Our thinking gets directed and structured without us being critically aware of it. The clearest example is loaded language, where words carry more than what they mean descriptively: there's an emotional content or a value judgement, which manipulates our responses without us being aware of it. In this way a writer can encourage us to accept her argument without us looking at it too closely.

> **Example: Spin**
>
> A commentator who wants to put a positive spin on someone refusing to budge on what he believes, might describe him as someone 'standing up for his principles', whereas another, who is not so sympathetic, might describe him as 'obstinate' or 'stubborn', perhaps even a 'hardliner'.

What can we do?
To avoid this happening in your own writing, use the following four strategies.

1   Separate the ideas from the language
Strip away emotionally charged language and unsubstantiated or irrelevant assumptions smuggled in without you realising it. If you then find that the situation is not as you normally describe it, ask yourself whether this is because the language you normally use has accustomed you to believe this, or if there is a substantive issue that has guided your judgement, which means there is good reason to think this way.

2   Translate
Take the passage you suspect might be loaded and translate it into neutral terms so you can see whether the argument is then so convincing.

3   An adjective audit
Count the adjectives in the passage and then see whether any convey unsubstantiated attitudes, rather than a line of thought. Can you do without the adjective? Does it affect the meaning of the passage? Adjectives are easy to attach, but they are dangerous if they have no basis in fact and express an attitude almost unnoticed. They slip beneath the rational radar more easily than just about any other word. Try to tune your radar for them as you read a newspaper or listen to the news.

4   Three-step technique

If you're not sure whether a word does convey substance and genuinely develops a line of thought, use the 'Three-step technique' we learnt in Chapter 8 and analyse the word. Ask yourself, 'But what do I mean by *X*?' This will unfailingly get to the bottom of things. It may take you a little longer, but you will be left in no doubt as to what is happening when you use this word.

Loaded language – 4 strategies:

1 Separate the ideas from the language.

2 Translate into neutral terms.

3 Do an adjective audit.

4 Analyse the word.

● Begging the question

If we're unclear about the implications of the words we use, we're likely to lose control over the direction in which our ideas develop. A good example of this is begging the question, which occurs when we accept as an assumption what we are arguing for as a conclusion. We manipulate readers without them knowing it by smuggling into the premises the conclusion about to be deduced. Strictly speaking, this is what we know as arguing in a circle or, more familiarly, the fallacy of the vicious circle. In other words, we use a premise to prove a conclusion and then use the conclusion to prove the premise.

Begging the question:	To accept as an assumption what we're arguing for as a conclusion.

Example: Sport

A friend might argue that she believes sportsmen and sportswomen are fitter than those who are not involved in sports. In response you argue that you know plenty of people who play sports, but they also drink excessively, smoke, are overweight and, in general, don't take good care of themselves. But your friend refuses to accept this as evidence against her theory, arguing that these people are not 'really' sports people. In effect she is using a definition of 'sports people' which already includes as one of its core elements someone who is fitter than those not involved in sports.

As this shows, the very issue that is in dispute is begged by the definition. Her argument, therefore, is only trivially true, as all examples of these arguments are. They are tautologies: your friend has made her argument true by definition and by no reference to anything outside it. And, of course, it's easy to persuade someone of anything if you're free to monopolise words and give them your own meaning. At best such an argument is useless: *A* in and of itself does not give us grounds for saying *A* is true.

Nevertheless, even though this seems obvious, they infect our thinking in various ways, so be alert to the following forms:

Begging the question
1 Common notions.
2 Moral words.
3 Verbal propositions.
4 Vague definitions.

1   Common notions

We hear these so often that they tend to go unchallenged: sentences that begin 'Everyone knows that . . .', 'It's common knowledge that . . .', 'It's all too clear that . . .' or 'It's obvious that . . .' So, challenge them and ask what evidence there is for what they claim.

2   Moral words

Even more subtle are moral words, like 'goodwill', 'honesty', 'generosity', 'promise' and 'murder'. Their meaning embraces not just a description of the facts, but a value judgement too.

Example: Honesty
When we say of someone that they are very honest, we are not just making a simple statement of the facts, but also passing judgement on their behaviour. The word 'honest' means not just someone who has a strong sense of justice and treats others fairly, but also that it is a good thing to be honest and bad to be dishonest.

So to argue that 'Generosity is a good thing' or 'Murder is wrong' begs the question, because the conclusions are already contained in the words themselves – they are tautologies. Generosity is good and murder is wrong by definition, so the statement says nothing substantive; it does nothing but unwrap part of the definition of the word.

3 Verbal propositions

An interesting variant of this is the 'verbal proposition'.

Example: Social workers and teachers

If you are a social worker you might be challenged by someone who asserts, 'You must admit that too much help for single parents is a bad thing', or if you are a teacher someone might insist, 'You can't deny that giving students too much freedom in the classroom is not a good thing.' And you cannot avoid agreeing, not because giving help to single parents or freedom to students is in principle a bad thing, but simply because of the meaning of the phrase 'too much'.

This is just a verbal proposition, not a factual one: 'too much' means 'a quantity so great that it is a bad thing'. We are presented with a mere tautology, nothing more significant than 'X is X', which is trivially true and cannot be used to prove a fact. Too much of anything is a bad thing, so the real point at issue is what do we mean by too much freedom or too much help, and this gets us back to questions of fact.

4 Vague definitions

As you can see, some of the most common ways in which we beg the question develop out of the role of definitions in the argument, particularly when these are used in a vague way. If someone uses a vague definition, it is likely to contain all they need to develop their argument. Then, when they are challenged by an example that doesn't fit and they're pushed towards a precise meaning, they try to save their case by insisting that the example isn't a 'real' sportsperson, musician or whatever the argument is about. But, of course, when you stretch the meaning so far in this way to defend a certain point of view the word ceases to do any real work and you end up making no point at all.

Clarity

1 Jargon

2 Abstractions

3 Loaded language

4 Begging the question

Summary

1 To develop our arguments consistently we must establish sharp, clear, constant meanings in the words we use.

2 Writing that is insulated from the concrete details of everyday life will be difficult to understand.

3 Resorting to jargon is a way of concealing the fact that we don't understand something or that our thinking has broken down.

4 Without concrete referents we can give abstractions any meaning we like.

5 Loaded language and begging the question are both ways of manipulating readers without them knowing it.

● **What next?**

However, clarity is just one half of the problem. Once we have pinned down our meaning clearly we must maintain it consistently throughout our arguments. In the next chapter we will learn how to recognise and deal with the problems this raises.

● Notes

1   Sir Peter Medawar, *Science and Literature in Pluto's Republic*, quoted in William Zinsser, *Writing to Learn* (New York: Harper & Row, 1989), pp. 62–3.
2   Helena Echlin, 'Critical Mass', in *Sydney Morning Herald*, 10 February 2001; the complete article appeared in *Areté*, www.aretemagazine.com
3   William Zinsser, *Writing to Learn* (New York: Harper & Row, 1989), p. 68.
4   *Sunday Times*, 18 January 1998.

33 Using language 2: Consistency

In this chapter you will learn . . .

1 that if we allow the meaning of the words we use to change in the course of an argument we will render the argument ineffective;
2 that the clearest example of this is equivocation, and the simple things we can do to avoid it;
3 what is meant by the fallacies of division and composition and how to avoid them.

As we develop our arguments, the way we move from one premise to another must be logically consistent. At times, even though we have taken great care to make sure of this, our efforts can be undermined by the flexibility of our language. And the more familiar we are with the terms we're using, the less likely it is that we'll see the mistake. The most common mistake is the fallacy of equivocation.

● The fallacy of equivocation

As we've seen, many of the words and expressions we commonly use have indefinite or changing meanings. When we use them in two or more different ways in the same argument, we commit the fallacy of equivocation, if that argument depends on the words maintaining constant meaning throughout. The argument itself may be valid, but we have no guarantee of its truth if the terms change their meaning in the course of it.

Example: Australian commercial

An Australian advertisement promoting concern for the environment has the presenter surrounded by people planting trees. He is clutching a handful of soil, which he allows to fall gradually through his fingers, while he tells us that those who fought for this (holding up the soil), their land, in the two world wars would be deeply disappointed by our generation, if we fail to protect it.

Those who wrote the commercial clearly sought to play on our inattention in not seeing that there is a difference between the 'Land' that we fought for, and the 'land' as in soil. By 'Land' we mean our culture, values and heritage, indeed our whole way of life, which might be threatened by an invader. This is quite different from the soil in which we plant crops. Clearly the persuasiveness of the argument rests on the equivocation of the concept 'land', which means different things at different stages in the argument.

What can we do?

The remedy, of course, is to ask whether the definition of the term at one point of the argument is the same as in the other and, if it isn't, replace the doubtful words with others. In the Australian advertisement the word 'land' with a small 'l' should be replaced with 'soil', but then this would rob the advertisement of its persuasiveness.

> So ask yourself . . .
> 1 does the persuasiveness of your arguments depend on similar equivocation?
> 2 have you been consistent in the way you've used words at different stages in your arguments?

● The fallacies of division and composition

Another equally common form of equivocation is found in the two fallacies of division and composition.

The fallacy of division

The fallacy of division is committed when someone argues that something, which is true only for the whole, is also true of its parts taken separately.

Example: Harvard

You might argue that Harvard University produces the best graduates in the country. So, John Smith, who recently got his degree from the University, must be an excellent person. But although the graduates of the best universities are generally excellent, to infer that any particular graduate is excellent merely because he attended one of these universities, would be an incorrect inference.

This fallacy can be found at the root of most forms of racism, in which someone is judged not on their own personal qualities, but by virtue of belonging to a certain ethnic group which is judged to possess certain characteristics. Still, in other situations we can argue quite validly that what is true of the whole is also true of the parts. I can argue that my computer is brand new, so all the parts are brand new.

The fallacies of division and composition

Division: whole ⟶ parts

Composition: parts ⟶ whole

The fallacy of composition
In contrast, as you would expect, the fallacy of composition is the converse of this: it is assumed that what is true of the part is also true of the whole.

Example: Football team

You might argue that because your favourite football team is made up of the best players in the game it must be the best in the country. But the fact that you might have the best players in your team does not ensure that you will have the best team. It will certainly help, but there are other important factors, like how well the players harmonise as a team and learn to work together, complementing each other's style, so that each player is able to play to his or her strengths and get the best out of themselves.

Consistency

1 The fallacy of equivocation

2 The fallacies of division and composition

Summary

1 Despite our efforts to create consistent arguments they are frequently undermined by the flexibility of language.

2 Our arguments are rendered ineffective if the meanings of words change in the course of them.

3 The two most common ways in which this occurs are equivocation and the fallacies of division and composition.

● What next?

We've seen in these two chapters that, while we might think language is just the vehicle for our ideas, it also exerts its own influence on them. As perception shapes what we see, language can shape what we think. An idea converted into words takes on a different form than we intended, while an argument put down on paper goes in a different direction than we expected. So we have to be aware of those forces that weaken our control over our ideas.

In all of these chapters on thinking there are tables you can photocopy and use to remind you routinely of those things you must work on to become a clear and consistent thinker. In Part 8 we will turn our attention to the practical things we can do to become better writers.

Part Eight

Writing your dissertation

34 **The first draft**

The success of a dissertation depends upon two things. First, there should be a clear rationale behind your research: your ideas and your strategy should make sense. Second, your dissertation should be written clearly and concisely in a style that is simple to understand and interesting to read. The first thing, a clear rationale, you established when you wrote your research proposal and then discussed it with your supervisor. We now come to the second.

● Start early

In the last two chapters we saw the importance of writing as the most effective way of gaining genuine control over our ideas and of working towards the centre of a problem. We can see our false starts, our inconsistent conclusions, our misuse of evidence and the unexamined assumptions that lurk unnoticed in the concepts we might otherwise use unreflectively. What's more, it engages our imagination, intellect and emotions, all of which are different ways of generating insights and developing our understanding.

In view of this, it makes sense to begin early. Record in your notebook and journal the constant dialogue you will be having with yourself on your ideas. Whenever a new idea comes to you, give yourself time to write it down and empty out your mind on it. This is your opportunity to express complex ideas and, in the process, form a deeper understanding of them, before you begin writing your first draft. In this way you will structure your thoughts, develop your arguments and evaluate your ideas as you go along.

- Writing gives us greater control over our ideas.
- We engage our intellect, emotions and imagination.
- So start early.

● The First Draft

Similarly, begin your first draft early, writing individual chapters as soon as they are ready. As with all forms of writing, it's better to start when the ideas are most familiar and vivid. Don't leave long periods between carrying out your research and writing it up; otherwise you might forget details and your impressions will lack the same freshness.

You'll also discover early whether you've got too much material or too little, and whether the results are turning out as you expected. If this means you will have to change your approach, it's better to know this early, rather than discover it when it's too late to do anything about it. So, if you conduct your interviews or read your primary material during the Christmas vacation, don't wait until the Easter vacation to begin writing up your impressions.

- Write when the ideas are familiar and vivid.
- Discover early whether you need to change your approach.

There are some things you can write from the very start. As soon as you've produced your research proposal and discussed it with your supervisor you can draft out the introduction, the literature review and the methods chapter. At this point all of this will be very familiar and you'll have all the material you need. It will also get you to the heart of these ideas before you set out on the actual research.

Then, after you've let your supervisor read the drafts, you can revise them immediately, while your discussion with your supervisor is still fresh in your mind. This way, not only will you write when you're most likely to produce your best work, but you'll avoid the dispiriting effects of seeing a mountain of work building up, all of which needs to be written and revised.

Write and revise from the start . . .
Introduction
Literature review
Methods chapter

● Planning

However, before you write any part of your first draft, you must plan the chapter as you would your essays. It's worth rehearsing your arguments thoroughly in detail before you write, to make sure they are truly yours; that you're genuinely at the heart of them.

Equally important, planning gives us the opportunity to sort out our ideas, so we can avoid the risk of omitting some important section or argument, which might be central to the issues we're discussing. We can identify the main points and how they break down into subsections and then down further into sub-subsections. In this way planning gives us the opportunity to create a clear structure through which our readers can navigate their way as they tackle our unfamiliar ideas and arguments. Without this it's all too easy to lose them, and if they can't see why our arguments are relevant, or they can't see what we're doing and why, we will lose marks.

- We make sure we're at the heart of our ideas.
- That we haven't missed anything.
- We create a clear structure, so we don't lose our readers.

The secret of planning lies in being able to put ourselves in the situation of actually writing the chapter without in fact writing it. In this way we're forced to make final choices as we work through two stages: editing, and ordering the ideas. If we fail to rehearse it in this sort of detail, we're likely to include in the chapter ideas and material that has no place in it. This will seriously weaken its clarity and logical structure, clouding it with unnecessary distractions that break up the logical sequence of our ideas.

The benefits of rehearsing our arguments in a detailed plan
1 We avoid losing our readers.
2 We avoid omitting some important section or argument.
3 We check that we have made the ideas our own.
4 We create a clear logical structure.
5 We check that our material is really relevant.
6 And that our ideas are clearly and consistently argued.

But most of all, by planning our chapters before we write we avoid doing the two most difficult things in writing both at the same time: that is, to summon up the ideas and plan the order in which they ought to be developed, and at the same time search for the right words and phrases to convey them with just the right strength and nuance, in order to develop the argument in the direction we've chosen. This is a task that is virtually impossible for all but the most familiar subjects that we've written about many times before.

> We avoid doing the two most difficult things in writing at the same time:
>
> 1 summoning up and planning our ideas;
> 2 choosing the right words and phrases to express them accurately.

● Write freely

Once the plan has been done, allow yourself to write freely as you follow it. Banish all fear of failure that what's going down might not be up to standard. Otherwise you might find yourself suffering from the legendary writers' block, which often comes from your internal editor stepping in to pass judgement on what you've done. Tell yourself this is only a draft: you're just sending out a reconnaissance party to see what you've got and how it shapes up.

The more you allow your words to flow onto the page without worrying at the moment too much about style and whether you've written complete sentences, the more your own voice will come through. You will find your own natural rhythm and there will be a lot more energy in your writing. Indeed, when you come to revision you will have to be careful not to kill this off. Too much editing can deaden your writing.

> • Discover your own voice.
> • Inject more energy into your writing.

To give you the space to do this, keep your inner editor at bay. We all have one; some are more persistent than others. They will try to intervene whenever they can, but particularly when you start your work, or when you complete a significant section and sit back to bask in the glow of your achievement. At moments like these you will be tempted to read it all through to allow your editor to give his or her approval. Editors are persistent and, if you allow them to come in too early, they will overpower the artist.

● Talk in print

The key to success here is to remind yourself that the best writing reads as though it is talk in print. The smoother the rhythm and the closer it is to our normal speech, the easier it is to read. You'll get your ideas across more effectively and you'll hold the attention of your readers.

> The closer it is to normal speech, the easier it is to read.

Of course it will still be more formal than the way you normally speak: you must avoid slang and colloquialisms. But that's not to say you can't use a familiar phrase we all use in daily conversation. If it conveys your meaning more accurately and concisely than a more formal phrase, use it. The problem with such phrases normally is that they reflect a 'habit' of thought, rather than real thought.

> So ask yourself . . .
> . . . does this phrase convey my idea accurately?
> . . . is there a better phrase?
> If it does and there isn't a better phrase, use it.

● Hang a question over what you write

Beware of the advice that tells you there should be *an* argument running though your dissertation that you must develop and defend. There will be many arguments running through it. Your work is not designed to defend opinions you arrived at *before* you began your research. This will only encourage you to tailor your evidence to your preconceived ideas much like an attorney will fail to mention, or will downplay or otherwise ignore any evidence that may weaken his case.

> Research is not about defending opinions you arrived at *before* you began.

The ideas you start with are provisional. You work beneath a set of questions to which you want answers. They drive your research. And like all genuine questions the answers could go in any direction. Your research may not reveal what you expect it will. So you must report this, not hide it.

Introductions, paragraphs and conclusions

By now, after many months of writing regular essays, you may not have any trouble with introductions, paragraphs and conclusions. But if you're still unsure, or you're not happy with the way you write these, look at Chapters 24, 25, 26 and 27 of *How to Write Better Essays* (Palgrave Macmillan, 2nd edition, 2008).[1] There you will find practical advice on how to improve them, simple steps to take and exercises you can practise.

Transitions

However, with the plan carefully rehearsed and structured the one remaining problem you will have to work on is how you're going to create fluent links between paragraphs that will signal to your readers the structure of your plan, so they will know what you're doing and won't get lost. For this you will need to have effective 'transitions' at the beginning of each paragraph to indicate the course of your argument. From this your readers should be able to see which way you're taking them. Transitions can be a short phrase, like 'As a result', or a single word, like 'Nevertheless'. They will help you create a taut, cohesive piece of work, with a clear connection between each paragraph.

> Transitions . . .
> - Indicate which way you're taking your readers.
> - Create a cohesive piece of work.

They work as 'logical indicators' telling your readers what you'll be doing. You might be striking a contrast with the previous paragraph ('In contrast',

'However'). You may simply be extending the argument you've already developed in a slightly different way ('Moreover', 'Therefore'). You may want to strengthen your argument by developing a point that reinforces it from a different angle ('Similarly', 'Likewise'). Or you may want to illustrate your point with an example ('For example', 'For instance'). In some paragraphs it will be obvious what you're doing and there will be no need to announce it, but if in doubt, use a transition.

> If in doubt, use one!

Nevertheless, in view of their importance, make sure your transitions do what you want them to do. Occasionally we find ourselves using weak transitions, which create only weak links and a weak structure. The worst are those we use for a list of points, words and phrases, like 'Also', 'Another point is' and 'In addition'. Moreover, transitions must do real work: avoid pressing one into service to create fluency that simply isn't there in the first place. If we haven't planned carefully enough, establishing clear intellectual links between paragraphs, very few readers will be fooled when we try to paper over the disjointed paragraphs with carefully chosen transitions. It will always sound false and manufactured.

> Make sure . . .
> . . . that they do what you want them to do;
> . . . that they do real work and don't just paper over the cracks.

As you come across transitions in your reading, note how other writers link their paragraphs. Keep a record in your notebook so you can use them yourself. Some of the most effective are the most simple, indeed so simple that we hardly realise they're there at all. Demonstrative pronouns, like 'this', 'these' and 'those', slipped into a topic sentence create a bridge between two paragraphs, while hardly disturbing the flow of ideas. In the table on page 332 you can see many of the most commonly used transitions and what they're used for. Photocopy it, pin it up near your computer and add to it when you come across new ones.

Similarities	In the same way, Likewise, Similarly, Correspondingly
Contrast	However, On the other hand, Yet, But, But at the same time, Despite, Even so, For all that, In contrast, In spite of, On the contrary, Otherwise
Illustration	For example, For instance, That is, In other words, In particular, Namely, Specifically, Such as, Thus, To illustrate
Extension	Similarly, Moreover, Furthermore, In addition, By extension, What is more, Above all, Further, In the same way
Conclusion	Therefore, Consequently, As a result, Thus
The next step	Then, After that, It follows
Emphasis	Above all, After all, Equally important, Especially, Indeed, In fact, In particular, Most important, Of course
Causal relations	As a result, Consequently, For that reason, So, Accordingly, Owing to this, Due to this, Because of this, Under these circumstances
Temporal relations	In future, In the meantime, In the past, At first, At the same time, During this time, Earlier, Eventually, Meanwhile, Now, Recently, Simultaneously
Summarising	Finally, In brief, In conclusion, In short, In simpler terms, In summary, On the whole, To summarise
Qualification	However, Nevertheless, Even though, Still, Yet
Alternatives	Alternatively, On the other hand, Rather
Explanation	That is to say, In other words, Namely, This means, To put it in another way, To put it simply

Summary

1   Start early. It will give you greater control over your ideas and engage your intellect, emotions and ideas.

2   Don't leave the first draft until later: write chapters as soon as they're ready.

3   Plan each chapter before you write, so you have a clear structure the reader can follow.

4   Write freely and keep your inner editor at bay.

5   Use transitions to indicate which way you're taking your readers.

 What next?

We now have a clear idea of how we should approach our first draft: writing freely within a well-structured plan without the intervention of our inner editor. So in the next two chapters we can turn our attention to the question of style and how we develop our own voice.

 Note

1   Bryan Greetham. *How to Write Better Essays*, 2nd edition (Basingstoke: Palgrave Macmillan, 2008).

35 Style 1: Finding your own voice

In this chapter you will learn . . .

1 how to find your own voice, even though you're having to use technical language;
2 how to ensure your writing is concise, direct and free of ambiguity;
3 of the importance of writing in the active form;
4 how to write lightly and produce a memorable, effective piece of prose.

A writer's individual style, his or her 'voice', most often develops through informal correspondence, like letters and journal entries, which envisage the reader as a friend or, at least, a friendly critic. More formal writing, aimed at some unknown, anonymous reader, encourages us to adopt a more universal and less personal form of communication. Unfortunately this often becomes cumbersome and clumsy. The further we depart from the rhythm of the spoken word, the more difficult it is to understand what we say.

● Technical language

For students this problem is particularly acute, because we're expected to use the technical jargon of our subject, which makes our writing more difficult to understand in terms of our everyday language. So, we must get the balance right. It helps if you can visualise your readers as a group of intelligent non-specialists, who might need just a little more translation of the technical aspects of your work. This helps you avoid the easy reliance on jargon and other literal shortcuts, forcing you into more complete explanations.

Jargon used without this sort of explanation turns your writing into a foreign language that must be translated before sense can be made of it. This will alienate readers, the cardinal sin in any form of communication, particularly writing. Write in a way that is accessible to any intelligent reader: you're not writing to be read by an exclusive set of code-breakers.

> Make sure you . . .
> . . . get the balance right between jargon and everyday language;
> . . . don't turn your writing into a foreign language.

● The first person

More difficult to resolve are the problems that come from the advice you're often given that your writing must be both impersonal and passive. Take the first of these. This means there's an embargo on all forms of the first person pronoun 'I'. You are then told that when you can't avoid it you must disguise your identity by talking about 'the author's opinion', 'in the opinion of the present writer' or similar hedging devices like 'It is thought that' and 'It has been suggested that'.

Yet then, when we're on the receiving end of this, much of our work as critical thinkers involves trying to get beneath this unhelpful subterfuge to distinguish between fact and opinion. We will want to know by whom it is 'thought' or 'suggested' and, if it is more than one, how many 'think' or 'suggest' it and what proportion: is it a majority, only a few or about 50/50?

> Critical thinking is our attempt to get beneath the subterfuge of hedging devices.

Unsubstantiated opinion

You are probably quite right in thinking this sounds like a ridiculous charade, an unconvincing subterfuge that flies in the face of everything we say about upholding the highest standards of academic integrity. If academic writers are expressing their own opinions they should uphold these standards of honesty and own up that this is 'my' opinion and you may not agree with it.

But the reason such advice is given is that our main focus in academic work is objectivity: we judge an argument on its consistency and how well it is supported by the evidence and not on the individual who has made the argument. So we cannot accept an argument that only rests on someone's subjective conviction.

> Objectivity: an argument is judged on its consistency and evidence, not on who made it.

Substantiated opinion

The offence this subterfuge is aimed at, then, is unsubstantiated opinion. But what of *substantiated* opinion? This advice appears to ignore the issues we discussed in Chapter 27 surrounding the principle of induction and the obvious epistemological truth that none of us have all the facts; that we must finally make a personal judgement after assessing all the evidence available. As Arthur Koestler so elegantly put it, 'The ultimate truth is penultimately always a falsehood':[1] there is always an evidential gap between the facts and our convictions, which we bridge by making a value judgement.

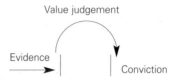

So, the common-sense advice would be to own up to your value judgements, rather than try to disguise them in these unconvincing ways. They are a necessary and unavoidable part of what we do. However, if the advice you receive from your department is to avoid the first person pronoun, you may have no other choice but to go along with this subterfuge.

● Passive writing

Equally worrying, this impersonal approach introduces unnecessary ambiguity into our writing. When you refer to 'the author' it's not clear if you're referring to the last mentioned reference or the writer of what's being read. The same is true of the passive form of writing. In the active form it's the doer of the action who is the subject of the sentence, rather than the receiver of the action, or the action itself, as in the passive form.

Active:	the doer of the action.
Passive:	the receiver of the action or the action itself.

In the active form we would normally say, 'I conducted an experiment', which is more precise than the passive form, 'An experiment was conducted.' This deliberately introduces ambiguity, leaving you unsure who conducted the experiment. By using a pronoun or noun to identify the person involved and an active verb to describe what she did, you can visualise the actual event in specific detail.

Passive:	Introduces unnecessary ambiguity.
Active:	Helps you visualise the event.

Not only does the passive form lack precision, but it is almost always less direct, positive and concise. For example, you might say,

> My first car will never be forgotten by me.

But when you convert this into the active form with the doer of the action the subject of the sentence, it is direct and therefore clearer and more concise:

> I will never forget my first car.

Unfortunately, this lack of clarity is a common feature of students' work. It expresses itself in a form of illiteracy unique to well-educated students, who struggle to express ideas in a language which is not theirs. Indeed, John Rodgers, a former professor of geology at Yale University, became so frustrated by it in his students' dissertations that he wrote a manifesto called 'The Rules of Bad Writing', among which were these two:

> Never use the first person where you can use ambiguous phrases like 'the writer' (especially when you've just mentioned some other writer) or, better still, 'it is thought' or 'it is considered', so that the reader can't be exactly sure who thinks what, or what – if anything – you do think.

> Never use an active verb where a passive verb will do. It pads out the sentence nicely and puts more distance between you and the facts – and the reader.[2]

So, to make your work clear and more direct, keep in mind the same principle we used in our research and in our analysis of abstract concepts, where we insisted that we must be able to cash in abstract words to see what difference they make in our lives; how they work in our experience. Wherever possible, use concrete words grounded in your everyday experience; don't distance your ideas from your readers' daily reality by using passive, impersonal, abstract forms. Otherwise, your arguments will be difficult to understand and, therefore, less persuasive.

● Writing lightly

You can now see that all this points to our one pre-eminent goal: to avoid all heavy, unreadable prose. If we can make our writing as light as our subject allows, our own voice will come through. The result is likely to be a more enjoyable experience for the reader and a memorable, effective piece of writing.

As we said in the previous chapter, the most effective writing – that which is the easiest to read – is nothing more than talk in print. Obviously, the closer we can get to our normal, everyday speech patterns, the easier it is to understand. Some of the best writing we've ever read seems to glide across the page as if it's just someone talking to you in the same room, even though the writer may be grappling with the most complex ideas and the deepest of emotions.

Summary

1 Balance technical language with everyday speech. Don't let your writing turn into a foreign language.

2 We must avoid introducing unnecessary ambiguity that comes from trying to avoid the first person and writing in the passive form.

3 Write as lightly as you can. Your own voice will come through and you'll produce a more effective piece of work.

● What next?

In the next chapter we will look at what this means in practical terms.

● Notes

1 Arthur Koestler, *Darkness at Noon* (1940; London: Vintage, 2005), p. 81.
2 Quoted in William Zinsser, *Writing to Learn* (New York: Harper & Row, 1989), p. 80.

36 Style 2: Simplicity and economy

In this chapter you will learn . . .

1 how to write clear sentences that readers can follow and understand;
2 how to use punctuation and logical indicators to get your ideas across without confusion;
3 how to use strong nouns and verbs to make your sentences sharper and clearer;
4 that knowing what to leave out is as important as knowing what to include;
5 how to declutter your sentences so the important words and your ideas stand out clearly.

The key to what we normally mean by a good style is learning to say what you want to say in the fewest possible words. It means simplicity and economy in the use of language.

● Simplicity

First, consider simplicity and how this influences the way we put together sentences and use words.

Sentences

When we write sentences our main concern is not to lose our readers. A complex sentence full of multiple clauses is difficult to follow. Not only are you likely to lose readers as they gingerly pick their way through it, but by the time they reach the end they will have forgotten your original point. To prevent this, try to do two things:

1 keep sentences relatively short; and
2 wherever it needs it, use a logical indicator ('but', 'if', 'however', 'therefore', 'moreover', 'similarly', etc.) to indicate what you're doing.

1 Length

Wherever possible, make your sentences short and their structure clear. Of course, sometimes it isn't possible just to use short, simple sentences. Occasionally, to develop a complex argument you can't avoid using a complex sentence structure. But if this is the case, beware of the dangers and do all you can to make sure the sentence can be negotiated easily, without any danger of confusion, by using logical indicators and the signposts of punctuation to indicate the structure.

Punctuation

Indeed, as you grow in confidence you will probably want to achieve more than this with your punctuation. Try to experiment, using the rhythm of your words and punctuation to convey the meaning. The 'white space' you create through your use of dashes, colons, semi-colons, full-stops (periods) and commas helps to create a rhythm that is nearer to the spoken word. Remind yourself, the nearer you can approach this the easier it is to understand what you've written.

> Make sure . . .
> . . . you indicate the structure of your sentence by using punctuation.

Different sentence lengths

In much the same way you can experiment using different lengths for your sentences to achieve different effects. Although shorter sentences are easier to follow, it's not necessary to make every sentence the same length. If your ideas are well thought out and organised logically – which they will be if you've planned the chapter – your sentences will have a rhythm of their own.

But remember, longer sentences tend to be soothing, while shorter sentences tend to be abrupt. So, if you want to get your point across in a way that makes the reader really think about it carefully, use a shorter sentence, particularly after developing an argument with a series of longer sentences. But beware of overdoing it – it easily devalues.

Short sentences:	Abrupt, good for grabbing your readers' attention and making them think
Long sentences:	Good for developing arguments

2   Logical indicators

As for logical indicators, the problem is not just that we fail to use them, believing that the reader can follow our train of thought without difficulty, but that they get lost in our sentences. When you read your work through, check that the logic is clear. If it isn't, try moving your logical indicator to a more important position in the sentence, say to the beginning.

> ## Sentences
>
> **1** Aim to create writing that is talk in print.
>
> **2** Don't lose the reader in long sentences.
>
> **3** Wherever possible use short sentences with clear structures.
>
> **4** Experiment with your punctuation, words and sentence length to create the rhythm of talk in print.
>
> **5** Make sure your logical indicators don't go missing.
>
> **6** Read it aloud to make sure it reads logically and smoothly.

Words

For the same reasons, we find words difficult too. More complex ideas demand as their vehicle more complex, even abstruse, language and a more subtle use of words. But this doesn't mean that we're driven to using a plethora of multi-syllabled words or the most convoluted sentences that conceal more than they reveal.

Don't settle for 'near enough'

We all know how difficult it is sometimes to find exactly the right word. So, instead, we reach for convenient jargon: it's near enough and we've heard it used often in our subject. However, if it's not right, don't use it. It will edge you still further from what you want to say and it might send your argument in a direction you don't want to go. Although you don't want to interrupt your flow of ideas and words, you must capture the idea well so that you can recall exactly what you were trying to say, when you come to revise.

If you fail to do this, your readers might conclude that you simply haven't got the intellectual determination to pin your ideas down precisely or, worse still, that you have few interesting ideas of your own at all. Either way,

> ## Settling for the wrong words
>
> **1** Can send you off in a direction you don't want to go.
>
> **2** Shows you haven't got the determination to pin your ideas down.
>
> **3** Suggests you have no interesting ideas of your own.

they're likely to assume that the words you've used mean one thing, when you really mean another.

Clichés

If you force yourself to search for exactly the right word, you're less likely to fall back on the familiar, reassuring, although empty, cliché. Like jargon, clichés are often a sign that you haven't pinned your idea down accurately, or that you haven't searched thoroughly for the exact word that will carry it perfectly. And yet, as most of us know, it's not always easy to avoid cliches. Indeed, it may not always be wise to. Cutting out all of them in your writing can often make your prose sound stiff and cumbersome. A familiar cliché, conveying just the right emphasis and meaning, will help you produce prose that is nearer to talk in print, with a natural rhythm that's not strained and difficult to read.

The problem is that all too often the impact is quite the reverse. An empty cliché, that does no real work beyond sounding cosy and familiar, can sap our writing of its life and vigour. If you want your ideas to have impact and your readers to appreciate that they are really interesting and original, avoid any word or phrase that doesn't do them justice, and this includes empty clichés.

> So ask yourself...
> . . . when a cliché comes to you in the middle of a passage, does this convey what I want it to, or is this familiar phrase encouraging me to adopt a thought structure that I didn't want?

Like everything else in your writing, if you use a cliché, mean to do it: have a clear reason, a purpose, for doing so.

Clichés

1 They can be familiar and reassuring, but empty.

2 Without them our prose can sound stiff and cumbersome.

3 Make sure they do real work: that they do justice to your ideas.

4 Ask yourself: does this convey what I want to say; does it take my argument in the direction I want to take?

Rely on nouns and verbs to carry your meaning

One indication of whether you've chosen the right word will be whether you're using adjectives to shore up your nouns, and adverbs your verbs.

Verbs

Wherever you can, try to build sentences around verbs that are specific and active. Weak verbs have to be shored up by adverbs and adverbial phrases that can water down the image. But beware of your choice: don't overstate the case by choosing a verb that is too strong. In the following sentences, by replacing the weak verb and its adverb with a stronger verb, the sentence is made sharper and its meaning clearer.

> Yet we still might be right in *thinking suspiciously* that behind all this information lies a covert message.

> Yet we still might be right in *suspecting* that behind all this information lies a covert message.

> Our desire for status and our respect for authority has given advertisers an effective way of *deceptively taking advantage* of our feelings to promote all manner of products.

> Our desire for status and our respect for authority has given advertisers an effective way of *exploiting* our feelings to promote all manner of products.

Nouns

In the same way, make sure your nouns are specific and definite, not general. They must produce a clear image. Like adverbs, if you have to use adjectives to shore up your noun, modifying or qualifying it, you've probably chosen the wrong one. The danger is your meaning will lose impact, or will be difficult to see, beneath the camouflage of adjectives and adjectival phrases. In the following sentences, by replacing the noun and its adjective with a single noun that is more specific, a clearer image is produced, one which carries much more meaning.

> By appealing to their *strong tastes* advertisers successfully by-pass the consumer's capacity to make rational choices.

> By appealing to their *passions* advertisers successfully by-pass the consumer's capacity to make rational choices.

It's not just tastes you're discussing, but passions, a particular type of taste.

They may give us information on the latest technology, but advertisers are also covertly suggesting that we can't afford not to keep up with the *latest developments*.

They may give us information on the latest technology, but advertisers are also covertly suggesting that we can't afford not to keep up with *progress*.

It's not just the latest developments, but the whole idea of progress and whether this is necessarily a good thing.

Replace prepositional phrases with prepositions

Like adverbs and adjectives, too many prepositional phrases water down your prose and obscure your meaning. Many of these we use in our normal speech simply because they give us more thinking time. But if you use them in your writing they will clutter up your prose and make it difficult for your reader to understand your meaning. Therefore, wherever possible replace prepositional phrases with simple prepositions.

> replace 'with regard to' with 'about'
> 'for the simple reason' with 'because'
> 'on the part of' with 'by'

This is not to say that such phrases are always inappropriate, but you should pose yourself the question, 'Can I replace these with a simpler preposition without any loss of meaning?' If you can, do it!

Is my subject just too complex for simple words and sentences?

Above all, resist the argument that says technical academic subjects are just too complex for simple words and sentences, so there's no point in trying. As we've said often enough, there is no subject that cannot be expressed simply, elegantly and clearly. Writing is a form of thinking, so if we can think clearly we will write clearly. In the best academic writing you will find:

1 Passages close to the spoken word with our normal clichés and rhythms of speech;
2 Words chosen to express precise meaning – vivid nouns, working adjectives and strong verbs;
3 No flab – authors saying what they want to say in as many words as they need and no more.

● Economy

This brings us to the second element of style, economy. Once you've thought your ideas through, your major concern thereafter should be to express them clearly, concisely, with an economical use of words. Each component of a sentence should have a reason for being there: it should have a clearly defined function. There should be no wasted effort: no unnecessary word or phrase that obscures the meaning of the sentence. Otherwise the clarity of your thought will be lost, leaving the reader wondering what it all means.

> There should be no unnecessary word or phrase to obscure your meaning.

The philosopher A. N. Whitehead described style as the ultimate morality of the mind. In other words, the mind should adjudicate rigorously on our use of words and our choice of phrases to ensure that:

1 each phrase has a well-defined function;
2 sentence structures are direct;
3 words are chosen for their absolute economy of expression.

Indeed, knowing what to leave out is as important as knowing what to include. Whitehead's ultimate morality of the mind is the art of knowing what not to do.

Therefore, if clauses and phrases can be summed up in a word, replace them. If they add nothing to the meaning of the sentence, delete them: words like 'ongoing progress' (progress), 'successfully avoided' (avoided), 'this moment in time' (this moment) and 'I will be fine going forward' ('will be' is the future tense so there is no need for 'going forward'). Start a list in your notebook and get into the habit of de-cluttering your work of all those wordy phrases:

Ahead of schedule – early
Arrived at an agreement – agreed
As a consequence of – because of
At the present time – now
Give an indication of – show/indicate
In close proximity to – near
Contributory factor – factor

Exactly identical – identical
Necessary prerequisite – prerequisite
Smooth to the touch – smooth
General consensus – consensus
Costs a total of – costs

You'll be surprised by the effect. It's worth having a sign near your desk reminding you constantly that the readability of your work increases in proportion to the unnecessary words you eliminate.

> The readability of your work increases in proportion to the unnecessary words you eliminate.

Equally important, the really significant words will no longer be smothered. Your points and arguments will no longer be obscured by unnecessary words and phrases. They'll stand out more, and they'll have impact to make the reader think and wonder. So, get into the habit of asking yourself, 'Is this word or phrase necessary and does it convey my meaning exactly?'

Summary

1 Avoid cluttering up sentences with unnecessary words that obscure your meaning.

2 When you use long sentences make their structure clear through logical indicators and punctuation.

3 Search for the right words; don't settle for convenient jargon.

4 Rely on nouns and verbs to carry your meaning and de-clutter your sentences of prepositional phrases.

5 Where phrases and clauses can be summed up in a word, replace them.

● What next?

As we've seen, most of our writing problems are, in fact, thinking problems. If we are clear about our ideas, the logical connections between them and about how we plan to develop our arguments, choosing our words, constructing sentences and writing fluently should come more easily. And even if we do make mistakes or our ideas develop in unexpected directions as we write, we still have the revision stage to give our ideas and arguments clearer form. First, though, in Part 9 we will learn how to cite our sources and acknowledge all the material we have borrowed.

Part Nine

Plagiarism, referencing and bibliographies

37 Plagiarism

In this chapter you will learn . . .

1 what exactly plagiarism is and why we should avoid it;
2 the reasons it occurs, often accidentally;
3 a simple 6-point code you can use to identify what you should cite;
4 the practical measures you can take to avoid accidental plagiarism.

Now that you have researched and written your dissertation you will be aware of just how much you have depended on the work of others. Much of the research we undertake involves us borrowing material in one form or another. Sir Isaac Newton famously acknowledged: 'If I have seen further it is by standing on the shoulders of giants' (in a letter to Robert Hooke, 5 February 1676). In one way or another we all have to stand on the shoulders of giants.

Consequently, we have an ethical obligation to acknowledge all those who have helped us by giving us material in the form of ideas, quotations, figures and anecdotes. Failure to cite their work will mean we have been academically dishonest: we have plagiarised. But why is it so wrong and what exactly is it?

● Why is it wrong to plagiarise?

There are two main reasons. To borrow somebody's work without acknowledging it might not be intellectual 'theft', after all it hasn't actually been taken away from them so that they can no longer use it themselves, but it is intellectual 'fraud' in that it involves trying to gain unfair advantage by passing off as your own the ideas or words of someone else. And whatever the offence, having invested so much thought and care in their work, those from whom we borrow deserve to be acknowledged, particularly when they have helped us by doing work that we might otherwise have had to do ourselves.

In contrast, the second reason is, quite simply, that it is just not in our interests. By passing off someone else's work as our own, not only could we fail on the grounds of having cheated, but there is little educational value in it. Copying work and presenting it as our own avoids the task of processing these ideas and making them our own by testing them against, and integrating them within, our own thought structures. If we fail to do this, there is little point in education at all.

> • Plagiarism ignores our ethical obligations.
> • There's no educational value in it.

What is plagiarism exactly?

There can't be many students at universities who don't know what it means, but still there are a number of things we do which we simply don't always recognise as plagiarism.

Few of us are in any doubt that our failure to cite the following constitutes plagiarism:

1 Direct quotations from someone's work.
2 A summary or paraphrase that is close to the original.
3 Statistics and other specific information and data.
4 Someone's unique ideas that have influenced our thinking.

But most examples occur in the grey areas and many are accidental. Students make mistakes because they fail to organise their work well enough, so that when they come to do their research they take notes in a rushed and careless manner, mixing passages they borrow with their own ideas. They fail to put these ideas into their own words, so that the paraphrases and summaries that find their way into their work are not sufficiently different from the original.

So, where should you draw the line?

With specific information or data, in the form of facts, statistics, tables and diagrams, it's easier to decide. You will have found them in a specific publication, which you will need to cite, so your reader will know who gathered the information and where to find it.

Distinctive contribution
The same applies to any information, or set of ideas, that have been organised in a distinctive way. The information may be known to you, but you

have never seen it presented in this form or argued in this way. And in this lies the crucial principle:

> Whenever the author has given something distinctive to the information or its organisation, cite the source.

In citing the source you are acknowledging the author's distinctive contribution. The same principle applies equally to a phrase or passage that you use verbatim. It has its own distinctive form, which you must acknowledge. Even cite a single word, if this is distinctive to the author's argument.

Common knowledge

But with many ideas and words the situation isn't so clear cut; there's nothing distinctive about them or their organisation. So you assume, quite reasonably, that although you got the ideas from a source you've read, you can use them without acknowledgement. One justification for this is that all knowledge in the public domain, all 'common knowledge', need not be referenced.

Still, this seems to do little more than give the problem a different name. So, what is 'common knowledge'? This brings us back to our original distinction. Common knowledge is all those facts, ideas and opinions that are not distinctive of a particular author or that are a matter of interpretation. They may be familiar ideas or just easily found in a number of common reference works, like dictionaries, textbooks and encyclopaedias.

Common knowledge:	Familiar or easily found in common reference works

It wouldn't even be necessary to give a reference for a distinctive contribution made by someone in a particular discipline, if this is well-known within that discipline. In politics or sociology, for example, it wouldn't be necessary to give a reference for Marx's concept of 'alienation', or in philosophy for Kant's 'categorical imperative', but if you were to refer to an author's particular interpretation of either, this would need a reference.

Example: Paradigm

The word 'paradigm' means a dominant theory in an area of study, which sets the conceptual framework within which a science is taught and scientists conduct research. It was first used in this sense by T. S. Kuhn in his seminal work *The Structure of Scientific Revolutions* (1962). Today the term has spread throughout the social sciences and philosophy. But in none of these areas would you be expected to cite the reference to Kuhn, if you were to use the term; so common has it become within each of these disciplines.

Other types of common knowledge come in the form of common or familiar opinion. It may seem to you undeniable that the vast majority of your fellow citizens are in favour of staging the next Olympic Games or the World Cup in your country, but no survey may ever have been done or referendum held. Similarly, it might generally be held that the elderly should receive special treatment, like free bus passes and medical help. In appealing to such common knowledge you would have to judge how familiar it is. The rule is, 'if in doubt, cite'.

Common knowledge

1 Familiar ideas found in reference works.

2 Ideas well-known within a particular discipline.

3 Common or familiar opinion.

● The six-point code

To make it easier for you to decide exactly when you need to cite, use the six-point code on page 355. This is another of those notes worth sticking to the side of your computer screen or pinning to the notice-board above your desk. Wherever you keep it, make sure it's just a glance away.

● Minimising the chance of an oversight

Nevertheless, even with this simple code and every good intention, there is always the possibility that you just might accidentally overlook the need to

When to cite

1 **Distinctive ideas**   Whenever the ideas or opinions are distinctive to one particular source.

2 **Distinctive structure or organising strategy**   Even though you may have put it into your own words, if the author has adopted a particular method of approaching a problem, or there is a distinctive intellectual structure to what's written, for example to an argument or to the analysis of a concept, then you must cite the source.

3 **Information or data from a particular source**   If you've gathered information from a source in the form of facts, statistics, tables and diagrams, you will need to cite the source, so that your readers will know who gathered the information and where to find it.

4 **Verbatim phrase or passage**   Even a single word, if it is distinctive to your author's argument – use quotation marks and cite the source.

5 **If it's not common knowledge**   Whenever you mention some aspect of another person's work, unless the information or opinion is widely known.

6 **Whenever in doubt, cite it!**   It will do no harm, as long as you're not citing just to impress the examiner.

cite a source. To reduce the chances of this, as you note material from your sources take two simple, practical steps.

1   Mark out clearly in your notes the ideas you borrow
To distinguish from your own notes the material you borrow, put it in a different colour, if not on different sheets of paper, or even in different computer files.

2   Record the details of the source to remind you that you are borrowing from it
Record at the top of the page the title of the text, the author's name, the page numbers and the date of publication. This will not only save you the nightmarish stress that comes from trying to track down a single reference to a quotation, or an idea, that you took down hastily, but it will also serve to remind you that you are working with a source.

© Bryan Greetham (2009), *How to Write your Undergraduate Dissertation*, Palgrave Macmillan Ltd

● Other reasons for citing

However, avoiding plagiarism is just one reason for citing our sources. Readers also need to be able to follow up the references to check that we have used our sources appropriately: that we've done justice to the author's claim to intellectual property and that we have drawn reasonable conclusions from the material. For similar reasons the information is also useful to us. If we want to follow up on our work in future, we will need to know where we got the material.

But perhaps even more important with our own self-interest in mind, extensive, thorough and detailed referencing also indicates that we have read widely over a range of different types of sources. It always gives examiners the confidence to award high marks, although this is no reason to inflate your references just to impress them. They will quickly spot a reference that does no real work.

Reasons for citing
1 To avoid plagiarising.
2 So readers can check that we've used the references well.
3 So we can follow up on our work in the future.
4 To show the examiners that we have read widely.

Summary

1 Not only is plagiarism unethical, but it is of no educational value to us.

2 Whenever the author has given something distinctive to the information or its organisation, we must cite it.

3 If it is common knowledge, there is no need to cite.

4 To avoid accidental plagiarism, mark out clearly in your notes what you have borrowed and the details of the source.

● What next?

Now that we know *what* to cite we can begin to look at *how* we cite.

38 Referencing and bibliographies

In this chapter you will learn . . .

1 the three cardinal objectives of all referencing systems;
2 the three elements and how you can organise them;
3 how to use the footnote and Harvard systems;
4 the advantages of each one;
5 about the importance of compiling a comprehensive bibliography;
6 how to compile a bibliography using one of the two most commonly used formats.

Now that we've dealt with the most difficult judgements about what needs to be cited we're left with the simpler problems of how we cite each reference and list its details.

● Departmental guidelines

The first thing you must do is check with your department to see if they have certain expectations, a system they would like you to use. If they have a style guide, make sure you follow it in every detail: the order in which you should arrange the details of the entry and the way you are expected to punctuate each reference and use capital letters, italics and underlining.

If they don't have a style guide, ask your supervisor or check the dissertations of previous years to see how other students did it. The important thing is to meet three cardinal objectives: it must be clear, accurate and consistent, so your readers have clear and sufficient detail to locate the exact reference for themselves.

> Three objectives:
>
> - Clarity
> - Accuracy
> - Consistency

In any referencing system there are three elements that you must decide how you're going to organise:

1 the extract from the source, which might be a direct quotation, a para-phrase or a statement of your own that you've derived from it;
2 the marker you insert into your text to direct the reader to the details of the source;
3 the actual details.

● Extracts

Incorporating paraphrases into your text presents no particular problem, but direct quotations often do, largely because we fail to observe certain conventions and this results in confusion. So, check your department's guidelines and if they don't insist on any particular style you'll find it helpful to use the simple rules listed on page 360.

● Referencing systems

As for the other two elements we must consider – the marker in the text and the details of the source – these are governed by the conventions of the different systems you or your department prefer to use. In some disciplines, like law and medicine, in the UK, USA and other English-speaking countries there are standard accepted systems, but for most it's yours or your department's choice.

Footnote system

This is variously known as the 'Footnote' or 'Endnote' or 'Number' system. It's probably the most familiar as book publishers tend to use it more than any other. It's also commonly used in the humanities, some social sciences and in law. The marker it uses is a small elevated number, a superscript, for each reference cited in the text. This refers to the details of the source found either in a footnote at the bottom of the page, or in a list of references at the end of the chapter or dissertation.

In this system the first reference to a **book** would appear as:

> P. Rowe, *The Craft of the Sub-editor* (Basingstoke: Macmillan, 1997), p. 37.

The place of publication is followed by a colon, after which come the publisher, a comma and then the date of publication. Later references to the same book can be abbreviated by shortening the title, if this can be done

Rules for using quotations

1 Short extracts

If they're no more than, say, three to four lines (30 to 40 words), incorporate them within your text and enclose them in quotation marks.

2 Long extracts

Indent them from both sides, or just from the left. Usually these are single spaced. With the quotation blocked in this way and separated from the main text there is no need to use quotation marks. With some style guides it's customary to reduce the font size, say, from 12 to 11.

3 Shortened extracts

3.1 When you shorten an extract to include only that which is relevant, indicate where you have taken words out by inserting three dots.

3.2 Where you have to insert your own words to ensure the shortened extract reads grammatically, enclose your own words in square brackets.

3.3 If a word which was formerly inside a sentence now begins it, enclose the first letter of the word in square brackets.

3.4 The one obvious rule that governs all these changes to the original text is that you must take care not to alter the author's meaning.

without losing details that mark out its distinctiveness, and by omitting the author's initials and publication details:

Rowe, *The Craft*, pp. 102–3.

A reference to a **journal article** would appear as:

Brian T. Trainor, 'The State, Marriage and Divorce', *Journal of Social Work*, vol. 9, no. 2 (1992), p. 145.

The title of the article comes between quotation marks. The name of the journal is given in full and, like the book title, is italicised. Then come the volume number, issue number and date. A later reference to the same article could be abbreviated by omitting the author's initials, the subtitle of the paper, if it has one, and the publication details. The journal name can either be abbreviated or, indeed, omitted.

> Trainor, 'The State', *JSW*, pp. 138–9.

Where there are several authors, full details of all their names and initials must appear in the first reference, but not in subsequent references. Where there are two authors you can give just their last names, but, if there are several, give the first author's name followed by the abbreviating *et al.* meaning 'and others'.

To save you from having to repeat the details of a text you might be using a lot, you can use three well-known Latin abbreviations. They may seem rather arcane, but once you've used them you will soon see just how much time and effort they can save. Say your first reference was as follows:

> 1. P. Rowe, *The Craft of the Sub-editor* (Cambridge, 1997), p. 37.

A number of references later you may want to refer to this text again. In this case you would use, along with the author's last name, the Latin abbreviation *op. cit.*, meaning 'in the work cited' for this author, instead of repeating the detailed description of the text, which you've already given. Let's say it was the fifth reference on your list:

> Rowe, *op. cit.*, pp. 102–3.

If, in the next reference, you wanted to refer to the same text again, this time you would use another Latin reference, *ibid.*, meaning 'in the same place' as in the previous reference:

> 6. *Ibid.*, p. 84.

If, then, in the next reference, you wanted to refer again to the same page of the same text, after *ibid* you would use the Latin abbreviation *loc. cit.*, meaning 'in the passage just quoted' – not just the same work, but the same passage:

> 7. *Ibid.*, *loc. cit.*

If you were referring to the same passage previously quoted in a text that appeared some entries earlier, then again you would use *loc. cit.*, but this time in conjunction with the last name of the author.

> 8. Trainor, *loc cit.*

Abbreviations

op. cit.	'in the work cited' for this author
ibid.	'in the same place' as in the previous reference
loc. cit.	'in the passage just quoted'

The Harvard system – the Author–date system

This system inserts into the actual text, enclosed in brackets, the author's name, the year of publication and the page numbers of the reference. These refer to the end of the dissertation, where readers can find a comprehensive list, a bibliography, of all the sources cited and used, with the full details of the texts to which these abbreviations refer. The following examples illustrate the various ways these references can be made in the text.

On some occasions you may decide that the author's name will appear in the actual text itself with only the year of publication and the page numbers in brackets.

> Perhaps artists need to feel politically motivated against oppressive regimes in order to etch their identity clearly against a social and political reality they deplore. In the words of Theodore Roethke, 'In a dark time, the eye begins to see' (1966, p. 239).

> Perhaps artists need to feel politically motivated against oppressive regimes in order to etch their identity clearly against a social and political reality they deplore. After all, 'In a dark time, the eye begins to see' (Roethke, 1966, p. 239).

> As Roethke (1966) points out, perhaps artists need to feel politically motivated against oppressive regimes in order to etch their identity clearly against a social and political reality they deplore. After all, 'In a dark time, the eye begins to see' (p. 239).

Paraphrasing

When you paraphrase an author's words, only the author and the year need to be included. For example:

> Certain diets that reduce the levels of serotonin in the brain appear to produce higher levels of aggression. Historically, periods of famine, and carbohydrate and protein malnutrition, have been associated with significant increases in crime and violence (Valzelli, 1981).

> Valzelli (1981) argues that those diets responsible for reducing the levels of serotonin in the brain appear to produce higher levels of aggression. Historically, periods of famine, and carbohydrate and protein malnutrition, have been associated with significant increases in crime and violence.

Your material may come from more than one source by the same author.

In this case arrange your sources chronologically, separated by a comma.

> Homelessness was shown to have increased as a result of the change in legislation and with the tighter monetary policy that doubled interest rates over a period of two years (Williams, 1991, 1994).

If the author has published more than one work in a single year, then cite them using a lower-case letter after the year of publication.

> Williams (1994a, 1994b) has shown that higher interest rates, while doing little to arrest the decline in value of the currency, have seriously damaged companies engaged in exports and increased the levels of home repossessions.

A reference may have more than one author.

When it has two or three authors, give all the surnames, separated by commas with the last one separated by the word 'and'.

> Recent evidence has shown that cinema attendance in the 1950s declined less as a result of the impact of television, than through increasing affluence and mobility (Brown, Rowe and Woodward, 1996).

Computer analysis has shown that the hundred most used words in the English language are all of Anglo-Saxon origin, even the first words spoken when man set foot on the moon in 1969 (Lacey and Danziger, 1999).

If there are more than three, cite them all the first time – for example: (Brown, Kirby, Rowe and Woodward, 1991) – but, when you cite them again, use just the first name followed by *et al.* (and all the others) – for example: (Brown *et al.*, 1991).

An author may cite another author.

In this case, if you want to use the comments of the cited author, then you acknowledge both authors, but only the author of the text in which you found the comments is listed in the reference list.

In describing recent studies that tended to show that men become dangerous when their personal aggressiveness is unnaturally contained, Masters (1997, p. 37) cites a comment by Anthony Storr, who says, 'Aggression is liable to turn into dangerous violence when it is repressed or disowned.'

Anthony Storr (cited in Masters, 1997, p. 37) argues that, 'The man who is able to assert himself in a socially acceptable fashion is seldom vicious; it is the weak who are most likely to stab one in the back.'

A number of authors may present the same idea.

In this case arrange the authors in alphabetical order, separated by semi-colons.

If a child does not receive love from its parents in the early years it will neither integrate their standards within its behaviour, nor develop any sense of moral conscience (Berkowitz, 1962; Farrington, 1978; Rutter, 1981; Storr, 1972).

Choosing a system

Footnotes
The main advantage of the footnote system is that it doesn't disrupt the text as much as the Harvard system. Entering the details of the reference in the

actual text itself clutters up the text, breaking the flow of ideas as you read, particularly when you have two or three citations at any point. This probably explains why almost all book publishers choose to use the footnote system. What's more, with the Harvard system, to follow up citations you have to search continually at the back of the dissertation for the full details.

The footnote system can also seem more flexible in that it allows us to add comments in a footnote, which we may not want to include in the text. These may be digressions from the main text which we think would be useful for readers, or they may be a list of references for readers to pursue if they are interested in a particular point or argument that may not be essential to the main focus of the dissertation. Still, the Harvard system doesn't preclude entirely the possibility of using some footnotes.

Footnotes – advantages

1 Avoids clutter in the text.

2 Flexibility of adding comments in a footnote.

Harvard system

The most obvious advantage of the Harvard system is that you don't have to compile, in addition to the bibliography, a separate list of references matching the sequence of citations in the text. However, as we'll see below, this is no longer a problem with modern automatic referencing programs.

The Harvard system means that we also don't have to worry about matching up footnote numbers in the text with the list, which could involve hours of re-writing the list each time we make changes to the text. It's quite simple to insert a new reference: just cite the source in the text and add it to the bibliography. But now, with modern automatic referencing programs, like *Procite*, *Endnote* and *Citation*, which automatically create and position footnotes or endnotes as well as compiling and changing the list as you make changes to the text, this is no longer a problem for the footnote system.

Harvard system – advantages

1 No separate list of references.

2 Don't have to match up numbers in the text with the list.

● Bibliographies

A reference list is all those works you've quoted or referred to in the dissertation, whereas a bibliography is a list of everything you've consulted, including sources you haven't quoted or referred to. Although this is essential with the Harvard system, it's not with the footnote system. Even so, it's useful to include one: it makes it easier to check what you've read without having to work through your footnotes. The aim of the bibliography is to tell your readers in the clearest possible way what you've used, so don't pad it out with items to impress them.

Primary and secondary material

If it's appropriate, divide the bibliography into primary and secondary material. Primary material includes government reports and statistics, research material, historic documents and original texts, while secondary material includes books, articles and academic papers, which usually discuss or throw light on the primary material. Arrange it in alphabetical order by authors' last names and where there is no author, as with some primary sources, use the first letter of the source's title.

Listing the sources – the formats

If you've been systematic from the start, the bibliography is quite easy to compile, particularly if you've adopted the habit of recording the details of your sources at the top of the page before you take notes, or, better still, using a computer database or a card-index with a separate card for each source, listing its details.

There are different conventions governing the way you list the texts, but as long as you are consistent and follow a regular sequence for citation, there should be no problem. In both of the following systems, where there is more than one entry by the same author arrange them chronologically under the author's name. Where a book or article has been written by two or more authors enter it into the alphabetical list according to the last name of the first author, but make sure you give full details of all the others.

1   Modern bibliographical format

This is used with the Harvard referencing system. It's slightly clearer than the alternative, because it's easier to see the alphabetical progression of the sources with the author's last name coming first, so it's probably wise to use it with the footnote system too.

For books and other free-standing publications:

Author's last name, first name and/or initials, year of publication (in brackets), full title of the work (italicised), place of publication and publisher (in brackets).

For articles:

Author's last name, first name and/or initials, year of publication (in brackets), full title of the article (in quotation marks), title of the journal (italicised), volume number (if published in volumes), issue number and page numbers.

> Author, N. (year of publication) *Title of Book* (place of publication: publisher).
> Author, N. (year of publication) 'Title of Article', *Title of Journal*, vol. 2, no. 1, pp. ••–••.

Examples

1. Alexander, Leo. (1949) 'Medical Science under Dictatorship', *New England Journal of Medicine*, vol. 241, pp. 39–47.
2. Ford, John C. (1944) 'The Morality of Obliteration Bombing', *Theological Studies*; reprinted in Wasserstrom, Richard A. (ed.), (1970) *War and Morality* (Oxford: Oxford University Press), pp. 1–18.
3. Robinson, R. E. and Gallagher, J. (1962) *Africa and the Victorians: The Official Mind of British Imperialism* (London: Macmillan).
4. Singer, Peter. (1979) *Practical Ethics* (Cambridge: Cambridge University Press).

2   Footnote system

For books and other free-standing publications:

Author's first name and/or initials, author's last name, full title of the work (italicised), place of publication, name of the publisher, and date (in brackets).

For articles:

Author's first name and/or initials, author's last name, full title of the article (in quotation marks), title of the journal (italicised), volume number (if published in volumes), issue number, year of publication (in brackets), and page numbers.

N. Author, *Title of Book* (place of publication: publisher, and date).
N. Author, 'Title of Article', *Title of Periodical*, vol. 2, no. 1 (date), pp. ●●–●●.

Examples

1. Leo Alexander, 'Medical Science under Dictatorship', *New England Journal of Medicine*, vol. 241 (1949), pp. 39–47.
2. John C. Ford, 'The Morality of Obliteration Bombing', *Theological Studies* (1944); reprinted in Richard A. Wasserstrom (ed.), *War and Morality* (Oxford: Oxford University Press, 1970), pp. 1–18.
3. R. E. Robinson and J. Gallagher, *Africa and the Victorians: The Official Mind of British Imperialism* (London: Macmillan, 1962).
4. Peter Singer, *Practical Ethics* (Cambridge: Cambridge University Press, 1979).

Summary

1 Follow your department's guidelines in every detail. If there are none, check dissertations from previous years.

2 Whichever system you choose, make sure you meet the three cardinal objectives: clarity, accuracy and consistency.

3 Although a bibliography is not essential for the footnote system, it is useful to have one anyway.

4 If it's appropriate, divide it into primary and secondary sources.

● What next?

Referencing and citing your sources may seem the least important of all the jobs you have to do, but not only is it important to acknowledge the help your authors have given you, but your care and thoroughness will help to confirm in the examiner's mind that this is a true reflection of all your work. The same impression will be created by a clear and comprehensive bibliography.

Now we turn to revision. Like compiling reference lists and bibliographies, the importance of this tends to be underrated and yet no other stage in producing your dissertation can have such a dramatic impact on the quality of your work.

Part Ten

Editing

39 Revision 1: The structure

In this chapter you will learn . . .

1 about the importance of revising in bringing to the surface the quality of your work and the extent of your achievements;
2 how to revise in a way that improves your work with each revision and doesn't endanger your best ideas;
3 how to revise with a purpose: first for structure and then for content;
4 how to revise the structure of the dissertation between each chapter and then within each one;
5 the importance of tying paragraphs in with introductions and conclusions;
6 how to ensure you've created and signalled a logical sequence of your ideas between and within paragraphs.

You may think that now the first draft is done the really important work is over. All that's left is to check the word count, spelling and grammar. But it's probably true that more marks are gained by each successive round of revision than by any other stage in the process. Writing the dissertation is only the beginning; revising it is when the quality really begins to shine through. So don't waste your research by settling for the first thing you can write. Give yourself plenty of time to redraft again and again to produce the sort of quality that reflects your abilities and your achievements.

> With each draft, the quality really begins to shine through.

Revision will determine whether you win or lose the reader. The first draft is for you: you are writing as you think, clarifying and developing your ideas. The second and subsequent drafts are for your reader: you work to make sure your ideas come through so clearly that someone who knows nothing about your research can understand it and feel the impact of your ideas as you do.

Academics place a lot of emphasis on carefully designing their research methods, but very little on researching the likely impact of their writing on the reader. It is very difficult to see it from someone else's perspective, so now is the time to think just of this.

- The first draft is for you.
- The second and subsequent drafts are for your reader.

● The writer and the editor

To do this effectively we must shift our focus from the writer to the editor: from the creative activity of converting our ideas into language to a more self-conscious focus on the way we've used words, phrases and structures. The editor inside us should be asking, how does it sound, is it fluent, does it move logically from one stage in the argument to another, are there sections that need more evidence, or more development?

The writer:	Creative activity converting ideas into language.
The editor:	Self-conscious focus on the way we use words, phrases and structures.

With this in mind, allow yourself a cooling off period, so your editor can surface. It's not that you're trying to create objectivity between yourself and what you've written as we so often think. This would endanger those rich insights you saw in your ideas when you first began to generate and develop them. It's these that first engaged your interest, and they're likely to engage your readers' too. So, if you were to revise in an objective, dispassionate frame of mind, you might kill the very thing that's likely to grab your readers and make them think. Nevertheless, approach your work as you believe your readers will and allow yourself to feel the impact of your ideas as you expect them to.

● Allocate plenty of time

As you revise, remind yourself that no-one should have to read one of your sentences twice to find out what it means. Such clear and simple writing comes through a continuous process of redrafting your work, until it is the best that you can get it. The effortless feel of talk in print that flows across the page in light, elegant prose only comes from a process that is continuous and cumulative as you edge closer with each draft to the clearest expression of your ideas. So avoid impromptu, unplanned revision.

> No-one should have to read one of your sentences twice to find out what it means.

● **Revise with a purpose**

This all sounds like a lot of work, but like most things it's not if you organise it well. The most difficult problem is that there seem so many things we ought to be looking out for. So, to simplify it, revise with a clear purpose. As you take each chapter revise it a number of times, each on a different level, looking for different things. The easiest way to organise this is to revise the structure first and then the content. And save each draft in a different file, that way if you lose your latest draft you won't have to start all over again.

● **Structure**

Structure means the thinking

When we talk about the structure of a piece of writing we're talking about the thinking that went into it: whether it is organised logically, whether the connections between our ideas are consistently developed and, of course, whether we have signposted these connections so our readers can see them clearly.

But, as we saw in previous chapters, beyond critical thinking, few of us are ever taught thinking as a set of distinct skills. What's more, we are rarely warned about the problems that arise from the tension between writing and thinking. So we must concentrate on this first and divide it into two parts:

1 the thinking in the dissertation as a whole, between each chapter;
2 and then within each individual chapter.

Between chapters

You might ask, why are we so concerned about structure? Well, structure is the product of pure thought – it is the scaffolding of our thinking, the way we connect and develop our ideas. So we must be concerned about two things: that we have developed our ideas logically and that we have communicated clearly the connections between them. This is always a problem with large projects done in different stages at different times separated by long periods. Discontinuities and contradictions are almost bound to occur.

> • Have we developed our ideas logically?
> • Have we communicated the connections between them clearly?

Consequently, we must pay particular attention to the way we link chapters and cross-reference them. Not only must these make logical sense, but we must signpost them clearly so our readers know which way we are taking them.

Research questions

The first thing is to check that the main research questions you mapped out in the introduction of your dissertation, or in the chapter on the research problem, are being picked up in the introduction of each chapter and then pursued consistently throughout, without irrelevant digression. Make sure you've let your readers know what is to come and how it relates to these research questions. Then, if you find passages that are not strictly relevant, remove them. What remains will stand out more clearly, particularly the structure.

> Make sure . . .
> . . . you show that you have fulfilled the promises you made in the introduction of your dissertation.

As you fulfil these promises in each successive chapter, let your readers know in the conclusion of the chapter that you have done so and then use the final sentences of the chapter to form a bridge to the next one. The same goes for the conclusion of the dissertation: show your readers that you have answered all the research questions that you promised to answer in the introduction.

> Introduction . . .
> • Map out the main research questions.
> • Let readers know what is to come.
>
> Chapters
> • Pick up the research questions in the introduction.
> • Pursue research questions without digression.
> • Let your readers know in the conclusion that you have fulfilled your promises.
> • Form a bridge to the next chapter.
>
> Conclusion . . .
> • Show your readers that you have answered all the research questions that you promised to answer.

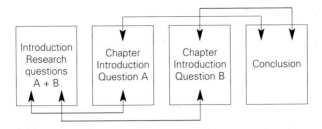

Within each chapter – the sections

Many students have a real struggle with structure, probably because they haven't set enough time aside to plan in detail each chapter, rehearsing their arguments before they write. So they have no idea, before and after, what the structure of a chapter might be. It comes across as a loose mix of ideas strung together in a way that is difficult to understand. If this is the case, at some point you will have to go through the dissertation, perhaps highlighting with a coloured pen the headings, subheadings and other structural features, so you can put them down on a sheet of paper and ask yourself whether these make sense.

> Highlight the structure and set it out to see if it makes sense.

Ask yourself whether what you've got in front of you is a set of consistent arguments, whether the connections are all there, that none are missing, that there are no irrelevant digressions. Make sure that all the arguments you develop are relevant to the introduction: that they pick up the issues you have mapped out there for your readers to follow. Then, after you've taken out those sections that are irrelevant, ask yourself whether each connection is clearly signposted, so the readers know what you're doing at each point and are in no danger of getting lost. In the conclusion, check that you've delivered on all your promises: that you have overlooked none of the issues you raised.

Ask yourself . . .
- Is it a set of consistent arguments?
- Are the connections all there?
- Are there irrelevant digressions?
- Do I pick up all the issues raised in the introduction?
- Are the connections clearly signposted?
- In the conclusion can I say that I have delivered on all my promises?

Literature review

As you work through the wealth of literature on your subject it's easy to lose sight of the central issues that form the focus of your research.

> So make sure that . . .
> 1 The articles and books you've included are all relevant to the issues your project is concerned about.
> 2 You highlight and abstract the structure to see whether the ideas are relevant and consistently developed.
> 3 It has a coherent structure and is not just a loose list of books and articles.

Research methods

A similar question dominates our revision of the research methods chapter.

> So, make sure that . . .
> 1 Your justification of the research methods you've chosen is clearly linked with the research questions you laid out in the introduction or in the research problem chapter.
> 2 This connection is perfectly clear.
> 3 Your readers are in no doubt why you've chosen these particular methods to answer the questions you're asking.

Conclusion/Discussion

In the conclusion of a theoretical, textual dissertation or the discussion chapter of an empirical dissertation, the conclusions we come to should relate directly to our findings. They should arise from the data and answer the questions and issues raised at the beginning. Like all good conclusions it must take us back to where we started and fulfil all our promises.

> So make sure that . . .
> 1 Your readers are able to see whether your hypothesis has been proved or disproved, or your research questions answered fully or not.
> 2 You've evaluated and explained in the conclusion the significance of your findings. They don't speak for themselves: they need to be analysed, evaluated and their importance revealed.

Within each chapter – paragraphs

Now we can move to the level of paragraphs, checking that our readers can see clearly the connections between them and the structure of the argument within each one.

Tying them in

To signpost your thinking, make clear the connection each paragraph has with the map of the chapter that you outlined in the introduction. Not every paragraph needs to be tied into the introduction in this way. Most of your chapters will be broken up into sections and the first paragraph of each section will do this. So then you need to make sure that each subsequent paragraph which makes up this section is tied into this first paragraph. If you find paragraphs are floating without any clear rationale, make sure the topic sentence (the first one that introduces the topic of the paragraph) ties it in to remind the reader of the structure of the chapter or section.

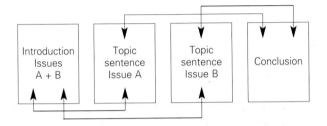

A logical sequence

Then ask yourself whether your paragraphs follow each other logically and fluently. If there seem to be no obvious connections or just abrupt changes of course, check to see if the paragraphs are in the right place. If they are, look at the transitions to see if there are better ones that would indicate more clearly the direction you want to develop the argument (see Chapter 34).

Structure within each paragraph

Within each paragraph, ask yourself whether the logical structure of the argument is consistent and clear from sentence to sentence. Some sentences you will be able to delete. In what remains, the argument will now be much clearer. With others you will just need to choose another logical indicator to make the development of your argument clearer, or move it to a more prominent position, usually to the beginning.

> Ask yourself . . .
> - Have I picked up the map of the chapter or section?
> - Do the paragraphs follow each other logically and fluently?
> - Is the logical structure of the argument in each paragraph consistent and clear?
> - Can I delete sentences to make it clearer?
> - Do I need new logical indicators or do I just need to move them?

Summary

1   Give yourself sufficient time to revise your dissertation to make sure your abilities and your achievements shine through clearly.

2   In each separate revision, revise with a clear purpose in mind.

3   Make sure the connections between each chapter and within them are consistent and clear to the reader.

4   We must ensure we've tied our paragraphs in with our introductions and conclusions to ensure we've created and signalled the logical sequence of our ideas.

● **What next?**

In this chapter our concern has been to ensure that the structure of our dissertation is consistent and clearly signposted for the reader. We can now turn to the content of each chapter and the tension between our thinking and writing.

40 Revision 2: The content

In this chapter you will learn . . .

1 how to revise our sentences and words to ensure we express our ideas clearly and develop our arguments consistently;
2 how to improve the flow and rhythm of our writing;
3 the different ways of reducing our word count;
4 how to ensure our final presentation displays our work to the best effect.

In revising the content, our concern shifts to the problems that can develop out of the tension between our thinking and writing. Do our words and sentences convey our ideas succinctly and clearly? Do they develop our arguments in the direction we want them to go or have we been pushed in a direction simply because we've chosen the wrong phrase?

● Sentences

Spelling and grammar

First check your spelling and grammar. Getting your spelling right is important: examiners may infer that if you haven't paid enough attention to this sort of detail, you are likely to have been careless elsewhere. For most writers proofreading your work can be difficult. The closer you are to it the more details escape your attention. So get a patient friend to do it for you, perhaps return the compliment by proofing his or her dissertation.

As for grammar, be sure that if you break the rules it's deliberate – that you're doing it for reasons of style, to produce a certain effect – and it's not the result of a lack of knowledge. Whether you keep to the rules or decide to break them, the key is clarity: it must be the best way of making your meaning clear.

Long sentences

The one problem you're bound to face is long sentences. If you leave them as they are you run the risk of confusing, even losing, your readers, who will then be unable to give you the marks you deserve. So cut up every long, complex sentence that can be reduced to two or more shorter ones.

Ask yourself . . .
- Is my spelling right?
- Have I broken the rules of grammar?
- If I've done it deliberately, is this the best way of making my meaning clear?
- Have I cut up all long sentences into shorter ones?
- Have I removed all unnecessary sentences?

● Words

Much the same advice goes for long words, although they have a different effect on your writing. They may not confuse your readers quite as much; nevertheless they can leave them wondering whether you really meant to say what you did, and they will often make your writing sound unnecessarily pompous. It makes sense, then, wherever possible to replace long obscure words with short and simple ones.

Strong nouns and verbs

Rather than drown your ideas in a sea of adjectives and adverbs that shore up weak nouns and verbs, check that you have used strong nouns and verbs with the minimum of modifiers. And constantly remind yourself that the fewer verbs you have to modify with adverbs, and nouns with adjectives, the better your writing will be. In the following sentence by substituting stronger, more specific nouns and verbs you can see how the sentence gains in clarity and directness.

> Theatre promoters are likely to comb through unfavourable reviews *looking carefully* for any isolated expression of a *favourable comment* that can be used to promote their plays.

> Theatre promoters are likely to comb through unfavourable reviews in *search* of any isolated expression of *approval* that can be used to promote their plays.

Ask yourself . . .
- Have I removed all unnecessary words?
- Have I replaced all long, obscure words with short and simple ones?
- Have I removed all unnecessary modifiers in favour of good strong nouns and verbs?

The active voice

Similarly, as we saw in Chapter 35, by using the active voice you will ensure that your ideas come through more clearly by making them more concise and direct. So wherever possible make 'the doer' the subject of the sentence. Still, there are some circumstances in which 'what is done', or 'the receiver of the action', is more important than 'the doer'. In the following example, what was actually done is more important than by whom. In these circumstances re-forming the sentence in the passive form makes the point more effectively.

> Professor Jenkins and Doctor Taylor of University College, London, last month achieved the most significant breakthrough yet in the treatment of colon cancer.

> The most significant breakthrough yet in the treatment of colon cancer was achieved last month by Professor Jenkins and Doctor Taylor of University College, London.

Ask yourself . . .
- Have I written in the active voice?
- Have I only used the passive voice when what is done or the receiver of the action is more important than the doer?

● Revising by ear

Finally, read your work through to see how it sounds. You're interested in its flow and rhythm. Hopefully, it should read like talk in print, with light effort-less prose that glides across the page with a pace and rhythm that holds the reader's attention.

Flow and rhythm

Unfortunately, most of us get so close to what we write and the thought patterns our sentences represent, that we find it difficult to read as another person would, so ask a friend to listen while you read it out loud or, better still, ask her to read it to you. If it doesn't come across fluently to someone who has never seen or heard it before, it will need to be changed.

It will certainly identify clumsy sentences or where you might have dealt with your ideas in an illogical order. You are also free to note where in your work it was difficult to understand the meaning of what was written. Failing that, record it and play it back to yourself as if you were listening to it for the first time.

Changing the pace

After this, you may want to change the pace of your work at certain times to make your points more effectively. You may want to speed up or slow down in some sections by varying the length of sentences. Longer sentences are very comforting and reassuring. They may be best suited to the development of the core elements of your arguments. But when you want to be abrupt, to grab your reader's attention with a vivid piece of detail, or with an insight you feel is a key point to get across, use a short sentence – don't let it get drowned in the words that surround it.

Ask yourself . . .
- Does it read well for someone reading it for the first time?
- Is the pace and rhythm right for the arguments I want to make?

● Word count

If, after this, you are above the word limit, look at the following things:

- **Repetition** – are their sections that say the same things but in different ways? Can you safely cross-reference them, rather than describe the same points again?
- **Less relevant sections** – are there sections that may be interesting, but won't earn you very high marks and could be left out? Ask yourself how relevant they are and how many marks they are likely to earn.
- **Unnecessary descriptions** – have you described material that you have also presented in a table? If so, think about scrapping the description and relying just on the inferences you draw from the table. In other places you might find that you have described data, so think about putting it into a table instead and using it from there.
- **Long quotations from literature** – they will earn you very few marks, so think about paring them down. Most of them can be edited while still doing the job you want them to do.

● Final presentation

First impressions count, however unfair this may seem. So, make sure your dissertation looks like the work of a fastidious person. Examiners should be able to scan it and see immediately how you have organised it.

Cover page

Keep your cover page simple, well arranged and easy to read. There are normally regulations about how it should be laid out, so check the official requirements. Usually it includes: the title, your name, the details of the module or course number, the degree that it's for and your university.

Title

Before you include the title it's worth reviewing it in the light of what you've done, to see whether it still accurately reflects your work. In Chapter 11 we pinned down the working title, now you might find there has been a change of perspective or a shift in emphasis. You may also find that you can express it more succinctly and directly. Check the following things:

1   **Key concepts and issues** – make sure they are included in the title.

In the dissertation on the study skills of undergraduates at university it may be important to include the concept of 'learning behaviour' or 'learning problems'. In the dissertation on the novels of George Eliot you would have to ensure that 'novelistic sympathy and distance' appeared.

2   **The context** – make sure you have carefully described the context of the research, to set clear limits on your study.

This may be a particular period in history, a location ('The effects of the government's smoking ban on pubs and restaurants in *Bolton*'), an author or group of authors, or a certain population of subjects ('undergraduates at university').

3   **Methodology** – although not necessary, you may find it helpful to include a short phrase indicating the methodology you've used.

It might be an 'analysis' of a writer's poetry, or a 'social geography' of football violence, or a 'case study' of the effects of the government's ban on smoking in public places.

4   **Perspective** – in some cases it might even be helpful to let the examiners know that yours is a study from a particular social, individual or philosophical perspective.

You might approach the study of the care of special needs children from 'the mother's perspective', or you might examine the influence of women's magazines from a 'feminist perspective'.

As we said in Chapter 11, it is often useful to state the main concepts or the main subject first and then add a subsidiary:

'Autonomy and dependency: the learning problems of undergraduates at university'

'The Hudson's Bay Company Archives: Gender and the Fur Trade' (University of Swansea)

'Themes and images in the female gothic novel: Ann Radcliffe, Jane Austen and Charlotte Brontë' (University of Sussex)

The abstract

Although this is often not required, it is well worth the effort. It will impress the examiners. Usually it comes after the acknowledgements (if any) and before the table of contents. About 200–300 words long, its main aim is to give a brief summary of your work. But it must make complete sense independently of the dissertation: there should be no reference to the text of the dissertation or to tables or figures. As a guide, use the following breakdown:

1 Principal objectives of the study
2 The context – a short description of the background to the issues
3 The particular research questions you examined
4 The main methods you used
5 Your key findings and conclusions
6 A brief note on the significance of your work

Keep your use of jargon and abbreviations to a minimum. If you want examples to guide you, have a look at a journal of abstracts, conference or journal papers, or a thesis.

Table of contents

Of course, this is much simpler to do, but make sure you list not only chapter titles, but subheadings, even sub-subheadings, along with their page numbers. You could also list in order of appearance your figures, charts and illustrations with their titles and page numbers. This could appear on the same page or separately on the following pages. If you've used appendices, you will have to list these too.

Acknowledgements

Although this, too, is not obligatory, it is a good thing to thank those who have been directly involved in your work or in supporting you: tutors, technicians and other students, the subjects of your research who volunteered their time and, perhaps, your long-suffering partner, who supplied you with endless cups of coffee as you toiled late into the night.

Summary

1   To avoid confusing and losing the reader we must split up long sentences and substitute short and simple words for long and obscure ones.

2   By reading our work aloud we can check the pace and rhythm of our writing to make sure it can be easily understood.

3   The final presentation should display our work to the best possible effect.

4   Examiners should be able to scan it and see immediately how we have organised it.

● To conclude

If you've worked your way through each of these levels of revision you should now have a text that carries your ideas clearly and does justice to your thinking. By now you will have realised that most of the quality that can be found in your writing has come from your revision. If you've met all the requirements of doing your dissertation and conscientiously worked at each stage of your research, it is more difficult to fail than pass. But if, in addition, you've worked carefully through each stage of revision, you will have a piece of work that has every chance of being awarded very high marks.

Conclusion

We began this book by explaining the importance of setting dissertations as a mode of assessment: that they give you the opportunity to do some genuine thinking and not just recycle the received opinions of those you regard as authorities. In the process they allow examiners to see not just *what* you think, but, more importantly, *how* you think.

So, although I'm sure it has involved a lot of hard work, I hope it has been a journey of discovery for you too. The most enduring thing I hope you have discovered, something that will shape your life more than any other aspect of your education, is that you will have learnt about yourself as a thinker. You have learnt about how creative you can be; how best to organise yourself to generate, capture and develop your own ideas; how to analyse concepts and problems so you see things more clearly; how to synthesise and manipulate ideas to find solutions to problems; and, of course, how well you can write, that you have a voice of your own, and how to organise your writing to let it come through.

Writing places us at the heart of our ideas. It offers us a way of crawling out from beneath the suffocating weight of other people's ideas to think for ourselves. Rather than just express what we think our teachers think we ought to think, we can think at a deeper level and express our own ideas. So, if you have followed the advice in this book, you will know that you can have original thoughts and you need not settle just for recycling the ideas of others.

Bibliography

Brande, Dorothea (1984) *Becoming a Writer* (London: Macmillan).

Buzan, Tony (1979) *Use Your Head* (London: BBC).

Chase, Stuart (1956) *Guides to Straight Thinking* (New York: Harper).

Dunleavy, Patrick (1986) *Studying for a Degree in the Humanities and Social Sciences* (Basingstoke: Macmillan).

Fearnside, W. Ward and William B. Holther (1959) *Fallacy: The Counterfeit of Argument* (Englewood Cliffs, NJ: Prentice-Hall).

Flew, Antony (1975) *Thinking about Thinking* (London: Fontana).

Fowler, H. and S. Winchester (2002) *Fowler's Modern English Usage* (Oxford: Oxford University Press).

Gowers, E. (1951) *ABC of Plain Words* (London: HMSO).

Greetham, Bryan (2008) *How to Write Better Essays*, 2nd edition (Basingstoke: Palgrave Macmillan).

Grix, Jonathan (2004) *The Foundations of Research* (Basingstoke: Palgrave Macmillan).

Stebbing, L. Susan (1961) *Thinking to Some Purpose* (Harmondsworth: Penguin).

Strunk, William and E. B. White (1979) *The Elements of Style* (New York: Macmillan).

Thouless, Robert H. (1958) *Straight and Crooked Thinking* (London: Pan).

Wilson, John (1963) *Thinking with Concepts* (Cambridge: Cambridge University Press).

Zinsser, William (1988) *Writing to Learn* (New York: Harper & Rowe).

Index

References to illustrations are printed in bold.

NOTES